MID-CENTURY GOTHIC

Manchester University Press

MID-CENTURY GOTHIC

THE UNCANNY OBJECTS OF MODERNITY IN BRITISH LITERATURE AND CULTURE AFTER THE SECOND WORLD WAR

LISA MULLEN

Manchester University Press

Copyright © Lisa Mullen 2019

The right of Lisa Mullen to be identified as the author of this work has been asserted by her in accordance with the Copyright, Designs and Patents Act 1988.

Published by Manchester University Press
Altrincham Street, Manchester M1 7JA, UK
www.manchesteruniversitypress.co.uk

British Library Cataloguing-in-Publication Data is available

ISBN 978 1 5261 3277 2 hardback
ISBN 978 1 5261 6025 6 paperback

First published by Manchester University Press in hardback 2019

This edition published 2021

The publisher has no responsibility for the persistence or accuracy of URLs for any external or third-party internet websites referred to in this book, and does not guarantee that any content on such websites is, or will remain, accurate or appropriate.

Typeset by Newgen Publishing UK

CONTENTS

Acknowledgements		*page* vi
Introduction: 'The world of things': an introduction to mid-century gothic		1

Part I: Agency

1	Rubble, walls and murals: the threshold between abstraction and materiality	17
2	Lost in translation: migrant bodies and uncanny skin	48
3	Machines and spectrality: the gothic potential of technology	80

Part II: Intimacy

4	Neophilia and nostalgia: the trouble with gentrification	121
5	Strange beauty: costume, performance and power in 1953	146
6	Bombs, prosthetics and madness: the painful nearness of things	183
	Conclusion: beyond the mid-century	208
	Bibliography	214
	Index	226

ACKNOWLEDGEMENTS

This work began at Birkbeck, University of London, with funding from the Arts and Humanities Research Council. I am immensely grateful to Luisa Calè and Esther Leslie for their wisdom, kindness and insight. I am also indebted to Tim Armstrong, Ben Highmore, Victoria McNeile, Terri Mulholland and Lisa Robertson, who read earlier versions of the manuscript, and whose comments were generous and incisive.

The book was completed while I was the Steven Isenberg Junior Research Fellow at Worcester College, Oxford University, and I am very grateful to the college for offering me the fellowship, and to Steven Isenberg and his family for their generosity.

Thanks also, as ever, to Ivy Mullen.

INTRODUCTION: 'THE WORLD OF THINGS': AN INTRODUCTION TO MID-CENTURY GOTHIC

> The new human type cannot be properly understood without awareness of what he is continuously exposed to from the world of things about him, even in his most secret innervations.
>
> Theodor Adorno, *Minima Moralia*[1]

Monsters and dreams stalked London's South Bank in 1951. The Festival of Britain site was a gothic space for a gothic time, visited by the sighing spectres of the Blitz, and the chain-rattling ghosts of modernism's promise of a brand new world. Carved out of a derelict warehouse district by the River Thames, it showcased new ways of living over 26 acres and 31 buildings, arranged around the Dome of Discovery's interplanetary statement of aluminium-clad futurism, and watched over by the towering Skylon, aimed like a missile to infinity. Inside each building was a throng of jostling and contradictory objects, ranging in size and gravitas from an entire aeroplane to a novelty violin made of matchsticks, and all broadcasting cacophonous messages about what Britain was or could be. The whole confabulation of architecture and exhibits had been conceived as an integrated, rhetorical declaration that would insist upon a frictionless continuity between the nation's glorious past and its confident future. Yet when this imaginary city sprang to life out of the post-war rubble, the exhibition's war-weary visitors – incomers from a grittier reality – became the ghosts who haunted its pavilions and precincts.

Like the mid-century decade that spawned it, the South Bank Exhibition proved to be a chaotic playground for unruly ideas. Its future-facing designs made an awkward frame for jingoistic celebrations of past heroic endeavour; modern art and technological utopianism bumped uneasily against whimsical displays of moth-eaten eccentricity and colourful kitsch. This midsummer dream-park was supposed to consolidate British post-war identity and potential, but its jumble of ambiguity and contradiction instead opened up uncomfortable dialogues with the grimy and battered infrastructure of real-life London. The idea of a clean articulation of the past and the future only served to highlight the disorderly and disarticulated reality of the present. And yet, against all odds and in the teeth of political and media hostility, the Festival was a roaring popular success. Its off-message dissonance was the perfect expression of a mid-century moment when the forward momentum of culture and progress was temporarily disrupted. Before the inrush of the briskly instrumental new structures of post-war consumer capitalism, old demons – war trauma, imperial over-reach, class antagonism – would need to be brought out into the open, examined and placated.

An anecdote recalled by the exhibition's Director of Design, Misha Black, summed up the way a spirit of resistance and liberation was invested in and expressed through the thing-world framed within this semantically supersaturated zone. Black describes a dinner laid on in the Dome of Discovery just before it opened to the public, organised as a morale-booster for the disgruntled workers who – like the post-war population at large – were labouring in difficult conditions to complete a project of regeneration that was essentially opaque in its intentions and outcomes:

> A few naked bulbs gave illumination, the dark areas were greater than the lit, braziers glowed with minimal warmth. The speeches of exhortation to greater effort and fewer trade-union disputes were dreary and misconceived. The atmosphere became as frigid as the night, when suddenly one man sent his paper plate (food eaten) whizzing across the void. In a moment a thousand plates were spinning, until the whole volume of the Dome was alive with white discs, as though invaded by flying fish. This was a magical moment.[2]

These abstract white discs were harbingers of a different kind of future – bracingly modern space invaders that hailed a new and unruly agency in the people who threw them. Repurposed as messengers of dissent and sent across the dark void, they also became uncanny in their moment of flight: animated by repressed emotions and impulses, they were an image of liberated potential, and spoke more eloquently than any of the carefully placed and exhaustively explained exhibits which would later fill the Dome. Answering the antinomian longings of the disgruntled diners, the plates staked a physical claim on the cultural space that the workers had laboured to bring into existence but from which they felt excluded. They subverted the gesture of disposal that mobilised them: instead of settling into place as abject rubbish, they took flight and performed an act of transformative magic.

The same spirit of recalcitrance also infused the South Bank site when it was opened to the public and began to operate as a dynamic system in continuous motion. Each idiosyncratic pathway chosen by each individual visitor through the maze of clamorous objects disrupted the integrity of the exhibition's sanctioned story – a story that was already teetering under its heavy discursive burden. In his reminiscences, Misha Black remembered 'screams of righteous indignation' from the pavilion architects as designers 'tried to cram their gallon of exhibits into the pint pot of the buildings'.[3] While the guide-catalogue claimed that the exhibition 'develop[ed] its themes by means of things you can see and believe', it proved impossible to codify the haphazardly curated displays in order to align them with a pre-planned message.[4] An approved 'way to go round' for visitors was illustrated in the guidebook by means of dotted lines, and accompanied by a neurotic emphasis on mapping and signposting on the site – but was generally ignored. Detailed captions and information boards were carefully composed, but, as Black put it, 'it is doubtful whether more than a single sentence lingered in the mind'.[5] Dylan Thomas, speaking in a BBC Radio broadcast, described how the chaotic subjectivity of the individuals passing through made the South Bank a playful and liberating space. 'Perhaps you will go on a cool, dull day, sane as a biscuit,' he wrote, 'and find that the exhibition does, indeed, tell the story of "British contributions to world civilisation in the arts of peace"; that, and nothing else. But I'm pleased to doubt it.' In practice, he observed, 'you see people go along briskly down the wide white avenues towards the pavilion of their fancy … and suddenly stop: another fancy swings and bubbles in front of their eyes'.[6]

Unintended meanings and harbingers of enchantment were conjured out of this swirl of competing fancies. Consumer goods, prominently displayed but impossible to buy, took on the character of fetishes. Open-sided buildings displaying the latest ideas in furniture recalled blitzed houses broken open by bombs. Bronze door handles in the showpiece Regatta restaurant were shaped like disembodied hands, so that the sculptor Barbara Hepworth 'refused to touch [them] as she associated them with amputation'.[7] This carnival of submerged affect erupted from a threshold moment. The lingering warscapes of the Blitz were still scarred by the bombers' radical acts of spatial defamiliarisation, while social upheaval threatened a culture untethered from its old assumptions and needing to define itself anew.

This is not a book about the Festival of Britain, but it seeks to examine and explain the gothic atmosphere that produced it, and other mid-century cultural artefacts. In particular, it seeks out uncanny objects which, like the paper plates in the Dome or the fractious domestic and industrial exhibits in the other pavilions, provided a focal point for human recalcitrance. As Adorno puts it in the quotation that opens this introduction, such objects offer secret insights into what was new about the people of the mid-century, and the ways in which the things around them demonstrated the powerful agency, and the suffocating intimacy, of a different kind of materiality. Such objects found their voice in mid-century novels, films and exhibitions, where they functioned as reservoirs of alterity and dissonance, and brought into focus the uncanny animations that acted on, or in concert with, human consciousness.

The literature and culture of the post-war decade have not received the same critical attention as the more easily classifiable eras of pre-war modernism or later post-modernism. Its in-between-ness has led some critics to the notion that the late 1940s and early 1950s marked the dying fall of a richer cultural milieu, or a regrettable retreat into aesthetic conservativism among chinking teacups which would be skittled away by Angry Young Men and 1960s counterculture.[8] Yet the years between 1945 and 1955 tackled distinctive and equally lively questions of their own, inspiring political and aesthetic experimentation in a generation moulded by dislocation, deprivation and aspiration towards a better life. In *The Four-Gated City* (written in 1969), Doris Lessing pointedly refutes the idea that 'everyone knows' 1956 was 'a watershed, a turning-point, a cross-roads' because it was the year of the Suez crisis and the Hungarian Uprising:

> It has become the year that everyone refers to: oh yes, that year of course! ... So that now, looking back, the people who lived through it say, for the sake of speed and easy understanding: 1956, and what is conveyed is the idea of change, breaking up, clearing away, movement.
> Yet the air had cleared well before 1956.[9]

Considering the period from 1945 to 1955 simply in terms of a dialogue with declining modernism, or with later avant-garde experimentation, is to ignore – among other things – the mid-century's gothicised experience of history. Salvaging modernity from the debris of modernism was not simply a case of shaking off the past, but of understanding its tendency to haunt the new material and popular cultures which were to become reservoirs of historiographical unease.

A schema of cultural hierarchies that had been powerful in wartime crystallised with a brittle sharpness at the moment when post-war socialism and the new materiality seemed to threaten age-old privileges. This moment also marks the point at which British modernism became anti-modern, as can be seen in T.S. Eliot's shrill and embattled appeal to cultural conservatism, 1948's *Notes Towards the Definition of Culture*, which sought explicitly to preserve the elitism of high modernism in the teeth of its post-war superannuation, insisting that firm delineations and stratifications must be the basis of any cultural salvation for Britain. Eliot asserts 'with some confidence' that 'our own period is one of decline' and that 'the evidences of this decline are visible in every department of human activity'.[10] His thesis is that connoisseurship is the essential arbitrator of cultural value, and is instinctively propagated by intimate networks of taste and knowledge. The process should be anything but commercial; the elite should be 'something much more organically composed', he writes, 'than a panel of bonzes, caciques and tycoons'.[11] His claim that civilisation springs 'from the soil' amounts to a theory of cultural *terroir*, with art cultivated like a wine which reflects the unique particularities of the vineyard.[12] Even the attempt to materialise this secret knowledge in the form of books is somewhat vulgar ('we read many books because we cannot know enough people').[13] He leaves it disdainfully to America to pursue the dissemination of culture via material goods, with Hollywood cited as major culprit:

> America has tended to impose its way of life chiefly in the course of doing business, and creating a taste for its commodities. Even the humblest material artefact, which is the product and the symbol of a particular civilisation, is an emissary of the culture out of which it comes: to particularise only by mentioning that influential and inflammable article the celluloid film; and thus American economic expansion may be also, in its way, the cause of disintegration of cultures which it touches.[14]

The interdisciplinary approach taken by this book is in part a refutation of Eliot's hierarchy of culture, which was already coming under sustained and intellectually serious attack by 1948, not only from the world of literature, but from the cinema, design and architecture. Scholars such as Ben Highmore and Richard Hornsey have suggested that these new cultural directions began to form a pattern of emergent dissidence in the 1940s; this book argues more particularly that narratives about upstart objects and disorderly commodities engaged with urgent questions about autonomy, self-determination and identity, and opened up a minatory, if fleeting, perspective on the workings of the new consumerist ideology which was to take hold in the economic aftermath of global conflagration.[15] By reappraising neglected post-war texts, including domestic, middlebrow and other non-canonical novels, and setting them within the wider contexts of visual art, film, and material and technological cultures, it will show how they reflected the sense of crisis and liminality which made the century's mid-point a gothicised, interstitial zone.

Post-war objects began to display a militancy which highlighted and problematised the onrush of a new type of consumerism far more assertive than its interwar iterations. In 1923, Georg Lukács had described the process of reification which the proletariat underwent when they were inculcated into the social relations required by industry, which treated them as functioning (or malfunctioning) units in a machine and robbed them even of the power to perceive their own reification.[16] After the Second World War, the rise of mass culture and advertising extended this process of reification to consumers, and not just workers; an ideal of *self*-commodification was promoted via an endless cycle of desire and imperfect fulfilment. In 1954, J.B. Priestley coined the term 'Admass' to describe the 'swindle' that had prevailed in the US for decades but had only come to Europe since the war:

> This is my name for the whole system of an increasing productivity, plus inflation, plus a rising standard of material living, plus high-pressure advertising and salesmanship, plus mass communications, plus cultural democracy and the creation of the mass mind, the mass man.[17]

For Priestley, this massification was a disaster for the individual: 'You think everything is opening out when in fact it is narrowing and closing in on you,' he wrote. 'You have to be half-witted or half-drunk all the time to endure it.'[18] The detrimental effect of mass consumption on individuality and personal agency coincided with the increasing sophistication of the new psychological techniques being used in marketing. In his 1957 book *The Hidden Persuaders*, Vance Packard identified the 'startling beginnings' that had been made since the war in an ongoing quest to mould consumers into the custom-built products of the advertising industry.[19] What he termed 'the depth approach' aimed to overcome 'the apparent perversity and unpredictability of the prospective customers' by making them identify with products on a psychical level, rather than offering them a logical rationale for purchase.[20] In one example, for instance, he described how a Chicago grocery chain decided to 'take on the traits "we like in our friends". Those were spelled out as generosity, courtesy, cleanliness, patience, sincerity, honesty, sympathy and good-naturedness.'[21] By identifying with the brand, consumers ratify and reinforce the norms it stands for, creating more and more pressure to conform and eliding the distinction between consumer and product. But if such theories aimed to enforce 'desirable' behaviour by flattening the distinction between subjects and objects, and ascribing personality, morality, autonomy and agency to the inanimate realm, then narratives about the recalcitrance of the thing-world offered a submerged revolutionary subtext: if uncannily subject-like objects could demonstrate the 'perversity and unpredictability' that consumer capitalism was designed to eradicate, then people, too – as uncannily object-like subjects – might also stubbornly refuse to conform to the programme.

Such cultures of economic unease and political insurrection have a natural affinity with the gothic – a form that arose in the eighteenth century as an expression of provocative intransigence towards Enlightenment rationality. In the early twentieth century, the imbrication of gothicism, modernism and materialism was central to Walter Benjamin's *Arcades Project*, which found currents of revolution in the ruins and discarded rubbish of Paris's consumer dreamworlds. As Margaret Cohen points out in *Profane Illumination*, his project amounted to a work of 'gothic Marxism' which was 'fascinated with the irrational aspects of social processes'. The Enlightenment, she points out, was 'always already haunted by its gothic ghosts, and the same can be said of Marxism from its inception'.[22] This revolutionary uncanny rediscovers a suggestive world of enigmatic, overdetermined symbols and psychological tensions in order to pathologise social relations and precipitate their rupture. But the hazy surrealism of Benjamin's interwar Paris had hardened, in post-1945 Britain, into something more prickly. Materialism was a battleground; socialism and the welfare state were pitted against a resurgent capitalism, and the things people needed or wanted were the weapons with which the war was fought. In this context, narratives about gothic objects not only expressed the psychological residues which attached to mid-century things, but carried a hefty cargo of political freight.

The terms 'gothic' and 'uncanny' connect this emergent critique of consumerism with a tradition of literary insubordination which goes back to Horace Walpole's *The Castle of Otranto*.[23] Freud's essay on 'The Uncanny' ('Das Unheimliche') was itself a critique of a gothic text, E.T.A. Hoffmann's 'The Sandman', and made explicit for the first time the way gothic literature had foreshadowed the psychoanalyst's attempts to make the mysteries of the psyche legible. After Freud, the culture of the gothic necessarily operates in dialogue with psychoanalysis, even if that dialogue is antagonistic. In *The Weird and the Eerie*, Mark Fisher called for a new critical vocabulary to illuminate the way twentieth-century culture responded to the gothic themes of fragmentation, doubling, hauntings, uninhibited sexuality and psychic spaces which produced the troubled, dislocated subject.[24] He proposed the term 'weirdness' to describe 'the presence of that which does not belong', which is often 'a signal that the concepts and frameworks which we have previously employed are now obsolete'.[25] The related quality of 'eeriness' is recognisable, according to Fisher, by 'a *failure of absence* or a *failure of presence*', the sensation that 'there is something present where there should be nothing, or is there is nothing present when there should be something'.[26] These categories differ from Freud's *Unheimlich*, he argues, because they do not stand in any kind of relationship with the homely: 'A sense of the eerie seldom clings to enclosed and inhabited domestic spaces; we find the eerie more readily in landscapes partially emptied of the human.'[27] In my opinion, however, Freud's *Unheimlich* always survives as the Ur-category into which such terms as 'weird' and 'eerie' are folded. I have been content to characterise the objects under discussion in this book as 'uncanny', even though my definition, like Fisher's, diverges somewhat from Freud. His conception of the *Unheimlich* depends on an analogical glitch in which something is both familiar and strange; close to, but not quite the same as, another object which has previously been smoothly assimilated into the cognitive homescape. In the mid-century, I argue, it is not the analogy between things and things, but between things and selves, that causes this cognitive glitch. All gothic objects combine semantic overdetermination with the disruption of authoritative narratives about the linearity of space and time. In mid-century gothic, however, the distinct personhood of the human self succumbs to fluid interactions with the thing-world; gothic objects are invested with economic and cultural power, but then exceed their allotted meaning and come to define, control or replace the people that make, own or use them. In this way, they challenge the integrity of the subject in one of two ways. First, they may exhibit an unwarranted *agency* and begin to pursue a thingly agenda that promotes their own survival and is indifferent to the historicity of the human; alternatively, the objects may achieve an uncanny *intimacy* by infiltrating the human and problematising his or her autonomy and individuality.

The six categories of uncanny objects collected together in this book express an insidious kind of otherness which resists commodification – a dialectic of objecthood and subjecthood which unseats fundamental categorical assumptions. Part I traces the enchanted agency of the mid-century object, which emerges first in the uncanny animation of the rubble and insubordinate detritus of wartime bomb sites; next, it appears in the aestheticisation of power, class and identity within the semiotic spaces of exhibition and spectacle; finally, it enables media hardware to command and undermine the subject's autonomous physical existence. In Part II, the intimate inhabitation of the human by the inhuman is exemplified, first, by the haunted junk of gentrification; next, by costumes and equipment which enable access to heterotopic forms of experience; and lastly by atomic bombs which disgorge vast zones of radioactive emptiness from their compact and inscrutable interiors. In postwar literature and culture, such disorderly objects not only provoke or sustain an impression of dislocation and refer to the eternal postponement of post-traumatic rehabituation, they also evade or complicate the smooth workings of economic and libidinal exchange. Whether they have been wrecked, salvaged and repurposed, or have become ritualised, intangible and unobtainable, their value and meaning remains disturbingly uncertain.

Such things differ from the modernist understanding of gothic objects typified in Benjamin's fragment-fetishising *Project*, or, for that matter, Virginia Woolf's short story 'Solid Objects', which describes how a man's obsessive attention to the thingliness of physical materiality leads to the breakdown of his human identity. When Elizabeth Bowen set out to define the qualities of post-war literature, she concluded that trauma must be the mid-century's primary subject, and that the interwar novel of the psychic interior 'did not finally diagnose the modern uneasiness – dislocation'.[28] Bowen was interested in the gothicisation of things and people who appear as uncanny apparitions in a post-traumatic world, out of place or out of time. The stream-of-consciousness approach was not sufficient to convey this new disruption of public/private priority:

> The salutary value of the exterior, the comfortable sanity of the concrete, came to be realised only when the approach of the Second World War forced one to envisage wholesale destruction. The obliteration of man's surroundings, streets and houses, tables and chairs, sent up, for him, their psychological worth. Up to now, consciousness had been a sheltered product: its interest as consciousness diminished now that, at any moment, the physical shelter could be gone.[29]

A lack of material safety had unpicked the modernist subject and – which perhaps amounts to the same thing – the modernist subject-matter. Tim Armstrong's *Modernism, Technology and the Body* has shown how modernism incorporated new technologies and objects into its aesthetic of proto-posthumanism; in the mid-century the tables were turned, and it was the human that had to be incorporated into an alien, and suddenly dominant, thing-world.

Theodor Adorno and Max Horkheimer's critique of mid-century mass culture identified the gothic undertow of the commodity economy in the 1940s. In *Dialectic of Enlightenment* (1944) they contrasted the instrumentality and rationalisation of capitalism with older cultural forms which could never be completely repressed.[30] They argued that independent thought and the idea of the unitary 'self' had been subsumed into a purist ideal of the Enlightenment 'subject', which could be understood and quantified by logic and economics: a subject cleansed of meaning, all the better to conform to the machinic regime of productivity and acquisition. Since, for Adorno and Horkheimer, ambiguity – which disrupts the sterile purity of reason – is the essential condition for meaning, then mass culture in the modern world poses an even greater threat than first-wave industrialisation, because it promotes the repression of the ambiguous self just as it strives to replace unruly things with objectively quantifiable products.[31]

During his wartime exile in California from 1938 to 1953, Adorno was profoundly affected by the strangeness of his American surroundings, which reflected his own strangeness as a displaced person in an alien culture. *Minima Moralia: Reflections from Damaged Life* held up a broken mirror to his own damage and his sense that a hostile materiality was stripping people of the cultural structures which had previously sustained them. For Adorno, modern design disrupted the proper balance between subjects and objects by indulging 'the implacable, as it were ahistorical demands of objects' that make 'gestures precise and brutal, and with them men'.[32] Thus, he observes that self-closing doors rob people of good manners by removing the responsibility of looking behind them as they pass through; sliding windows normalise the practice of shoving; and cars suggest, by their very existence, the possibility of mowing down innocent pedestrians. Adorno follows this observation to its savage conclusion: simple interactions with the thing-world, he warns, will become so coarsened by the 'unresting jerkiness' demanded by modern objects, that human subjects will be brought steadily closer to the baked-in brutality of the fascistic mindset.

As mid-century literature and culture attempted to resituate the self in relation to this totalising thing-world, the gothic return of repressed enchantment offered a dialectical remedy. By highlighting the auratic autonomy of newly re-mythologised objects, gothic narratives suggest ways of reintroducing the autonomous self at the expense of the reified subject, so that consumerism is problematised. The whole project of reification is endangered by objects which themselves stake a claim to selfhood and irrationality. Such objects offer – to borrow Isobel Armstrong's resonant phrase – a 'moment of difficulty', an impediment to the frictionless transit of the subject through the machine of economics.[33] If we accept Adorno's distinction between independent self and chained subject, and borrow the distinction that Bill Brown drew in his 'Thing Theory' between intransigent things and obedient objects, we can see that, whereas the economic arbitrage of *subject* and *object* is an attempt by each to gain decisive mastery over the other, the fluidly ambiguous relationship between *self* and *thing* is liberatingly dialectical, and offers a way out of the self's imprisonment in rational subjecthood.[34] Thus, human disobedience and resistance can be modelled and expressed by the unruliness of uncanny things.

Marghanita Laski's 1949 novel *Little Boy Lost* directly addresses the superannuation of pre-war modernism and the post-war mood of dislocation, and invests simple objects with the power to disrupt old habits of mind.[35] It recounts the anguished wanderings of a modernist poet, Hilary Wainwright, who goes looking for the baby son he lost during the Nazi occupation of Paris. Secretly, Hilary dreads being reunited with his lost son because he believes that he will then have to settle into a new life of humdrum responsibility with his dull fiancée, and be subsumed into the kind of sclerotic domesticity he himself grew up in, and which he escaped by adopting the urbane attitudes of modernism. Navigating the affectively supercharged bombscapes of post-war France – a gothic 'wilderness of desolation' – he is forced to confront his own neurotic intellectualism as well as questioning his self-identification as a member of an international modernist clique supposedly immune to parochial, bourgeois concerns.[36] In contrast to Hilary's spasms of aesthetic superannuation, the boy he tracks down, Little Jean, is the model citizen of the new modernity: full of hope and optimism despite his abject state, he is not oppressed but grounded by the battered objects he has gathered around him – 'a pinecone, a stone marble with nearly all its colour rubbed away, a used American stamp, and a tiny little celluloid swan with its head broken off and a dirty piece of rag tied round its neck for a bandage' – and his teacher remarks, rather curiously, that his intellect is distinguished by a superior 'sense of causation', which seems to give him a foothold in history.[37] Jean sees the proper value in solid things, which has nothing to do with the post-war discourse of consumerism, but everything to do with what Bill Brown calls 'the dialectic by which human subjects and inanimate objects may be said to constitute one another'.[38] Most importantly, Jean demonstrates an effortless hybrid identity, entirely fluid and contingent on context: right up until the end of the novel, he might be Hilary's son, or he might not be. Finally, it is a modern, mass-produced object – a cheap toy dog which Jean remembers from his infancy and correctly names – that holds the key to the true relationship between the man and the boy. But by then, it is clear that Hilary will only survive by holding tightly on to this child – whatever his identity – and heading towards the future that he represents.

While Jean is a mid-century native, Hilary has to be awakened from his modernist stupor before he can cross over into the new post-war reality, and this means he must experience the full emotional impact of the trauma that has befallen Europe. It is possible to hear in the novel an echo of all the lost and broken families of the Holocaust, the emotional wreckage of loss, anger, guilt and denial and the physical wrench of dislocation and homelessness. Like the toy dog, Jean is also a kind of uncanny object, capable of cathecting the terrible cataclysm that Hilary wishes to pretend never happened. History's thresholds must be crossed, and the moment of difficulty at the point of transition represents an opportunity for recuperation. As we will see in a later chapter, Laski repeatedly places her characters in such contested spaces; stuck on the wrong side of the war, on the hingepoint of the century, the supposedly modernist Hilary is simply not modern enough to realise that the ambiguity *is* the meaning.

The mid-century was a time of inversion: inside became outside; old became new; modernity became historical; junk became treasure. But while this sense of topsy-turvy possibility conferred a freshness and novelty not otherwise available to an essentially conservative and cash-strapped nation, it brought with it a nagging anxiety. Would the norms of society survive? Would value and authenticity lose their meaning? Would codes become illegible? Would objects break free of the meaning ascribed to them and begin to bleed history?

In a *Vogue* article on the Festival of Britain, Laski described the ubiquitous tapered shape that appeared in furniture, souvenirs, typography and the buildings themselves, and became its defining design emblem. She asked:

> What are we to deduce from the ubiquitous shape in the Exhibition, the top-heavy pillar, the triangle on its apex, the inverted cone? ... Since we have lately been told that its converse shape, the obelisk, is a phallic symbol, have we here its antithesis, an unconscious symbolism of the decline of the west? Or does it symbolise an airy indulgence in fancy, an aspiring imagination no longer earthbound?[39]

Her speculation ends on a warning note that the optimism of novelty might suffer its own reverse:

> Over everything hangs the shadow of the most important question of all – shall we remember the Festival as the beginning of the future it promises, or as the last pleasant dream before the nightmare?[40]

This book attempts to explore both the dream and the nightmare – and to answer the question of what happens after the dreamer wakes up.

NOTES

1 Theodor Adorno, *Minima Moralia: Reflections on a Damaged Life*, trans. E.F.N. Jephcott (London: Verso, 2005), p. 40.

2 Misha Black, 'Architecture, Art and Design in Unison', in Mary Banham and Bevis Hillier, eds., *A Tonic to the Nation: The Festival of Britain 1951* (London: Thames & Hudson, 1976), pp. 82–85 (p. 85).
3 Black, 'Architecture, Art and Design in Unison', p. 84.
4 *South Bank Exhibition London: Festival of Britain* (London: HMSO, 1951), p. 9.
5 Black, 'Architecture, Art and Design in Unison', p. 84.
6 Bevis Hillier, 'Introduction', in Banham and Hillier, *Tonic*, p17. Quoting Dylan Thomas, *Quite Early One Morning* (New York: New Directions, 1954), p. 220.
7 Black, 'Architecture, Art and Design in Unison', p. 83.
8 See for instance Alan Sinfield, *Literature, Politics and Culture in Postwar Britain* (Berkeley: University of California Press, 1989) and Jed Esty, *A Shrinking Island: Modernism and National Culture in England* (New Haven: Yale University Press, 2013).
9 Doris Lessing, *The Four-Gated City* (London: Paladin, 1990), pp. 307–08.
10 T.S. Eliot, *Notes Towards the Definition of Culture* (London: Faber and Faber, 1948), p. 19.
11 Eliot, *Culture*, p. 85.
12 Eliot, *Culture*, p. 19.
13 Eliot, *Culture*, p. 86.
14 Eliot, *Culture*, p. 92.
15 See Richard Hornsey, *The Spiv and the Architect: Unruly Life in Postwar London* (Minneapolis: University of Minnesota Press, 2010).
16 Georg Lukács, *History and Class Consciousness*, trans. Rodney Livingstone www.marxists.org/archive/lukacs/works/history/ [accessed 28 January 2018].
17 J.B. Priestley and Jacquetta Hawkes, *Journey Down a Rainbow* (London: Heinemann-Cresset, 1957), pp. 44–45.
18 Priestley and Hawkes, *Journey*, p. 45.
19 Vance Packard, *The Hidden Persuaders* (London: Penguin, 1960), p. 16.
20 Packard, Hidden Persuaders, p. 17.
21 Packard, *Hidden Persuaders*, p. 47.
22 Margaret Cohen, *Profane Illumination: Walter Benjamin and the Paris of Surrealist Revolution* (Berkeley: University of California, 1993), p. 2.
23 Horace Walpole, *The Castle of Otranto: A Gothic Story* (Oxford University Press, 1996).
24 Mark Fisher, *The Weird and the Eerie* (London: Repeater, 2016).
25 Fisher, *The Weird and the Eerie*, p. 61; p. 13.
26 Fisher, *The Weird and the Eerie*, p. 61. Emphasis in original.
27 Fisher, *The Weird and the Eerie*, p. 11.
28 Elizabeth Bowen, 'English Fiction at Mid-Century', in *People, Places, Things: Essays by Elizabeth Bowen* (Edinburgh: Edinburgh University Press, 2008), p. 322.
29 Bowen, 'English Fiction', pp. 322–23.
30 Theodor W. Adorno and Max Horkheimer, *Dialectic of Enlightenment*, trans. John Cumming (London: Verso, 1997).
31 Adorno and Horkheimer, *Dialectic of Enlightenment*, p. 31.
32 Adorno, *Minima Moralia*, p. 40.
33 Isobel Armstrong, *Victorian Glassworlds: Glass Culture and the Imagination 1830–1880* (Oxford: Oxford University Press, 2008), p. 12. See Chapter 3 for a discussion of Armstrong's theory of glass.

34 Bill Brown, 'Thing Theory,' *Critical Inquiry*, 28:1 (Autumn 2001), 1–22.
35 Marghanita Laski, *Little Boy Lost* (London: Persephone, 2001).
36 Laski, *Little Boy Lost*, p. 80.
37 Laski, *Little Boy Lost*, p. 94; p. 154.
38 Bill Brown, 'The Tyranny of Things (Trivia in Karl Marx and Mark Twain),' *Critical Inquiry*, 28:2 (Winter 2002), 442–69 (p. 446).
39 Marghanita Laski, 'The visionary gleam: thoughts on the South Bank Exhibition,' *Vogue*, June 1951, pp. 73–78 (p. 78).
40 Laski, 'The visionary gleam,' p. 78.

PART I
AGENCY

1

RUBBLE, WALLS AND MURALS: THE THRESHOLD BETWEEN ABSTRACTION AND MATERIALITY

> In the first days of bombing ... one marvelled at pure debris; but soon this became usual and to lift the human interest it took a bare tree gibbeted with hanging scarecrows from a blasted old-clothes shop, or an unbroken mirror hanging high-up on the façade of rooms disappeared.
>
> William Sansom, *The Blitz: Westminster at War*[1]

It is impossible to account for the material turn that characterised mid-century culture without examining how it developed out of the experience of the Second World War. The Blitz, in particular, exploded people and things out of their familiar contexts: an arbitrary redistribution of the personal, the meaningful and the mundane blurred the distinctions between these categories, while the sudden and widespread visibility and banality of dead bodies, or body parts, meant that objects and human forms became uncannily interchangeable. The writer William Sansom, who worked as a fireman in Westminster during the Blitz, describes such 'freakish effects' of the defamiliarised city, the 'strange light and strange textures' of the bombscape:

> [W]ith the pale plaster crumbled out on the street, with the puppety figures of rescue workers in their flat bowlerish hats covered also with pale dust, with the dead and wounded collapsed and unmoving – there was some of the atmosphere of the doll-shop, the shop for making plaster figures or people of wax.[2]

Just as clothes blasted into a tree might become quasi-human amid this strange new scenery – either as scarecrows or even the 'gibbeted' victims of an execution – so people here become uncanny simulacra of human forms which are only hazily defined ('puppety', 'bowlerish'). Perhaps because Sansom was putting out fires in the West End, he found that bombed buildings conjured up a sense of gothic theatricality:

> Here a pantomime was afoot, in the empty street a sudden festival booth had been erected and the play was on. At the root of this appearance lies something of the sympathy between *grand guignol* and the clown. Both, though one may laugh, are festivals of the macabre, of torchlit, painted terror.[3]

Such descriptions as these suggest the limitations of considering the Second World War bombsites as spaces that fit comfortably into the cultural narrative of ruins; of what Leo Mellor has called the 'ever-present interest in the ruin and the fragment, the incomplete or decayed structure that offers an implicit dialogue with the past through its very continued existence'.[4] The ability of bombsites to access both the restless scope of history and a frozen moment of sudden cataclysm certainly accounts for some of their uncanny quality, but their supercharged power derives from the macabre pantomime that Sansom describes – the sense that these are transitional spaces where a transformation, or even an inversion, of normality is performed. This chapter will argue that the interaction between bombsites and time becomes even more complex when one takes into account the temporal (and indeed socio-cultural) vertigo of the human subject who haunts these contemporary ruins.

Mellor cites the stopped clock 'still affixed to a wall in a bombsite' as the paradigmatic bombsite object, underscoring his argument that bombsites are broken timepieces which no longer relate to human temporality.[5] Yet when Sansom wanted to describe a similarly telling detail, he chose 'an unbroken mirror hanging high-up on the façade of rooms disappeared'.[6] Sansom's mirror is a subtly different metaphor, suggesting that these resonant bombsite objects offer to reflect back the plight of the subject, even while they appear to rise haughtily above human concerns in their 'unbroken' indifference. Later still, he suggests, even 'the unscathed mirror or picture hanging exposed on the wall became platitudinous – and it then took a row of ten grey Ascot toppers exposed in their open cupboard to raise an eyebrow'.[7] Sansom considered such objects, because they map so closely onto the particular idiosyncrasies of vanished individuals, more interesting than the 'pure debris' which was itself a marvel in the first days of bombardment; but in this chapter I want to place such metonymic personal possessions back, as it were, into the rubble, and look more closely at the thingly residue of the walls on which reflective objects – and in particular art-objects – precariously hung. A piece of rubble, I would argue, is the Blitz's Ur-object, utterly abject and empirically meaningless, yet nevertheless freighted with narrative; it tells the story both of the building from which it derived, and of the catastrophic moment of its transliteration from coherent wall to disorderly debris. Rubble, in its blunt materiality, contains within it a narrative of catastrophe and wreckage; yet it is also an abstracted form, blasted out of history into a pure and irreducible eternity, remote from its former spatial and personal meaning.

By accessing eternity in this way, bombsites became a refuge for those who wanted to escape from modernity, and so a theme of conflict with modernism often characterises the cultural examples in this chapter. Modernism, with its enthusiasm for bricolage and fragment, seemed to have predicted the ruinscape of the 1940s, but I would argue that, as a way of looking at the world, it was put under strain by the sudden actualisation of its metaphors. In the wake of the First World War, high modernism had implied a promise to pull both the world and the word apart in order to make experience new, but for those who had lived through the Blitz, the Second World War seemed to have completed only half the job. The dialectical machinery of historical renewal had malfunctioned: the kaleidoscope had been shaken, but no new picture had formed.

In this chapter, the search for this picture – for an aesthetic ratification of the suffering and destruction of the war – will be traced through six different cultural responses to rubble and the walls from which it derives. Murals, in particular, are evoked as a special category of art-object, one that had gained popularity under modernism but which now seemed to mark a point of conflict between implacable materiality and the fugitive abstract idea. Strikingly, the murals of the mid-century seem to presage or bring about the destruction of the very walls on which they are painted, and these tumbling walls become an image of revolutionary remaking which responded to the uncanny power of art.

'A WALL WILL FALL IN MANY WAYS': WILLIAM SANSOM'S WAR STORIES

For someone with William Sansom's experience as a Blitz fireman, the idea that walls and buildings were possessed of both agency and animation was self-evident – under bombardment, they were not solid but moved, writhed, lashed out with deadly force at the human beings in their ambit. In 'Building Alive', Sansom gives an hallucinogenic first-person account of being inside a bombed building and knowing that another flying bomb is on its way.[8] He notes the arbitrary nature of these robot-bombs' deathly, machinic force: 'It could drop anywhere. It was absolutely reasonless. It was the first purely fatal agent that had come to man for centuries, bringing people to cross their fingers again, bringing a rebirth of superstition.'[9] A feral intent motivates the building's eerily inorganic ecosystem, with its 'creakings, a groan of wood ... A legion of plastermice ... pattering up and down the walls.'[10] In the devastated cityscape 'all the laborious metropolitan history had been returned to its waste beginning', but something post-apocalyptic and post-human was beginning to stir amid the tangle of broken pipework:

> Only the little sounds sucking themselves in hinted at a new life, the life of leaden snakes, hesitating and choosing in whispers the way to blossom. ... A new growth was sprouting everywhere, sprouting like the naked plumbing, as if these leaden entrails were the worm at the core of a birth, struggling to emerge, thrusting everything else aside.[11]

The narrator survives this encounter with living architecture only by chance – he watches as the building opposite collapses instead, crushing a man on a stretcher who has only just been pulled out of a different bombsite.

The horror of being buried by rubble is a frequent theme of Sansom's wartime stories. In 'The Wall' – a story written during the Blitz and originally published in Sansom's 1944 collection *Fireman Flower*, his fireman narrator finds himself entranced by the pattern of symmetrical rectangles in a wall which is suspended over him, on the brink of falling. Like the flying bombs, walls are awesome in their inhuman arbitrariness:

> A wall will fall in many ways. It may sway over to the one side or the other. It may crumble at the very beginning of its fall. It may remain intact and fall flat. This wall fell as flat as a pancake. It clung to its shape through ninety degrees to the horizontal. Then it detached itself from the pivot and slammed down on top of us.[12]

The fireman is transfixed by the moment, 'hypnotised, rubber boots cemented to the pavement' with 'ton upon ton of red-hot brick hovering in the air'.[13] He finds himself 'immediately certain of every minute detail' of the wall and its windows, where 'alternating rectangles of black and red ... emphasised vividly the extreme symmetry of the window spacing: each oblong window shape posed as a vermilion panel set in perfect order upon the dark face of the wall.'[14] Sansom's characters frequently experience a kind of sensory bleed at such moments of extremity, a dreamlike merging of distorted vision, haptic sensation and emotion: 'The oblong building, the oblong windows, the oblong spacing. Orange-red colour seemed to *bulge* from the black framework, assumed tactile values, like boiling jelly that expanded inside a thick black squared grill.'[15] Yet these bulging fiery rectangles are what save him when time finally moves again and the wall 'detache[s] itself from the pivot and slam[s] down on top of us'. Although buried under rubble, he and two colleagues survive because they have 'been framed by one of those symmetrical, oblong window spaces'; it is the wall's Victorian patterning, its manmade, cultural symmetry, that provide a hiatus in its merciless material force – a recess in which the men can shelter.[16] The firemen can slip between the chunks of masonry because, at the moment of their most dangerous agency, such walls prove porous. In the postwar period, as we will see in Chapter 6, bombs would become the archetypal technological object capable of exploiting the porosity of the human subject; here, with the war still being fought, Sansom's stories show the human subject exploiting the porosity of the bombed object.

'A GOOD WALL WILL PAINT ITSELF': JOYCE CARY'S *THE HORSE'S MOUTH*

In Joyce Cary's novel *The Horse's Mouth*, published in 1944, the same year as *Fireman Flower*, walls problematise the primacy of materiality in a different way. Although set just before the onset of war, it responds to the frightening instability of the fabric of London's blitzed cityscape with a fable about mural-painting, the commodification of art and the uncanny agency of the thing.

The narrator of Cary's novel is Gulley Jimson, an ageing painter whose artistic vision constantly threatens to overwhelm his sensory engagement with the object world. Whereas Sansom's characters experience aloof materiality as a threat to the physical existence of a vulnerable, mortal human, Gulley has little interest in his own bodily form, and indeed strives towards the condition of pure abstraction that exists inside his head. But an artist must make art, and he struggles constantly to realise these concepts; not only because of the gap between idea and expression, but because his lack of money means he is forced to steal or swindle goods or artists' materials simply to live and work. Gulley's madness, Cary implies, originates in the persistence of his belief that such recalcitrant materiality can somehow express the transcendental truths that exist inside his head.

Despite enjoying critical success early in his career, Gulley is, in old age, a liminal character, unable to function according to the codes and rules of society. Frequently arrested and jailed for petty crimes, he is pushed to the spatial margins too, working first in a derelict boathouse by the Thames in west London, and then being forced to move to a dosshouse and paint on any surface he can access. Through his eyes, the reader finds everyday life receding to a dull background roar as his imagination intuits the world as a series of sublime shapes and colours and converts them into wildly ambitious visual compositions. He processes the natural world platonically; he conceptualises his paintings in the first instance as pure, eternal form, then struggles to understand what they might represent:

> [I] knew what I wanted to do. That blue-grey shape on the pink. The tower. The whatever it was, very round and heavy. Something like a gasometer, at full stretch without its muzzle. Or possibly an enamel coffee-pot. And chrome-yellow things like Egyptian columns or leeks or dumb-bells or willows or brass candlesticks, in front.[17]

As he works, however, he finds these shapes demand to be expressed figuratively, as animals, plants and human flesh which aspire to live and breathe. He is only satisfied when they manage both to exceed life and to embody it; when their thingly aloofness from petty human frailties combines with a vigorous sense of agency and vitality.

His self-image as a Romantic seer is backed up by his obsession with William Blake, whom he quotes incessantly as part of the internal monologue of his imaginative practice; but unlike Blake, Gulley has no social or revolutionary philosophy underpinning his spiritual visions. He is unmoved, for instance, by the political arguments of his friend Plantie, who organises anarchist meetings; Gulley only comments drily that 'I don't like converters. You never feel safe with them. They've always got some knuckleduster up their sleeve.'[18] In the end, however, it is Gulley who uses violent force against others. When he kills his former wife and muse, Sara, because she won't give him back a sketch he did of her (which he wishes to sell in order to fund his next project), the once-charming, mystical aesthete is revealed as a narcissistic psychopath who sees Sara, finally, as just another material obstacle in the way of his totalising artistic vision.

The novel continually reiterates the tension between abstraction and materiality; Gulley's artistic practice is both enabled and confounded by the thing-world through which he moves. The book's enigmatic title is reflected in a metaphorical motif which runs through the narrative, with Gulley using horse imagery whenever he encounters a problem with the authenticity of art and its ability to materialise abstract form. Early in the book, for instance, when he is working on a depiction of the Fall of Adam and Eve and groping towards representation as the conduit of meaning, the equine image comes at the epiphanic moment:

> I can do something with the foreground now, it's as empty as a beer jug with the bottom knocked out. ... And all at once I made a thing like a white Indian club. I like it, I said, but it's not a flower, is it? What the hell could it be? A fish? And I felt a kick inside like I was having a foal. Fish. Fish. Silver-white, green-white. And shapes that you could stroke with your eyebrows.[19]

In the 1970s, Edward H. Kelly argued that the novel's title is a reference to the story of the artist Apelles (which Horace attributed to Petronius) 'who, when in despair because he could not satisfactorily paint the foam on Alexander's horse's mouth, angrily dashed his brush against the canvas, and by mere accident or luck achieved that which had eluded his painstaking care'.[20] In Kelly's reading, Cary's novel thus becomes a meditation on the role of luck, or divine intervention, in the creative process; yet, given that the Apelles anecdote depends as much on the intervention of the brush as it does on the will of the gods, it could just as easily be seen as a gloss on Gulley's fraught relationship with the thing-world. In general, critics in the two decades after the novel's publication tended to read it in terms of questions about free will and the author's attitudes to his amoral protagonist.[21] Read from the perspective of mid-century attempts to grapple with the agency of the thing, on the other hand, Gulley's outrageously anti-social behaviour become instead the portrait of an artist dehumanised by his preoccupation with the auratic power of art. Yet despite Gulley's endless meditations on philosophical and aesthetic abstraction, the material world continually reasserts itself; like Apelles's brush, Gulley's materials have an agenda and an aesthetic project of their own, which will be pursued no matter what the cost to Gulley. In the end, his artistic expression depends on his ability to grasp this material world: to buy or steal paints and brushes, unearth reusable canvases in junk shops, find walls with the right texture and surface and – in all cases – on his ability to preserve and hold on to these things through the storm of incident which swirls around him.

Gulley is aware of the fact that, as soon as he gets his ideas down in paint on walls or canvas, he renders them precarious; either they will suffer the depredations of materiality and be vulnerable to theft and damage, or they will be absorbed into a commodity system in which they will once again become abstract and fluid. With other objects, he has come to accept this; after each spell in prison, he expects to find his possessions have 'just melted' (as Marx warns everything solid will do in a commodity culture),[22] although he is shocked when his artworks fall prey to the same process:

> I hadn't expected to see the frypan and kettle again. You can't leave things like that about for a month in any friendly neighbourhood and expect to find them in the same place. But [the painting of] the Living God with his stretchers and stiffeners weighed a couple of hundredweight. ... Someone said the landlord took it for the rent. The landlord swore he had never seen it. I daresay he had hidden it somewhere in an attic, telling himself that it might be worth thousands as soon as I was dead.[23]

Throughout the novel, Gulley's canvases will revert to their status as vulnerable material objects – they are variously stolen, vandalised with an air-gun and a knife, used to patch a leaking roof, or simply lost – but his bitterest complaint is always that they may have been sold for inflated sums without his permission and without any financial benefit trickling down to him. Paradoxically, however, despite his repeated attempts to retrieve past paintings and sketches in order to sell them to a collector he has met, he never quite manages to do so, partly because he understands all too well that the market turns solid objects into abstractions and that retrieving their value in fact devalues them:

> What do you mean, for instance, when you say a picture is worth five thousand pounds or five hundred or five bob? A picture isn't like chocolate, you can't eat it. Value in a picture isn't the same thing as the value in a pork chop. ... For instance, one might say that pictures haven't got any value at all in cash. They're a spiritual value, a liability. Or you might say that they hadn't got any real value till they're sold. And then the value keeps on going up and down.[24]

Typically, Gulley delivers this speech at the very point when his friend Coker is attempting to help him by ensuring he receives some cash for his work: on this occasion, Gulley is determined *not* to be paid. In *Dialectic of Enlightenment*, published the same year as *The Horse's Mouth*, Theodor Adorno and Max Horkheimer pinpointed the same paradox which skewers Gulley: 'Pure works of art,' they wrote, 'which deny the commodity society by the very fact that they obey their own law, were always wares all the same.'[25] Gulley's answer is to commit a series of wilfully self-sabotaging acts whenever he comes close to a profitable engagement with the social and financial systems he despises. None of the paintings he begins over the course of the novel is finished – the implication being that he deliberately avoids the moment when the completed artwork will break free of his creative authorship and realise its own potential autonomy. But in any case, this autonomy is inevitably compromised as soon as the work changes hands as a commodity.

This is clearly the case with the sketch that provokes Sara's murder. This is an early study for Gulley's single acknowledged masterpiece – a portrait of Sara in her bath – and as such it records the exact moment of the encounter between artist, muse and art-object which led to his consummate artistic achievement. The sketch remains a powerful object, but only as long as it stays in Sara's possession, where it continues to articulate a truth about the particularity of its moment. Despite this, owning it brings her no happiness; she admits to looking at it often, though 'not for pleasure. It makes me so sad I could cry.'[26] For her it is a souvenir of her disastrous marriage to Gulley and her lost youth and beauty: her emotional history is congealed within it. For Gulley, who finished with it, and her, long ago, it has become a dead thing, at best a frozen moment of technical virtuosity, and perhaps merely a token of potential financial value. When they look at it together, Sara admires her own youthful body, while for Gulley her beauty is inextricable from his skill at rendering it. 'Look at the vein there,' he says, 'just a drag of the brush across the grain. Yes I could handle paint then.'[27] They fight over the sketch until Gulley threatens to cut Sara with a box-opener – foreshadowing her later death when, determined to take possession of the sketch, he will cosh her and throw her down a flight of stairs. At the end of this first struggle, however, Sara gets the better of him: offering to wrap the picture for him, she secretly switches it for a bundle of old newspaper. This deception fittingly reveals the sketch as a shape-shifting mid-century object: recalcitrant, demotic and uncannily ambiguous. Because it has meaning for Sara, she sees it clearly and is bound to it, even though it speaks of her grief. On the other hand, reduced to a mere chattel in Gulley's eyes, the picture easily slips out of sight and away from his grasp.

As Gulley's model, Sara was the primary witness to, and victim of, the violence of artistic objectification. Indeed, Gulley's first vision of 'The Bath' came to him the first time he hit Sara – subjugating her flesh in the service of spirit and Ideal form, as he interprets it:

> As Billy [Blake] would say, through generation into regeneration. ... Materiality, that is, Sara, the old female nature, having attempted to button up the prophetic spirit, that is, Gulley Jimson, in her placket-hole, got a bonk on the conk, and was reduced to her proper status, as spiritual fodder.[28]

Gulley's sense of authorial entitlement – the artist bending people and things interchangeably to his will – reveals the radically dehumanising processes of modernity to be as much aesthetic as economic. The painted Sara that Gulley 'could handle ... then' becomes confused with the ageing, vulnerable, real-life Sara who stands in his way now; her murder arises from her exposure to the ruthless inhumanity of art and artist; it is not merely a crime of acquisition produced within the superstructure of a commodity system.

Gulley's hallucinations and delusions express the cognitive aporia generated by the tension between his notion of pure art and the commodity culture within which he must practise; and from the dissonance between his natural affinity with destitution and his aspirations to bourgeois acceptability. As the 'pork chop' speech quoted above points out, he knows that an artwork is a poor vessel for a would-be capitalist's reservoir of exchange value, because its price is so volatile and subject to fashion. This potential abjection of the commodified art-object is most starkly illustrated when Gulley visits a junk shop in search of old canvases he can paint over. Junk shops appear in narratives of midcentury memory and value with remarkable frequency, and will be discussed in more detail in later chapters; this early example gives clear indications of how the trope will develop as a critique of commodity culture in the 1950s. Here, already, is the archetype of a shop that fails to function as a shop; and Gulley is the archetypal customer who fails to behave as a customer. Indeed, the shopkeeper is equally dysfunctional; Cary presents her/him as a hazily defined fixture ('a widow like a cottage loaf'; 'a little man shaped like a flower-stand')[29] doomed to be destroyed by the eternally cursed premises:

> Ikey's is a shop that never has any luck. It changes hands about every six months. It has murdered more people than even the haberdashers opposite. ... I walked in and bought a fine junk-shop Romney with a few holes, etc., and some boot-marks on the lady's face, for two and sixpence. Of which the two was not perhaps altogether British mint silver. But the young gentleman was in such an excited state ... that you could have paid him in a Bank of Engraving note and taken change. I often wished I had, for a week afterwards he hanged himself over the stairs.[30]

The shop's current incumbent, however, is more circumspect; Gulley fails to con him out of the large canvas he has seen there ('Fifteen by twenty. Birth of Moses, by Antonio Something, 1710. Italian style, turnips and gravy'), and which has inspired him to plan a new version of *The Fall*.[31] Crucially for the novel's denouement, his failure to procure it leads him to revert instead to his favourite medium: walls themselves. It is not that he believes walls to be more permanent than canvases – walls 'fall down or get knocked full of holes by charwomen's brooms', he declares, whereas 'canvas is more portable. All the National Galleries like you to paint on canvas. They can't hang walls.'[32] Rather, it is the brute materiality of walls which attracts him, despite their lack of portability and durability. When he is invited into the home of a smart art collector, Beeder, Gulley soon contrives to take up residence while his host is abroad, and immediately sees the potential of the walls as a site for his own art. The satirical point is implied: collectors want authentic art-objects to hang in their fashionable 'studio' flats, but in this case Gulley turns the space – through a process of stealing, pawning or destroying all Beeder's possessions – into an authentic artist's studio – impoverished, half derelict, invaded by the destitute, and covered in paint.

> When I took down the water-colours in the studio to have a look at the other walls, I made a discovery. A good wall is often ruined by pictures, and I have found most excellent material in unexpected places, for instance behind a collection of old Masters. And this was a gem. ... A good wall, as they say, will paint itself. And as I looked at this beautiful shape, I saw what it was for. A raising of Lazarus.[33]

Like his previous obsession, *The Fall*, and his final project, *The Creation*, Gulley's Lazarus picture takes the relationship between matter and eternity as its subject. While *The Fall* depicts divine beings transforming into mortals, and Lazarus crosses the threshold between death and life, *The Creation* – which Gulley paints on the wall of a derelict chapel – not only features the creation of matter by a supernatural force, but wields a supernatural force of its own, acting with uncanny agency on its creator:

> I used to wake at night shivering all over, thinking the vampires were eating my toes; but it was only the Creation sticking its great beak into me. I used to laugh all at once and jump up in the street ... but it was only because I felt cold hands down my back, hands of Creation.[34]

In *The Creation*, Gulley at last believes that he will be able to marry form and meaning together, since he has found a way to make art itself the subject of his painting. 'This set [of forms] came up nearly complete. Not a gap anywhere,' he says, though he must still negotiate the gap between conception and materialisation:

> As every mural painter knows ... the line that is as lively as spring steel in the miniature, may go as dead as apron string on the wall. And what is a living whole on the back of an envelope can look as flat and tedious as a holiday poster, when you draw it out full size.[35]

The scale of the mural is a corollary of its implacable materiality: just as the falling wall towered over the fireman narrator in William Sansom's story, so this wall dwarfs Gulley, who has to crawl about on its vertical surface via a complex system of pulleys and moving platforms. This is a dangerous encounter for the artist. Gulley had earlier condemned his painting of Adam and Eve because 'it didn't hit you hard enough. It wasn't solid enough': 'What was the Fall after all. The discovery of the solid hard world, good and evil. Hard as rocks and sharp as poisoned thorns. And also the way to make gardens.'[36] It is inevitable, then, that he should be drawn not only to the solidity of a wall as an artistic medium but also to its potential to lash out violently at the human subject. Indeed the chapel's solidity is as illusory as Gulley's authorial jurisdiction over the artwork he creates: the chapel has been condemned as unsafe even before Gulley applies the first stroke of paint, and as he continues to work it is literally demolished around him. When he finally succumbs to a fall of his own (echoing both Adam and Eve's and Sara's fall down the stairs), he is working on the large, black form of a whale, which dominates the composition and symbolises the painting's power to swallow Gulley as if he were the Biblical Jonah. In the novel's final scene, whale and wall become one as the fabric of the building cracks open under the paint, and the spectacle of Gulley as the mad artist is revealed to a waiting audience of curious onlookers, reminiscent of figures in a Stanley Spencer painting:

> And just then the whale smiled. Her eyes grew bigger and brighter and she bent slowly forward as if she wanted to kiss me. ... And all at once the smile broke in half, the eyes crumpled, and the whole wall fell slowly away from my brush. ... When the dust began to clear I saw through the cloud about ten thousand angels in caps, helmets, bowlers and even one top hat, sitting on walls, dustbins, gutters, roofs, window sills and other people's cabbages, laughing. That's funny I thought, they've all seen the same joke. God bless them. It must be a work of eternity, a chestnut, a horse-laugh.[37]

For Adorno and Horkheimer in *Dialectic of Enlightenment*, laughter marks the triumph of the culture industry over art: 'Laughter ... always occurs when some fear passes ... It is the echo of power as something inescapable':

> To laugh at something is always to deride it, and the life which ... in laughter breaks through the barrier, is actually an invading barbaric life, self-assertion prepared to parade its liberation from any scruple should the social occasion arise. Such a laughing audience is a parody of humanity.[38]

As his art crumbles, Gulley seems to be transmuted into mere entertainment, like the cartoon character who (in Adorno and Horkheimer's terms) epitomises barbaric mass culture by demonstrating that 'the breaking down of all individual resistance is the condition of life in this society'.[39] Gulley's fall creates a dialectic of laughter, the hilarity of his audience echoing the 'horse-laugh' of eternal artistic divinity and turning the masses into 'ten thousand angels' who, like Benjamin's description of the Angel of History, are onlookers to an inevitable pile-up of rubble.[40] This fatal encounter, in which wall, mural and artist are simultaneously destroyed, coincides with the collapse of materiality and produces a shattering moment of revelation, a glimpse of the semantic fluidity in which art and meaning are eternally deferred. Gulley's attempts to bluff, evade and negotiate his way through a commodity system could be read as a protest *against* reification: as Adorno and Horkheimer argue, only through imprecision and semantic fluidity can an alternative to the deadening conformity of enlightenment rationality be glimpsed. Thus, Gulley's artistic vision becomes garbled and fragile in the process of taking material form, and this final gesture towards ambiguity enables his art to escape the instrumentality of mere representation. Yet as an artist, Gulley's brush with inhumanity does not offer him redemption, but aligns him with atrocity.

The novel finishes with Gulley seriously ill in hospital, muttering to an uncomprehending nurse that laughter is the same as prayer. His transcendental epiphany at the brink of death coincides with the impending loss of his own materiality: matter, for Gulley, turns out to be a matter of death, not life. But it is not just Gulley's life, art and autonomous selfhood that are at stake at this threshold moment: culture itself is confronting the onset of war and the material wreckage it will cause. Gulley's apprehension of art as essentially a violent attempt to wrestle abstraction into materiality extends to claiming authorship of the impending conflagration. 'For me to paint a wall on any building,' he says as he begins work on the chapel painting, 'is as good as asking it to catch fire, or get struck by lightning, or fall down. And as this thing I'm doing is the biggest I've done yet, it will probably bring up an earthquake or a European war, and wreck half the town.'[41] While Gulley races to complete *The Creation* before he is arrested for Sara's murder, and before the chapel's demolition is completed, the reader perceives another looming deadline – the declaration of war and the Blitz, which really will 'wreck half the town'.

'All wars are due to modern art … That's the trouble. It's a disturbing influence,' Gulley says, ascribing the rise of fascism to the fact that Hitler 'never could put up with modern art. It's against his convictions.'[42] Yet shockingly, by the end of the novel, he has become so engulfed by his own totalising aesthetic that he wants to incorporate Hitler's gaze into his final, death-dealing mural. 'All at once I saw Hitler's blue eyes fixed on me. So that's it, I thought. Yes, that's what the whale's wanted all the time.'[43] This contradiction – Hitler is opposed to modern art, and yet essential to Gulley's definition of it – not only confirms Cary's profound distaste for his protagonist, but pinpoints the superannuation of interwar definitions of modernism and modernity as the battleground of mid-century ideology. In his Epilogue to 'The Work of Art in the Age of Its Technological Reproducibility', Walter Benjamin countered the Futurists' manifesto of '*Fiat ars – pereat mundus*' (Let there be art – let the world perish) with the charge that mankind's 'self-alienation has reached such a degree that it can experience its own destruction as an aesthetic pleasure'.[44] In Gulley, Cary creates a portrait of the artist as alienated both from his own humanity and from pleasure itself. He sees art's annihilating power as analogous to fascism because both are doomed attempts to manifest abstract concepts, and by implication must end in violent, destructive failure. If, as Benjamin pointed out, fascism does not so much despise modern art as create it through its nihilistic interventions, then trivialisation and laughter may be the most effective antidote. Gulley's assessment of the man he calls 'Artist Hitler' provides a provocative gloss on modernism as aestheticised violence. 'He's got ideas that chap,' he says. 'And he wants to see them on the wall.'[45]

'AN IVY-CLAD RUIN IN THE FOREGROUND': THE MURALS OF *BRIDESHEAD REVISITED*

Evelyn Waugh's *Brideshead Revisited* is another story of a painter who makes pictures on walls only to see his art threatened by the impermanence of its material context. Its milieu is far removed from the dosshouses frequented by Gulley Jimson, yet it is just as haunted by death and destruction. It is, indeed, haunted by ruins, both actual and potential, and both literal and metaphorical. At the beginning of the novel, Charles Ryder, the bourgeois agnostic who has struggled all his adult life to read the indecipherable codes of the aristocratic and Catholic Marchmain family, arrives at their house, Brideshead Castle, with his army unit, unaware until that moment that the house he once knew as a bastion of elite privilege has been commandeered for war-use. The scenes set in 1944 frame the main narrative of the novel, and lend an elegiac air to Charles's first-person narration of his youthful friendship with the alcoholic Sebastian Flyte and his later engagement to Sebastian's sister Julia. The shoddy current state of the house is contrasted with the baroque glories of its heyday earlier in the century; the ruin of Brideshead crystallises the growing hostility to modernity which Charles has internalised over the years, as he has succumbed to the allure of the Marchmains' traditions and beliefs.

It is telling that he first finds his artistic vocation, as a young student in the 1920s, while painting a mural of a gothic ruin in a disused garden room at Brideshead – a room which was itself now 'derelict'.[46] Like Gulley Jimson, Charles finds artists' materials taking on an uncanny autonomy at the moment when inspiration strikes: first a tin of old paints appears in the room and gives him the idea of decorating the walls; and when he begins he finds that 'the brush seemed somehow to do what was wanted of it'.[47] Charles is not attempting to access a lofty stratum of metaphysical truth with his art, but instead seeks to tether in material form a vision of the picturesque, creating a wistful mural of hermetically sealed unreality featuring 'a landscape without figures, a summer scene of white cloud and blue distances with an ivy-clad ruin in the foreground'.[48]

In the novel's final chapter Charles learns that this room has been ruined for a second time: his commanding officer comments that 'it was a signal office and they made absolute hay of it; rather a shame'.[49] Like all muralists, Charles must accept the symbiosis between his supposedly timeless ruinscape and the temporal exigencies of its context. Mural-painting epitomises the immersive possibilities of material art – which can superimpose one location and temporality onto the fabric of another – but also its fragility. While the building stands, a mural creates a counterfactual parallel space to trick the eye; but should the building fall, the trick fails and the illusory vistas are snuffed out along with the fantasy of timelessness which they are meant to suggest. The eternity Charles wants to access is entirely different from the sublime vision experienced by Gulley during his near-death epiphany. Charles, in contrast, is engaged in an anti-modern project to create a well delineated but counterfactual reality, in which aristocratic privilege and taste will not be demolished by time.

As Waugh concedes in his preface to the 1959 edition, however, the novel's intended theme – the supposedly imminent ruination of the kind of house that Brideshead represents – never in fact transpired, thanks to the National Trust and a turn in post-war fashion towards the nostalgic:

> It was impossible to foresee, in the spring of 1944, the present cult of the English country house. It seemed then that the ancestral seats which were our chief national artistic achievement were doomed to decay and spoliation like the monasteries in the sixteenth century.[50]

Waugh is sheepish about the novel's overwhelming nostalgia for an architectural legacy he assumed would soon disappear, but which, embarrassingly, persisted into the post-war period. 'I piled it on rather, with passionate sincerity,' he admits. 'Much of this book ... is a panegyric preached over an empty coffin.'[51] In hindsight, he presents the novel itself as an anachronistic curio:

> It would be impossible to bring it up to date without totally destroying it. It is offered to a younger generation of readers as a souvenir of the Second World War rather than of the twenties and thirties, with which it ostensibly deals.[52]

Thus, like the buildings whose demise he anticipated, the book is overlaid with a sense of its own potential or actual ruin; its destruction has been averted, but only through a temporal sleight of hand, so that it becomes a memorial of a more complex kind, with the once-urgent moment of its creation folded into the sense of general nostalgia. The extra-textual post-hoc analysis contained in Waugh's preface tacitly acknowledges the dialectic of ruin and nostalgia which runs through the novel; historical linearity turns out to be circular. As modern war creates new kinds of ruins and a new attitude to the past, the very idea of ruins – and their symbolic correlative – is threatened with superannuation.

By mentioning sixteenth-century monasteries, Waugh draws an explicit comparison between the demolished country seats of the aristocracy and the gothic ruins of the Romantic imagination – the kind of ruins Charles painted onto Brideshead's walls. In his mature artistic career, he also paints ruins, but ruins which haven't yet come into being: he specialises in capturing the likenesses of large houses which have been earmarked for demolition or redevelopment, beginning with Marchmain House, the London home of Sebastian's family. This first house painting is as important for his aesthetic development as the first garden-room mural, and once again, Charles is temporarily transported out of self-consciousness as the paints begin to work autonomously:

> I could do nothing wrong, At the end of each passage I paused, tense, afraid to start the next, fearing, like a gambler, that luck must turn and the pile be lost. Bit by bit, minute by minute, the thing came into being. There were no difficulties; the intricate multiplicity of light and colour became a whole; the right colour was where I wanted it on the palette; each brush stroke, as soon as it was complete, seemed to have been there always.[53]

His inspiration comes from the fact that he is working 'against time, for the contractors were only waiting for the final signature to start their work of destruction'.[54] Yet as his fame as a house-painter grows, this antagonism towards time binds him into the very progress of destruction which he deplores:

> I was called to all parts of the country to make portraits of houses that were soon to be deserted or debased; indeed, my arrival seemed often to be only a few paces ahead of the auctioneer's, a presage of doom.[55]

Charles is caught in a temporal paradox; by seeking to arrest progress and lock himself into an archaic fantasy, he becomes an unwilling harbinger of modernity. He goes in search of a gothic ahistoricity, hoping to engage with a past aesthetic that might persist into the present. But he cannot call it into being at will because he is too determined to pin it down; instead he encounters something more uncanny – the agency of his own painting materials and of other objects – but is blind to its import. His failure as a mid-century artist arises from his unwillingness to understand the new gothicism, in which the objects of modernity, as abject and unauthenticated as they may be, can engage the human subject in accessing a new kind of meaning about the circularity of time and history. No wonder that, in despair, he decides to leave this successful house-painting career behind to seek alternative ruins which are – in his narrow terms – properly distant, both in time and space. Travelling in Central America, Charles

> sought inspiration among gutted palaces and cloisters embowered in weed, derelict churches where the vampire bats hung in the dome like dry seed-pods and only the ants were ceaselessly astir tunnelling in the rich stalls; cities where no road led, and mausoleums where a single, agued family of Indians sheltered from the rains.[56]

As Marina MacKay points out in *Modernism and World War II*, the only character in *Brideshead* who remains unconvinced by Ryder's colonial neo-Romanticism is the 'modernist survivor' Anthony Blanche, who first appears in the novel broadcasting Eliot's 'The Waste Land' from an open window, and who glories in his outsider status as a homosexual who is 'part Gallic, part Yankee, part, perhaps, Jew; wholly exotic'.[57] He is Ryder's only critic, decrying his gentlemanly art for its dead-eyed insularity, and comparing it to 'a dean's daughter in flowered muslin'.[58] He cuts straight to the inauthenticity of Ryder's attempt at exotic gothicism, calling it 't-t-terrible t-t-tripe' ('Where, my dear Charles, did you find this sumptuous greenery? The corner of a hothouse at T-t-trent or T-t-tring?').[59] MacKay finds Waugh's simultaneous sympathy both for Charles's nostalgia and for Blanche's contempt 'perverse' and the sign of a novel 'rebelling against itself', and arguably this conflict is a factor of the mid-century moment in which it was created.[60] Charles adopts the air of a 'would-be modernist' though there is little evidence of this modernism in the novel;[61] as MacKay notes, he is paralysed by his inability to come to terms with progress. His love for Julia is bound up with his desire to possess Brideshead as an aristocratic time-capsule: his wish to marry her only arises with the revelation that she, not her brother, will inherit the house. Even sexual intercourse with Julia is described, chillingly, in terms of house ownership: 'It was as though a deed of conveyance of her narrow loins had been drawn and sealed,' Charles muses. 'I was making my first entry as the freeholder of the property I would enjoy and develop at leisure.'[62]

Yet he loses the deeds to both Julia and Brideshead by the end of the novel, robbed by the very tradition which so beguiles him: Julia rejects him in favour of a return to Catholicism. At this moment, Charles finally capitulates his one remaining modern attitude, the agnosticism which has defined him and which has set him apart from the family. Charles loses something once central to his identity, but finds comfort in his newfound faith because through it he can finally access eternity and escape from time. He has been battling time ever since he came to Brideshead and was overwhelmed by the tantalising inaccessibility of the past, which persists in the objects and fabric of the building but cannot be experienced except by an imaginative dissociation from the haptic present, with all its urgent bodily and material requirements. The property motif finds its way into his experience of the onset of religion, too: in an extended metaphor, Charles imagines the emergence of Julia's (and ultimately his own) faith through the image of a hut engulfed in an avalanche:

> Quite silently a great weight forming against the timber; the bolt straining in its socket; minute by minute in the darkness outside the white heap sealing the door, until quite soon when the wind dropped and the sun came out on the ice slopes and the thaw set in a block would move, slide, and tumble, high above, gather weight, till the whole hillside seemed to be falling, and the little lighted place would open and splinter and disappear, rolling with the avalanche into the ravine.[63]

This brutal wipe-out leaves no ruin behind. Through Catholicism, Charles hopes – like Gulley Jimson – to be released from materialism, not through a vision of the sublime but by walling himself into a frozen version of history.

The contemporary ruins of the Blitz are curiously absent from this 'souvenir of the Second World War', but they make a tangential appearance, perhaps, in Charles's disgusted contemplation of a half completed housing estate, which he sees through the gaze of a future archaeologist:

> The Pollock diggings provide a valuable link between the citizen-slave communities of the twentieth century and the tribal anarchy which succeeded them. Here you see a people of advanced culture, capable of an elaborate draining system and the construction of permanent highways, over-run by a race of the lowest type.[64]

These unfinished buildings appear like bombsites, porous and readable, but what Charles sees there is not the glory of a lost civilisation but a hollow reduction of modern culture to mere systems of waste disposal and transport, while his snobbish (and indeed racist) disgust at the 'tribal' beings into which he imagines humanity will degenerate is reminiscent of H.G. Wells's time traveller encountering the barely human Morlocks of the distant future. As is fitting for a character who wishes to reverse time so that he might become a present-day ghost who haunts the past, his vision of the destruction of humanity does not have to wait for an apocalypse in the distant future because it has, to all intents and purposes, already happened. Charles ends the book drifting around Brideshead like a ghost, muttering '*Quo modo sedet sola civitas* [how lonely the city stands]. Vanity of vanity, all is vanity.'[65]

'A PLACE OF STILLNESS, A PLACE APART': HUGH CASSON AND THE BOMBED CHURCHES OF LONDON

While Charles Ryder was vilifying the suburban schemes which had been interrupted by the war, an idealistic young technical officer at the Ministry of Town and Country Planning was busy drawing up more plans for cheap, quick solutions to the housing crisis. But Hugh Casson was, in his way, also preoccupied with ruins. In 1945, several years before his emergence as a respected architect, he wrote an illustrated booklet called *Bombed Churches as War Memorials*.[66] It elaborated an idea which had first been proposed the year before in the *Architectural Review*, and was supported by a letter to *The Times* signed by, among others, John Maynard Keynes and T.S. Eliot – namely, that a number of war-damaged City of London churches should be selected for preservation as ruins, with gardens designed around them which would provide urban spaces for 'relaxation, contemplation and remembrance'.[67]

The fact that he assumed they would not simply be rebuilt and used for worship indicates how far the role of churches, bombed or not, was changing at this time. Nine years later in 1954, Philip Larkin would write 'Church Going' in which he wondered 'When churches fall completely out of use | What we shall turn them into' and then concluded, much like Casson, that people would still haunt these places of 'grass, weedy pavement, brambles, buttress, sky' because they are somehow 'proper to grow wise in, | If only that so many dead lie round'.[68]

The church, as we have seen, is a common motif in these mid-century ruin-narratives: the deconsecration of Lady Marchmain's Art Deco chapel at Brideshead, for instance, marks a key point in Waugh's novel, while in the last scene, set in 1944, Charles finds comfort in the reanimation of the chapel, which now shelters 'a Blitzed RC padre ... jittery old bird, but no trouble' who conducts masses for any soldiers, including Ryder, who want to worship.[69] A similarly jittery blitzed priest will haunt the ruins of Rose Macaulay's *The World My Wilderness* – discussed later in this chapter – and find no comfort there; but both the elaborate chapel at Brideshead – all 'angels in printed cotton smocks, rambler-roses, flower-spangled meadows, frisking lambs, texts in Celtic script, saints in armour'[70] – and the derelict chapel reduced to rubble by the uncanny power of Gulley Jimson's *Creation* in *The Horse's Mouth*, attest to the affinity of spaces which house art and religion. Church architecture, like art, attempts to materialise an abstraction, and thus sits in a dangerously liminal zone where ideas are transubstantiated into things. Like Cary and Macaulay, Casson placed ruined churches at the vanguard of a new approach to meaning and memory. As Gaston Bachelard wrote in *The Poetics of Space* (1958): 'Space contains compressed time. That is what space is for.'[71] He was theorising domestic rather than public space, but his concept of topoanalysis – 'the systematic psychological study of the sites of our intimate lives' – is just as applicable to the idea that church ruins could provide both a material link with personal memories, and a sanctuary in which to house them.[72] The war and its ruins haunt Bachelard's notion of domesticity and homeliness as an absent presence; Casson's pamphlet was an attempt to devise new architectural treatments of bombsites within a process of cathexis for traumatised Londoners, reframing them in a way that anticipates Bachelard's argument that, in material spaces, 'our memories have refuges ... All our lives we come back to them in our daydreams'.[73]

The *Bombed Churches* pamphlet was part of a wider acculturation of London's new bombscapes. Elizabeth Bowen was already incorporating ruins into the psychic landscapes of characters struggling to come to terms with peace (discussed in detail in Chapter 3), while Lorenza Mazzetti's *Together* (1956) (discussed in Chapter 2) and the Ealing comedy *Hue and Cry* (1947) commandeered bombsites as playgrounds of imaginative possibility.[74] Casson's crucial point was that the transformation of bombed churches into war memorials should involve a transformation of the object-witnesses of the Blitz – the fallen stones themselves – into a particular type of art: 'Preservation ... involves an understanding of the ruin *as* a ruin, and its re-creation as a work of art in its own right, keeping the essential forms but enhancing them with an imaginative and appropriate background.'[75] This definition of art implicitly rejects the model suggested by the Duchampian readymade, for instance – ruins are not 'found', but are to be understood as art only once they have been 'enhanced' by the application of a carefully designed contextual frame. Like the neo-Romantic artist John Piper, who created a series of melancholy, enigmatic bombsite paintings, Casson's ruins are not to be perceived as modernist harbingers of upheaval and atomisation, but as the kind of Romantic objects Charles Ryder would have recognised, in which the sublime, the picturesque and the gothic coalesce. Yet the ruins of London in 1945 were not isolated, distant features in visual dialogue with nature, but part of an extensive and ugly streetscape of rubble; and they did not provide imaginative access to the sweep of history through the longevity of their survival, but offered a snapshot of a moment of sudden, recent devastation. Casson nevertheless insists that they partake of the charisma of 'creepered and bird-haunted' places like Tintern Abbey or Raglan Castle:

> Even though a ruin to-day is as common a feature of the street scene as a pillar-box, it still has this power to stir the heart. Even though we live and work among ruins, they still possess the beauty of strangeness.[76]

Just as nature provides a backdrop which enhances the impact of old ruins, Casson imagines that a new material context will enhance the strangeness of the bombed churches once the city has been rebuilt around them:

> Against the scale of our century the churches would acquire a new meaning as monuments, small, intimate, and informal, contrasting frankly and not competing with the giant facades surrounding them. The simplicity of the modern style of building is particularly suitable to act as a screen against which old buildings with their more intricate and more human forms look their best.[77]

Thus the churches' aesthetic legitimacy – which contradicts their practical redundancy – depends on the shortcomings of modernity: like Waugh, Casson fears that the future city may have no room for ancient architecture; it is taken for granted that the gigantic new buildings surrounding the ruined churches will be anything but intimate or human, and will need to have their bombastic blankness softened by contiguity with something old and intricate.

Casson argues that the new city must make room for the past within aestheticised 'communal' spaces which must not, for all their communality, succumb to everyday banality.

> In its neighbourhood then should be placed the memorial, close enough to be touched by the friendly atmosphere, but not so near that its quiet is disturbed by the bustle of daily life. A memorial should not be remote, but it should be withdrawn a little from the noise and distractions of human contacts. It should be a place of stillness, a place apart.[78]

This memorial space replaces acts of worship with a different form of imaginative and emotional work. As well as remembrance, the purpose of this space is to absorb trauma – to circumscribe and contain it and, by materialising it outside the suffering human subject, to cathect it. This is not an act of forgetting; indeed, the very language Casson uses emphasises continuity with the painful past. The 'stillness' of the memorial space recalls the motionlessness of death, while its 'apartness' evokes, not only physical separation, but also fragmentation, the memory of buildings and lives falling apart under bombardment, which is also materialised literally in the ruins themselves. The very stones become uncanny cyphers for human suffering: 'They are aloof,' he writes, 'but have not lost contact with us, and with us they have undergone the physical trials of war, and bear its scars.'[79] For Casson, this function is even more important than religion because these object witnesses are inoculated against time and contingency by the very fact that they continue to exist. A church is, he argues, 'even when scarred and broken, a piece of architecture, sometimes perhaps a masterpiece. Every stone – whether fallen or in place – is a fragment of the past, part of the pattern of history.'[80] Art, architecture and spirituality are conjoined here to a particular definition of history structured by an underlying anti-teleological rationale. It is not just the scars of war that Casson's aloof stones must bear witness to: modernity itself is destroying old masterpieces. In 1948, Casson published an article (with G.M. Kallmann) called 'Metropolis in Transition' which described the changing demography of London brought about by new transport links and ribbon developments stretching out into the suburbs. He blames urban sprawl on 'building societies, and the BBC ... chain stores and 50-shilling suits ... cinemas and the Green Lane' and mourns the fact that 'London stretches over most of SE England. Metropolis has become Metroland.'[81] Moreover, the article claims that London's transformation involves a shift towards the material objects of mass culture and away from the fetishised, metaphysical commodities of a bourgeois, 'Metropolitan', economy presided over by a middle-class elite of which Casson might well count himself a member:

> Metropolitan activities ... are largely of the mind. They are concerned with the abstract notions of business and finance, with the ramifications of politics, with fashion, entertainment and learning. The carrier of city culture is the intellectual, the aesthete, the professional man, and the politician.[82]

For Casson (like T.S. Eliot in *Notes Towards the Definition of Culture*), culture must be mediated – indeed aestheticised – by an elite if it is not to lose touch with its proper purpose. He describes, in *Bombed Churches*, the kind of time-honoured communal space he hopes to emulate, in which a fantasy of social cohesion and harmony exists because it has arisen organically from within the community:

> Every city and village has some such place which has been naturally selected by those who live there as a focus and meeting-place for the community. It may be the city square, it may be a certain group of trees, or just a patch of well-worn grass. It

is a place chosen, as a rule, not for its beauty but for its associations. The children play there, the young people meet there, the old remember it.[83]

The political assumptions underpinning this idyllic scene are revealed, however, when it is set beside a description of Leicester Square in the 1948 article, which acts as a gloss for the rose-tinted nostalgia of the earlier pamphlet:

> The monstrous club-foot of the Odeon towers over Leicester Square where all the visual horrors of the modern metropolitan scene can be found in their most degraded form. Against this fantastic scenery of neon and hoardings, even the trees seem an unwelcome intrusion and the patch of trampled grass, hemmed in by the circling traffic, becomes a corral for morons instead of a promenade for citizens.[84]

Placing this reactionary polemic beside the romanticism of *Bombed Churches* highlights Casson's contempt for the 'degraded' mass of human subjects who might intrude upon his bourgeois vision of the ruins. Indeed, in many of the illustrations that accompany his essay in the pamphlet, human figures are absent, or retreat to the margins of the spaces. Romantic ruins, he reminds us, are places we have traditionally 'made expeditions' to; they maintain their sublimity by shrugging off the human desire to inhabit and define them. Casson's post-war church-ruin-garden-memorials are similarly to be grasped by the mind, as a symbol of remembrance – not necessarily experienced directly by bodily occupation, and definitely not trampled by the masses.

The spectral quality of these spaces is addressed more generously in the pamphlet's final section, written by Czech émigré Jacques Groag, and detailing his suggested architectural treatment of St Anne's in Soho. While Casson had depicted the churches as largely depopulated spaces, Groag's sketches contain numerous human figures, shown relaxing on a bench or leaning over a balustrade to contemplate a water feature, chin in hands. People are especially visible in the interior views, in which mournful, shadowy figures haunt the memorial chapel housed in the ruin's basement. In his design, this is approached via a low-ceilinged, dark passage covered with a mural which 'should have some of the terror of medieval cycles of the Dance of Death: death in battle, death in the midst of pleasure, death coming suddenly from the sky, and death coming as a solace to the wounded'.[85] The figures in the mural and the living visitors are sketched in the same scale and with a similar vagueness, so that they merge together, emphasising the elision of life and death, artwork and subject, within this dark, crypt-like space punctured with sudden shafts of daylight from above.

In the end, St Anne's was not remodelled as a memorial ruin, and nor were the other churches alluded to in the pamphlet. Casson's idea had numerous opponents, including the distinguished architect Herbert Baker, who had designed a number of war cemeteries and memorials after the

1914–18 conflict. In a letter to *The Times* he condemned the idea outright, arguing that 'a war memorial should lift up our thoughts to the hills of loving remembrance' while 'a war-blasted church left in ruins would surely lower them to the inferno where hate and revenge dwell'.[86] Another correspondent to *The Times*, L. Munday, called such preserved ruins 'a morbid commemoration of a successful assault by the forces of evil upon the Christian faith' and suggested that, 'surmounting the wreckage, the only appropriate finial would be the swastika in substitution of the overthrown cross'.[87] The church authorities, meanwhile, largely ignored the proposal. The Bishop of London's Commission on the Future of the City Churches produced a report in 1946 which placed the twenty bombed churches of the Square Mile into three categories: eleven were to be restored, five should be demolished and the land sold, and four should be demolished and the sites used for alternative church purposes 'with the primary object of administering to the needs of youth'.[88]

Yet some church ruins *were* preserved as war memorials; most famously, a new Coventry Cathedral was built beside the bombed remains of the old. Even among the City of London churches, room was finally found for fragments of preserved ruins, although not in any schematic way: the churchyards of Christchurch Greyfriars, St Dunstan-in-the-East and St Swithun London Stone remain as public gardens, as does the footprint of St Mary Aldermanbury, although that church's ruins were transported wholesale to Fulton, Missouri in 1966, where they were rebuilt as a memorial to Churchill. Other remnants have been adapted for modern use: useable parts of Christchurch Greyfriars and St Augustine Watling Street were listed for preservation in 1950, and the tower of St Alban Wood Street is now a private home, and sits alone on a traffic island, dwarfed by office blocks, perhaps belatedly fulfilling Casson's vision of an intimate antiquity in dialogue with the inhuman scale of its modern context – and only to be experienced directly by the privileged few.

'THE NATURE OF THE WALL'S SURFACE': RUINS AS REFUGE IN *THE WORLD MY WILDERNESS*

By coincidence, the same artist – Barbara Jones – illustrated the covers of both Casson's *Bombed Churches* pamphlet and the first edition of Rose Macaulay's post-war novel set amid London's bombsites, *The World My Wilderness*.[89] Jones's work as a curator is examined in the next chapter, but these illustrations demonstrate that she had a keen eye for the combination of horror and mundanity which characterised blitzed bombsites and also informed her practice as a collector. Both covers are deceptively simple pen-and-wash sketches which combine the immediacy of contemporaneous record with a romantically idealised vision of sunlit and picturesque decay. Macaulay's novel contains a crucial scene which takes place in a bombed City of London church, St Giles Cripplegate – one of a number of ruins adopted as an alternative home by a population of drifters and troublemakers. These include the novel's teenage protagonist, Barbary, who has been transplanted into London from her wild, barefoot childhood in Provence, and who is traumatised in equal measure by her experiences at the fringes of the French resistance, her guilt over her collaborationist stepfather's execution, and by this sudden attempt to turn her into a civilised English art student.

Rose Macaulay would have agreed with the critics of Casson's scheme; 'bombed churches and cathedrals', she wrote in *The Pleasure of Ruins* (1953), give us 'nothing but resentful sadness'.[90] Her own house was destroyed by an incendiary bomb in 1941, and she felt that the Blitz had changed the meaning of ruins for her contemporaries:

> *Ruinenlust* has come full circle: we have had our fill. Ruin pleasure must be at one remove, softened by art ... or centuries of time. Ruin must be a fantasy, veiled by the mind's dark imaginings: in the objects that we see before us, we get to agree with St Thomas Aquinas that *quae enim diminutae sunt, hoc ipso turpia sunt* [things that are lacking in something are thereby unsightly], and to feel that, in beauty, wholeness is all.[91]

She admits, however, that these 'wholesome hankerings' may simply be 'a phase of our fearful and fragmented age', and she balances two temporal perspectives in her account of contemporary bombsites.[92] In the present, they lack meaning, displaying only a 'catastrophic tipsy chaos'. They seem promiscuously candid and available, buildings broken apart by bombs offering the cheap melodrama of a 'domestic scene wide open for all to enjoy'.[93] She follows the gaze of spectators who have come to witness the interiors of a 'drab little house' transformed into something 'bright and intimate like a Dutch picture or a stage set' and who are both fascinated and repelled by the idea that they too may undergo such a squalid – or perversely glamorous – transformation:

> Tomorrow or tonight, the gazers feel, their own dwelling may be even as this. Last night the house was scenic; flames leaping to the sky; today it is squalid and *morne*, but out of its dereliction it flaunts the flags of what is left.[94]

In contrast to this chaotic and conflicted rush of emotion, she looks forward to a future time when human lives will be irrelevant and 'the ruin will be enjungled, engulfed' as 'trees [thrust] through the empty window sockets'. She writes: 'All this will presently be; but at first there is only the ruin; a mass of torn, charred prayer books strew the stone floor; the statues, tumbled from their niches, have broken in pieces; rafters and rubble pile knee-deep.'[95] In *The World My Wilderness*, Macaulay presents London, through the eyes of Barbary, as if this 'enjungling' had already taken place. But Barbary is, like Charles Ryder, on the run from history; she may not haunt these spaces, as he does, as a would-be time traveller seeking an aesthetic and conceptual conduit to the past, but instead she sets herself up as the prototype of a new type of ruin-dweller who might inhabit the stones in an eternal future tense which does not require her to undergo any process of recuperation and renewal.

As an artist, Barbary refuses to make any claims about meaning in art; she can't take her studies at the Slade seriously but likes to paint postcards of bombsites to sell to the citizens who come to gawp at them. Like Gulley Jimson, she paints a mural on a church wall, but this intervention takes place long after the building's ruin, rather than bringing it about, and lacks any of the destructive power of Gulley's paintbrush:

> Barbary and Raoul stood before the east wall, whereon a Judgment Day painting now faintly burgeoned: God the Father, with the blessed souls smiling on his right hand, on his left the wicked damned taking off for the leap into the flames. They were pleased with this painting, which had admirable clarity of design, though, owing to the nature of the wall's surface, the colours did not stand out very distinctly.[96]

Later in the same scene, an agitated vicar suddenly enters the church and insists on saying mass – a service which ends with an anguished sermon about his own personal hell:

> Fire creeps on me from all sides; I am trapped in the prison of my sins ... The flames press on; they will consume my body, but my soul will live on in hell, forever damned ... Trapped, trapped, trapped there is no hope ... For this is hell, hell, hell.[97]

A younger clergyman arrives and explains that Father Roger has been traumatised by being pinned under a beam in his burning church. 'I'm afraid he frightened you,' he apologises. 'No,' Barbary replies. 'Not more than I was already.'[98] Without access to her own history and the chance to come to terms with it, Barbary lives in a state of perpetual fear; unlike in Casson's pamphlet, the burnt-out church is not a sanctuary or a site of therapeutic remembrance, but an actively frightening place which threatens to trap its inhabitants in a perpetual loop of unresolved trauma. Like Sansom's fireman, this clergyman understands that walls enclose a space where you can be 'trapped, trapped, trapped' and find yourself erased from the world; but for Barbary, the aftermath of catastrophe is a space of freedom, full of voids and absences. Barbary's solution to trauma is to accept this sense of emotional and physical wilderness, just as she and Raoul accept that 'the nature of the wall's surface' – its pocked and fire-blasted ruination – will define their painting of Judgement Day.

The novel's vivid descriptions of London's shattered post-war landscape as an enchanted jungle of weeds and greenery empties them of people and any sense of urban life: when Macaulay writes that 'the paths ran like streams and the ravines were deep in dripping greenery that grew high and rank running over the ruins as the jungle runs over Maya temples, hiding them from prying eyes' she is herself painting a kind of mural on top of the bombsites, creating a counterfactual space-within-a-space and turning a few overgrown streets into a vast landscape. Like the Mexican ruins among which Charles Ryder attempted to find some essence of ahistoric profundity, Macaulay's fecund bomb sites have a hellish quality of damp decay, reflecting Barbary's perception of herself as a lost sinner without hope of redemption. Yet she is willing to embrace novel forms of escapism, as long as they do not demand any self-examination or acknowledgment of her troubled past; indeed, her perception that the ruins are a place where 'one belongs more'[99] makes her more, not less, amenable to the idea of turning herself into a consumer, the ideal prototype of emotionally unencumbered ahistoricity. Naturally, however, she accesses this new realm of nihilism via criminal rather than economic activity. She is egged on in this project by a street-smart shoplifter called Mavis. Disguised under a thick layer of make-up, Barbary trawls a department store for things she might steal in order to create a new sense of a future in which history and authenticity will no longer exist:

> She saw much. Galaxies of desirable objects, glittering into the focus of attainability, shone with a new moonish lustre, as of fruit ripe for plucking and within reach. They slid like dropping peaches into her bag ... She was carried away by the bounty of opportunity and the ease of performance.[100]

Barbary's physical transformation into the painted image of a consumer with 'rouge on her cheeks, crimson lipstick on her mouth, and scarlet polish on her nails' is a carefully staged illusion; like Sansom's sense of Blitz 'pantomime' or Macaulay's own description of bombsites as a 'stage set', Barbary understands instinctively that these transitional places require a greasepaint performance. The sense of lush possibility she finds at the shops echoes the alien fecundity of the bombsites, and her newfound acquisitiveness is real: 'Barbary said she would like to keep some of the things, such as a musical-box, a yellow scarf decorated with black kittens, a paint-box, a canary with a whistle, a cushion with a handle, and a small alarm clock.'[101] Suddenly burdened by possessions which might be lost or stolen, she calls on the 'sly secrecy of the maquis' and hides them among the ruins;[102] and Macaulay pauses at this crucial turning point for an extended meditation on the commercial history of the streets through which Barbary travels with her stolen goods, reflecting that they had recently been 'stately with ingenious men who had manufactured hats, mats, ties, underwear, accounting books, typewriters, fancy goods, gloves and buttons';[103] these merchants have been 'blown sky high' and in their place 'the new traders, the pirates, the racketeers, the black marketeers, the robber bands, roam and lurk'.¹⁰⁴ Indeed, it quickly transpires that Barbary's wartime cunning will be no match for the blunt bullying tactics of the spiv Horace, who has followed her to her hiding place and effortlessly relieves her of her spoils.

Barbary has learnt a sharp lesson about post-war consumerism: things 'glittering into the focus of attainability' may prove as ephemeral as the commodities 'blown sky high' by the war. Barbary's drift from the anarchism of the unmediated ruins to the trap of consumerism and the lure of objects of desire leaves her little choice but to retreat even further into her fantasy that she is still in Provence and on the run from the Gestapo, rather than fleeing British policemen hunting for spivs and shoplifters. When Barbary undergoes her own seemingly inevitable fall, 'plung[ing] steeply down a chasm into the stony ruins of a deep cellar', it is not – like Gulley Jimson's – an epiphanic escape from materiality, but a definitive re-entry into the world of things:

> [She] lay still beneath a thorn apple bush, among the medieval foundations of Messrs. Foster, Crockett and Porter's warehouse. They – Messrs. Foster, Crockett and Porter – had been used to make surgical instruments, which were what she would now require.¹⁰⁵

'EXPLODING THE REGATTA RESTAURANT': MURALS AT THE FESTIVAL OF BRITAIN

When Macaulay's novel was published, plans were already well advanced to channel the memories of blitzed citizens into the desires of modern consumers on a population-wide scale, via the South Bank Exhibition of the 1951 Festival of Britain. Six years after his work on *Bombed Churches*, it was Hugh Casson who took on responsibility for the architecture of the Festival. In the 1940s, he had wanted to imagine a new metropolis built on abstract ideas, where a middle-class elite could process the trauma of war via a return to the picturesque and the soothing notion that the past could be preserved in a carefully framed aesthetic space dedicated to memory. By the 1950s, he had realised – or been forced to accept – that London's transformation would be demotic and dynamic, with wartime relics and residues reimagined in a collective *Traumarbeit* which enabled the population to re-embrace the idea of modernity. The Festival pavilions he commissioned combined clean lines and bold forms with exactly the kind of humane details and a friendly sense of proportion and scale which he had warned would be missing from the new builds in the city. Like ruins, these spaces incorporated voids and openings which made them porous and accessible, but unlike the reverent historicism of the *Bombed Churches* proposal, the South Bank site invited not remembrance, but wonder. And whereas Barbary's dreamspace was the site of nightmares, a perpetual future tense in which both past and present were nothing more than traps, the South Bank Exhibition sought to provide its visitors with a sensorium that actualised a progressive future in tangible form.

The Regatta Restaurant, designed by Misha Black, was the first building seen by many visitors crossing from the river's north bank, and it immediately confronted them at point-blank range with an uncompromising architectural statement in International Style, visually detonated by a large-scale spiral mural by Victor Pasmore.[106] Rather than being painted, this design – consisting of graphic black swirls on a white background – had been fired onto ceramic tiles and used as the building's cladding. William Feaver, writing in 1976, called Pasmore's mural 'the most positive contribution by a painter to the South Bank', and described its 'roughcast textures and cosmic overtones' as a key Festival motif.[107] Pasmore had carefully considered the relationship between his work and the building where it would be displayed; he wanted to make a case for 'the purely abstract style' and its 'validity … when brought to bear emotionally on the cubic and utilitarian functionalism of modern architecture'. Disdaining the option of 'reinforcing [the architecture] harmonically by repeating its forms', he wanted to 'transform it optically by means of contrast'.[108] As a recent convert to abstraction, he was rejecting the idea of the figurative mural as a counterfactual scene obscuring its architectural host; instead, he imagined the confrontation between wall and artwork as a moment of crisis – a deliberate statement about fragmentation in a piece Pasmore based on 'the idea of "exploding" the Regatta Restaurant'.[109] For newly landed inhabitants of old London, all this contributed to a kind of defamiliarising cinematic jump-cut from their war-damaged capital into the shiny micro-city of the future, where fragmentation and confusion could be a deliberate design strategy rather than (or as well as) a traumatised Blitz memory. Rather than cling to a Romantic idea of ruin and loss, which must be aestheticised within a picturesque conceptual and physical landscape, the South Bank Exhibition rebooted the idea of an exploded building as a legitimate modern statement about materiality and abstraction.

Around a hundred murals in total were commissioned for the South Bank, most of which were destroyed at the end of the Festival.[110] John Piper's *The Englishman's Home*, which made walls both the subject of the work and its medium, was a rare survivor. Commissioned for the southern façade of the Homes and Gardens Pavilion, the painting shows a collection of monumental buildings – including a Moorish mansion, a Palladian edifice, the suggestion of Tudorbethan gabling and some bricky Victorian gothic – jumbled together in a parade of architectural styles which never quite amount to a sense of wholeness or safety. Inside the pavilion, stylish room-sets staged an ideal of modern domesticity, but outside, the buildings in Piper's mural made a dark statement about the impenetrability of the English mindset. As they soar to the top of the mural, they seem to shoulder each other out of the way, jostling to command the foreground. A dead white tree reaching hand-like into a fiery red sky makes a gothic statement on the left of the picture, and various examples of a fortress aesthetic – railings, turrets, a heraldic shield – remind us that an Englishman's home is a place to be defended at all costs. None of the windows and doors depicted seems to be a real opening, and even in places where perspective suggests you could walk in, the way is barred by thick shadows. A courtyard walled with topiaried yew hedging is filled with swirling murk lightened only by puffs of smoke. And in the sky, adrift amid the gathering storm clouds, hangs a wispy streetscape of back-to-back terraces: this is a statement about class too. If the enigmatic blocks inhabited by the bourgeoisie are all too substantial and impassive, these working-class streets are barely real, clinging precariously to the idea of form as they mingle with the dark and tumbled sky.

Six months later, the South Bank was itself a ruin, the pavilions dismembered and the site sold off to developers. Its passing was publicly mourned by Casson, who appeared in a film, *Brief City*, in which he stalked through the wind-blown debris while reminiscing about the Festival's success.[111] The mournful figure of Casson – contrasted with footage of the crowded Festival in full swing during the summer – emphasises the loneliness of the desolate, wintry site and returns the viewer to the idea that architecture somehow invites its own destruction. In its ruined state, the South Bank completes the cycle begun by the Blitz: it is transformed from a chaotic place of communal possibility into a self-contained unit of space, entirely explicable (at the very moment when it slips into absence) by Casson as the figure of the artist pronouncing magisterially on its definitive meaning. Yet this idea of the human subject describing and defining the art object was already insufficient; as the next chapter will show, objects at this time were beginning to describe, define and materialise missing human subjects in their turn.

NOTES

1 William Sansom, *The Blitz: Westminster at War* (Oxford: Oxford University Press, 1990), pp. 12–13.
2 Sansom, *The Blitz*, p. 75.
3 Sansom, *The Blitz*, pp. 75–76.
4 Leo Mellor, *Reading the Ruins: Modernism, Bombsites and British Culture* (Cambridge: Cambridge University Press, 2011), p. 3.
5 Mellor, *Reading the Ruins*, p. 6.
6 Sansom, *The Blitz*, p. 13.
7 Sansom, *The Blitz*, p. 13.
8 William Sansom, 'Building Alive', in *Something Terrible, Something Lovely* (London: Hogarth Press, 1948), pp. 172–76.
9 Sansom, 'Building Alive', p. 174.
10 Sansom, 'Building Alive', p. 173.
11 Sansom, 'Building Alive', p. 175.

12 William Sansom, 'The Wall', in *Stories* (London: Hogarth Press, 1963), pp. 13–18 (p. 16).
13 Sansom, 'The Wall', p. 14.
14 Sansom, 'The Wall', p. 15.
15 Sansom, 'The Wall', p. 15, emphasis in the original.
16 Sansom, 'The Wall', p. 16.
17 Joyce Cary, *The Horse's Mouth*, in *Triptych* (Harmondsworth: Penguin, 1985), p. 652.
18 Cary, *The Horse's Mouth*, p. 558.
19 Cary, *The Horse's Mouth*, p. 533.
20 Edward H. Kelly, 'The Meaning of "The Horse's Mouth"', *Modern Language Studies*, 1:2 (Summer, 1971), 9–11 (p. 10). The story derives from an account by physician and philosopher Sextus Empiricus in *Outlines of Pyrrhonism*, trans. R.G. Bury (Cambridge, MA: Harvard University Press, 1933), p. 19.
21 See for instance Alvin J. Selzer, 'Speaking Out of Both Sides of "The Horse's Mouth": Joyce Cary vs. Gulley Jimson', *Contemporary Literature* 15:4 (Autumn, 1974), 488–502.
22 Karl Marx and Friedrich Engels, *Manifesto of the Communist Party*, trans. Samuel Moore, section 1, paragraph 18, lines 12–14, www.marxists.org/archive/marx/works/1848/ communist-manifesto/ch01.htm#007 [accessed 28 January 2018].
23 Cary, *The Horse's Mouth*, p. 506.
24 Cary, *The Horse's Mouth*, p. 592.
25 Adorno and Horkheimer, *Dialectic of Enlightenment*, p. 157.
26 Cary, *The Horse's Mouth*, p. 670.
27 Cary, *The Horse's Mouth*, p. 669.
28 Cary, *The Horse's Mouth*, p. 542.
29 Cary, *The Horse's Mouth*, p. 598; p. 599.
30 Cary, *The Horse's Mouth*, p. 598.
31 Cary, *The Horse's Mouth*, p. 597.
32 Cary, *The Horse's Mouth*, p. 598.
33 Cary, *The Horse's Mouth*, p. 674.
34 Cary, *The Horse's Mouth*, p. 739.
35 Cary, *The Horse's Mouth*, p. 718.
36 Cary, *The Horse's Mouth*, p. 653.
37 Cary, *The Horse's Mouth*, p. 766. The description of onlookers as angels may refer obliquely to Spencer's 1920 painting *Christ Carrying The Cross*.
38 Adorno and Horkheimer, *Dialectic of Enlightenment*, pp. 140–41.
39 Adorno and Horkheimer, *Dialectic of Enlightenment*, p. 138.
40 Walter Benjamin, 'Theses on the Philosophy of History', in *Illuminations*, trans. Harry Zorn (London: Random House, 1999), pp. 245–55 (p. 249). Benjamin's revolutionary vision pictured an angel of history hurled backwards through the never-ending storm of progress, which 'keeps piling wreckage upon wreckage and hurls it in front of his feet'.
41 Cary, *The Horse's Mouth*, p. 738.
42 Cary, *The Horse's Mouth*, p. 755.
43 Cary, *The Horse's Mouth*, p. 757.
44 Walter Benjamin, 'The Work of Art in the Age of Its Technological Reproducibility', in *Selected Writings*, trans. Marcus Bullock and others, vol. 4 (Cambridge, MA: Harvard University Press, 2003) p. 270.

45 Cary, *The Horse's Mouth*, p. 559.
46 Evelyn Waugh, *Brideshead Revisited: The Sacred and Profane Memories of Captain Charles Ryder* (London: Penguin, 2000), p. 74.
47 Waugh, *Brideshead Revisited*, p. 74.
48 Waugh, *Brideshead Revisited*, p. 74.
49 Waugh, *Brideshead Revisited*, p. 322.
50 Waugh, *Brideshead Revisited*, p. x.
51 Waugh, *Brideshead Revisited*, p. x.
52 Waugh, *Brideshead Revisited*, p. x.
53 Waugh, *Brideshead Revisited*, p. 204.
54 Waugh, *Brideshead Revisited*, p. 204.
55 Waugh, *Brideshead Revisited*, p. 212.
56 Waugh, *Brideshead Revisited*, p. 213.
57 Marina MacKay, *Modernism and World War II* (Cambridge: Cambridge University Press, 2007), p. 129; Waugh, *Brideshead Revisited*, p. 27.
58 Waugh, *Brideshead Revisited*, p. 254.
59 Waugh, *Brideshead Revisited*, pp. 251–52.
60 MacKay, *Modernism and World War II*, p. 131; p. 129.
61 MacKay, *Modernism and World War II*, p. 128.
62 Waugh, *Brideshead Revisited*, p. 243.
63 Waugh, *Brideshead Revisited*, p. 291.
64 Waugh, *Brideshead Revisited*, p. 5.
65 Waugh, *Brideshead Revisited*, p. 325. The Latin verse is from the Bible, Lamentations 1. 1; the whole reads, 'How lonely the city stands that was full of people'. The second quotation is from Ecclesiastes 1. 2.
66 Hugh Casson, 'Ruins for Remembrance', in Hugh Casson, Brenda Colvin and Jacques Groag, *Bombed Churches as War Memorials* (Cheam: Architectural Press, 1945), pp. 5–22.
67 'Ruined city churches: preservation as memorials', *The Times*, 15 August 1944, p. 5.
68 Philip Larkin, 'Church Going', in *The Less Deceived* (London: Marvel, 1977), pp. 28–29.
69 Waugh, *Brideshead Revisited*, p. 321.
70 Waugh, *Brideshead Revisited*, p. 33.
71 Gaston Bachelard, *The Poetics of Space*, trans. Maria Jolas (Boston: Beacon, 1964), p. 8.
72 Bachelard, *The Poetics of Space*, p. 8.
73 Bachelard, *The Poetics of Space*, p. 8.
74 See, for instance, Elizabeth Bowen, *The Demon Lover and Other Stories* (London: Jonathan Cape, 1952) [1945] and *The Heat of the Day* (London: Vintage, 1998) [1948]; *Together*, dir. by Lorenza Mazzetti (Harlequin Productions and BFI, 1956); *Hue and Cry*, dir. by Charles Crichton (Ealing Studios, 1947).
75 Casson, 'Ruins for Remembrance', p. 15, emphasis in the original.
76 Casson, 'Ruins for Remembrance', pp. 17–18.
77 Casson, 'Ruins for Remembrance', p. 15.
78 Casson, 'Ruins for Remembrance', p. 21.
79 Casson, 'Ruins for Remembrance', p. 11.
80 Casson, 'Ruins for Remembrance', p. 11.

81 Hugh Casson and G.M. Kallmann, 'Metropolis in Transition', in A.G. Weidenfeld, ed., *The Changing Nation: A Contact Book* (London: Contact, 1948), p. 1.
82 Casson and Kallmann, 'Metropolis in Transition', p. 1.
83 Casson, 'Ruins for Remembrance', p. 21.
84 Casson and Kallmann, 'Metropolis in Transition', p. 5.
85 Casson et al., *Bombed Churches as War Memorials*, p. 35.
86 'Ruined churches as memorials: the emotional effect', *The Times*, 22 August 1944, p. 2.
87 'Ruins of bombed churches' *The Times*, 19 August 1944, p. 5.
88 See 'Future of the city churches: commission's final report', *The Times*, 2 October 1946, p. 7.
89 Rose Macaulay, *The World My Wilderness* (London: Collins, 1950).
90 Rose Macaulay, *The Pleasure of Ruins* (London: Weidenfeld & Nicholson, 1953), p. 454.
91 Macaulay, *The Pleasure of Ruins*, pp. 454–55. The Latin sentence is from Thomas Aquinas, *Summa Theologiae*, 1. 39. 8; it should read 'diminuta sunt', not 'diminutae' as Macaulay has it.
92 Macaulay, *The Pleasure of Ruins*, p. 455.
93 Macaulay, *The Pleasure of Ruins*, p. 454.
94 Macaulay, *The Pleasure of Ruins*, p. 454.
95 Macaulay, *The Pleasure of Ruins*, p. 453.
96 Macaulay, *The World My Wilderness*, p. 165.
97 Macaulay, *The World My Wilderness*, p. 167.
98 Macaulay, *The World My Wilderness*, p. 167.
99 Macaulay, *The World My Wilderness*, p. 181.
100 Macaulay, *The World My Wilderness*, pp. 178–79.
101 Macaulay, *The World My Wilderness*, pp. 178–79.
102 Macaulay, *The World My Wilderness*, p. 179.
103 Macaulay, *The World My Wilderness*, pp. 181–82.
104 Macaulay, *The World My Wilderness*, p. 183.
105 Macaulay, *The World My Wilderness*, p. 195.
106 The Regatta was designed by Mischa Black and Alexander Gibson of the Design Research Unit.
107 William Feaver, 'Festival Star' in Banham and Hillier, *Tonic*, pp. 40–57 (p. 49).
108 Victor Pasmore, 'A Jazz Mural', in Banham and Hillier, *Tonic*, p. 102.
109 Pasmore, 'A Jazz Mural', p. 102.
110 See Lynn Pearson, '"Roughcast Textures and Cosmic Overtones": A Survey of British Murals 1945–1980', *Decorative Arts Society 1850-the Present*, 31 (2007), 116–37 (p. 119).
111 *Brief City: The Story of London's Festival Buildings*, dir. by Jacques B. Brunius and Maurice Harvey (Observer Films, 1952).

2

LOST IN TRANSLATION: MIGRANT BODIES AND UNCANNY SKIN

In the early summer of 1939, amateur archaeologist Basil Brown began excavating a large mound in the grounds of Edith Pretty's East Anglian estate at Sutton Hoo.[1] Having investigated three other mounds nearby the previous year, he was not expecting to find much more than some minor evidence of a looted grave, but when he unearthed a single iron rivet he began to realise that he had found a rare Anglo-Saxon ship burial. Not only that, but it soon became apparent that the ship contained an undisturbed burial chamber. The excavation eventually yielded a magnificent hoard of gold, silver and finely wrought, jewelled regalia, evidence that a powerful king had been interred there. Or had he?

Early accounts of the find naturally focused on the idea that the items were ritually buried alongside a king or chieftain's corpse – the sword was 'by his side'; there was a 'deliberate placing of precious objects for the man's use and enjoyment in another life.'[2] Then on 23 February 1940 *The Times* reported a lecture given by a Cambridge academic, Charles Phillips, to the Society of Antiquaries, which contradicted these speculative conclusions in the light of the absence of any human remains on the site. The 'remarkable feature of the deposit was that it was not associated with a body ... The whole had the character of a cenotaph for a great man whose body could not be recovered, possibly through being lost at sea.'[3] Yet while this lost body clearly resonated with wartime fears for sailors missing in action, the elaborate grave of 'Britain's Tutankhamun' also evoked gothic mythologies about reanimated corpses, haunted relics and the penalties of disrupting the boundaries between past and present.

The excavation itself was carried out in a hurry as war with Germany became inevitable. Charles Phillips had taken over from Brown as head of the excavation after it became clear that the find was substantial. His 1956 account of the dig shows how impressed he was by the glamorous objects he unearthed, and how clearly they spoke to him. He recounts the first visit made to the site by Thomas Kendrick, then keeper of British and Medieval Antiquities at the British Museum (a post later taken over by Phillips), and his excitement at sharing the treasure with an expert in Anglo-Saxon art:

I went to meet him at Woodbridge station and took with me one of the best of the small jewelled buckles, carefully wrapped, in a tobacco tin, so that he could have an advance idea of what he was to see when we reached the main treasure at Mrs Pretty's house. It was a dramatic moment when I drew him into the waiting room to show the buckle, and the scale of the discovery became clear to him.[4]

This was an intimate encounter; by placing the buckle in a humble tobacco tin and pocketing it, not only was Phillips staking a personal claim to it, he was instinctively transforming it from a dead relic into a modern object. His action may have been dubious in terms of archaeological practice, but it exemplifies the regenerative subject/object exchange inherent to an archaeologist's relationship with his finds. Phillips, by turning it into his private accessory, was both bringing the buckle back to life, and expropriating its power and articulacy by making it speak on his behalf. Other objects, too, seemed to come uncannily alive for Phillips during the dig: he remembers the 'daunting look' of a huge and elaborately decorated whetstone sceptre, for instance, with its 'sinister-looking bearded human heads' projecting up out of the earth.[5] Even a humble stack of upended silver bowls was observed to give 'the most odd performance': 'It stood quietly in the rays of the setting sun for some time and then suddenly heaved upwards slightly with a metallic click', Phillips wrote. On examination, it turned out that the bowls had been corroded and compressed by the weight of the sand and soil, and 'as the mass dried out with the overlying weight of sand removed, it sprang apart like an opening concertina'.[6] As these long-dormant objects blossomed into subjecthood without the burden of soil and time to restrain them, they also brought their missing owner uncannily into the present day, where he could be called upon to betoken a timely expression of national identity.

In a 1951 article on Sutton Hoo in *Scientific American*, Rupert Bruce-Mitford, who was to spend many years examining and documenting the Sutton Hoo collection at the British Museum, pointed out that the early Anglo-Saxons 'left no temples, no pyramids, no cities, roads, aqueducts or colossal figures, no written documents; its archaeology was "an archaeology of little things"'.[7] With the discovery of Sutton Hoo, such 'little things' brought an unknown culture vividly out of the darkness, acting once again – as they had done in their former existence as the ritual signifiers of royal status – as the incontrovertible material evidence of a hard-won yet still precarious power. This process resonated with the mid-century-gothic imaginary by updating the kind of antiquarian horror-narratives inspired by the curse-craze of the 1920s which had followed the excavation of Tutankhamun's tomb. In those tales, vengeful mummies killed off over-curious Europeans with mysterious diseases, or broke out of their sarcophagi to wreak havoc in the book-lined studies of academics; but now, the uncanny reanimation of the Sutton Hoo king did not respond to scholarly overreach, nor manifest itself as a walking corpse. Its gothic energy was conceptual rather than palpable, and its codes were cultural rather than hieroglyphic.

In the absence of their putative owner, the grave goods took on an uncanny potency: the lost subjecthood of the dead king seemed now to reside in the objects which had once embodied his sovereignty and wealth. It is true that later, more sophisticated analysis of the site would indicate that the burial *had* in fact once contained a body, which had dissolved in the acidic local soil; but when the Sutton Hoo treasure was exhibited for the first time in 1946 – having spent the war in the depths of Aldwych tube station – it was presented unambiguously as the avatar of a missing Anglo-Saxon, who, despite being 'lost', could be conceptually reconstructed from the traces his absent body left on the world in the form of his weapons, armour, and symbols of power.[8] To the post-war population, this was a powerful idea. The supposed cenotaph seemed to provide historical backing for a modern shift in ideas about identity and material culture. If Anglo-Saxon things could achieve so much charisma and meaning that they could ritually materialise their missing owner, what did this say about the objects of modernity?

The charismatic modern objects which surrounded and interpellated the consumer were everyday 'little things', often cheaply mass-produced, but increasingly important to definitions of self and culture – two concepts that were sharply contested in the post-war decade. For some, the evocation of a quasi-mythical past in which gold-plated overlords bestrode the Anglo-Saxon fenlands might provide ammunition in a revolt against post-war socialism and the loosening of aesthetic and social hierarchies; in *Brideshead Revisited*, as we saw in the last chapter, Charles Ryder's vision of disgusted archaeologists from the future picking over the detritus of the 'Pollock diggings' displayed the kind of class panic that was interlaced with nostalgia for the pharaonic glamour of the Sutton Hoo hoard.[9] Yet the England which these bejewelled relics evoked, although magnificent, was indisputably a foreign place. The exotic flavour of Anglo-Saxon material culture, with its strange zoomorphic motifs and evidence of pre-Christian theology,[10] acted as a reminder of Britain's heritage as a nation of immigrants – 'one of the most-mixed people in the world' as the Festival of Britain South Bank Exhibition guide put it.[11] In that guide's partial and potted version of the history of the nation, the Anglo-Saxons were sketched in as alien disruptors, 'pirates' who 'rushed in to rub out all traces of the Roman touch'; 'barbarians' who settled only when they 'could find no more cities to sack'.[12] Sutton Hoo provided an aesthetic riposte to this brutish characterisation; an anonymous archaeology correspondent writing in the *Manchester Guardian* argued that the relics' non-European design elements were cheering proof that 'art knows no frontiers':

> Insular Britain owes the first impetus of its Saxon art to the style which had already over twelve hundred years of life in the Middle East. The Sutton Hoo finds, if for no other reason, are of the highest importance to the history of our art because of this.[13]

Thus, Sutton Hoo's dead king could be both the original Englishman and – simultaneously and, to some, disturbingly – a harbinger of cultural colonisation from abroad. This undertow of ethnic ambiguity was acutely pertinent at a time when colonial hegemony had been thrown into reverse by the collapse of the British Empire, and national identity abruptly redefined by an influx of British subjects from the Caribbean and South Asia. In his study *The Mummy's Curse*, Roger Luckhurst notes that the kind of 'imperial gothic' which gave rise to tales of archaeological and antiquarian horror around the turn of the twentieth century gained much of its uncanny frisson from its emphasis on the porosity of national borders and the implied possibility of 'reverse colonisation': trade routes are 'pathways that generate transits of story and superstition,' he writes; thus, gothic narratives about plundered tombs and reanimated pharaohs

> refigured the structural violence of the colonial encounter in tales of insidious natives, long-buried curses, haunted museums and mysterious, vengeful objects ... What the British had inherited from the untold centuries leaked out in disfigured allegory from the very stones.[14]

Like a rampaging mummy, the uncanny museum object materialises the problematic of transnational plunder, as the exploited and colonised subject is first reified into an inanimate, fungible commodity, and then later reverts alarmingly to autonomous agency, and sets out to exact its historical revenge. In mid-century gothic, however, such objects no longer ooze a univocal history of foreign misadventure and misappropriation; instead, they may speak of value misconstrued at any time or place – or across any class or cultural border. Lizbeth Paravisini-Gebert has traced the process by which Caribbean authors successfully appropriated the gothic and turned its Eurocentrism back on it, 'reconfigur[ing] the standard tropes of the genre' in order to address, among other things, the horrors of slavery.[15] 'The colonial space,' she writes, 'is by its very nature a bifurcated, ambivalent space, where the familiar and unfamiliar mingle.'[16] This gothicised interchange between oppressed and oppressor can also illuminate the emergent recalcitrance of both immigrant and working-class cultures at the mid-century. Collections of aestheticised things, both in fiction and in exhibitionary practice, echo the uncanny animation and agency of the objectified bodies of post-colonial gothic: they instantiate absent subjects through their implacable presence, and complicate assumptions about time, space and identity. This chapter will trace the connections between culture, nationality and the uncanny, bringing together two different but mutually illuminating strands of enquiry. First, we see how Barbara Jones's 1951 exhibition of 'British popular art' at the Whitechapel Gallery, *Black Eyes and Lemonade*, explored the gothic potential of practices such taxidermy and tattooing, celebrating them as exemplary forms of working-class self-expression, and also finding in them domesticated echoes of colonial (mis)adventure. Meanwhile, traces of post-colonial gothic also find their way into Sam Selvon's novel *The Lonely Londoners* (1956), where skin is not a canvas for decoration (as it is in tattooing) nor the raw material of an uncanny resurrection of the dead (as it is in taxidermy), but instead becomes the problematic marker of alterity by which a disenchanted generation of African-Caribbean migrants find themselves forcibly defined.[17] In both cases, a distinctively mid-century gothic register exposes the way both time and space have become congealed and entangled with the contested quasi-objects of post-industrial modernity. Like the exhumed and expropriated mummy or the repatriated trophy-object of colonial exploitation, the reified physicality of the exploited factory labourer (whether spectrally materialised within the spectacle of consumerism, or forced into visibility as a migrant worker of colour venturing into the public spaces of post-war white culture) becomes a locus of political, social and aesthetic critique. Bringing Selvon's novel into dialogue with the problematics of post-colonial gothic literature, and with Jones's uncanny curatorial practice, reveals how the corporeal absence framed by the Sutton Hoo 'cenotaph' was filled in the post-war years by new definitions of identity and culture.

'THINGS THAT OPPRESS OR PLEASE': *BLACK EYES AND LEMONADE*

When Barbara Jones was called upon to define the parameters of something called 'British popular art' for her Festival of Britain exhibition at the Whitechapel, an element of gothic estrangement seemed essential; it was this aspect, she felt, which gave the theme its contemporary flavour. An earlier exploration of traditional decorative objects, Noel Carrington's 1945 *Popular Art in Britain,* had focused conventionally on folk curios like horse brasses, smocking patterns and elaborate ironwork hinges, and had expressly placed them outside the system of taste, thus inoculating visitors from any exposure to aesthetic insubordination.[18] Carrington want so far as to prescribe a moratorium on rational critique as the best strategy for appreciating such handwork: 'To classify and rationalise too far will not prove rewarding,' he stated airily.[19] Jones's project was, in contrast, urgently critical and political; she wanted to demolish old hierarchies of taste by engaging with mass-produced, factory-made ephemera, which would be placed alongside artisanal, hand-crafted one-offs in order to expand the realm the 'authentic':

> To draw a rigid line between hand and machine-made works of art is unrewarding ... Somewhere there is a dividing line between tool (allowed as hand) and machine, but it is very difficult to say exactly where, and so far the human brain has always

dictated just what the machine shall produce. It will be interesting to see what popular arts are produced by cybernetics.[20]

Jones saw factory production and technological mediation, not as the gloomy end-point of traditional craft, but as an exciting new efflorescence in the arabesque progress of the vernacular, with the products of man and machine on a continuum of decorative and creative possibility, which would bring to light the deeply buried emotions that popular art alone could access.

In *The Unsophisticated Arts*, the book she wrote to accompany the exhibition, she asserted that the objects she had collected together were doing valuable psychical work by tackling subjects that 'serious' art was not addressing, namely the discomfort and even horror produced by the surreal juxtapositions of everyday life. 'Behind the arts as practised and enjoyed by the cultivated,' she wrote,

> there remain always the vernacular arts, and in these the less sophisticated people work out of their minds the things that oppress or please them. Two subjects are pre-eminent, containing emotions and linked themselves: horror, and ... the counterfeiting of man.[21]

Indeed, a whole section of her exhibition was devoted to the uncomfortable frisson created by 'Man's Own Image': here, visitors were greeted by hairdressers' models with wigs, a ventriloquist's doll, a phrenologist's bust, a carnival head and, presiding over the whole section, two waxworks from Madame Tussauds.[22] Jones intended these imposing figures to evoke a particularly uncanny agency: in waxworks, she wrote, the suspicion of malevolent intent is always implied by their 'staring stillness', and the 'stiff and waxy ones', in particular, acquire 'their own nasty life and move a little in the corner of your eye ... Never could it be a kindly action that any waxwork would move to perform.'[23]

Jones was always interested in harnessing the disruptive power of things that wriggle into life just beyond the limits of normal looking. Having studied mural-painting at the Royal College of Art in the 1930s, she often worked at the intersection of public and commercial art, and was also a much-commissioned book illustrator and graphic designer. By the time she was invited by the Society for Education in Art (SEA) to curate this exhibition, she was already a passionate observer and collector of the unruly objects of everyday life. Indeed, she exceeded the SEA's brief spectacularly, conceiving *Black Eyes and Lemonade* in terms of an explicit re-education of the art establishment within she worked. Gillian Whiteley, in her essay 'Kitsch as Cultural Capital', tracks evidence of an increasingly heated debate between the SEA on one side, and Jones and Hugh Scrutton of the Whitechapel Gallery on the other.[24] The SEA had originally agreed that their aim was 'to develop the imagination and creative powers of the whole rising generation and to establish an indigenous expression of art in the everyday life of the community which is based on common experience and interest in the environment.'[25] Once Jones had begun sourcing her exhibits, however, they became nervous, protesting that

> the lowest levels of taste are not worth exhibiting and bring the exhibition down to a trashy level. We need not bring in greenish hairdressers models and fluffy kittens – still less the dull and ugly enamelled tin advertisements which are not even the result of popular taste, but sordid practical commerce.[26]

In the light of this evidence, Jones's catalogue introduction reads as a somewhat pointed retort:

> There are a number of ways in which an exhibition of popular art could have been arranged: historically, sociologically, geographically, by categories of materials used, by occupations, by artistic themes, and so on. But it was finally decided to set up a series of arbitrary categories which reflect most forms of human activity without creating bogus sociological implications, and which also did make the exhibition physically possible to arrange.[27]

Jones's instincts were correct: the show proved to be a hit with the public, with a total of 30,754 visitors making it the most successful exhibition at the Whitechapel in the 1950s.[28]

Many of the pieces on display came from her own private collection, and all of them were selected according to the personal and idiosyncratic preferences of Jones and her co-organiser Tom Ingram ('It will ... be noticed that we are prejudiced in favour of cats and commerce,' she joked in the catalogue's introduction).[29] She recalled how she and Ingram bought an old London taxi and toured Britain following opportunistic leads and scooping up things which caught their eye. They discovered a warehouse on the Regent's Canal in London crammed with advertising material from Thorley's Agricultural merchants:

> The latest discards were near the door, clean and new, but beyond them far to the back were rolls and bundles thickly black with London grime. We peeled off the top layers to find more than a century's advertising: posters, tin plates, leaflets that unfolded to show chicks bursting from the egg, and portraits in oils of prize animals fed on Thorley's. The collection filled a whole room of the gallery.[30]

This anecdote reveals within the cheerful opportunism of Jones's curatorial practice an echo of an archaeological methodology: digging up this buried subculture, she finds it teeming with uncanny new life, like the paper chicks which spring up from the superannuated leaflets. The *Black Eyes* exhibition made visible the synchronic continuity of popular taste which is endlessly refreshed and renewed but retains its essential character; to understand it required a rejection of traditional hierarchies and the adoption of new type of seeing. Jones draws a distinction, in the catalogue, between the instinctive good judgement of the 'popular eye' which 'arranges stripes on butcher's aprons and lobsters and soles on the fishmonger's slab'[31] and the 'museum eye' achieved by education within an elite cadre of connoisseurs – connoisseurship which 'must be abandoned' if the visitor is to understand the collection of objects at the Whitechapel as an exhibition of *art*, and not a deluge of everyday kitsch.[32] Both the catalogue's cover and its poster featured strong graphic representations of unblinking eyes arranged, not horizontally as on a face, but vertically, as if to emphasise that a reoriented gaze will be required by the exhibition's visitors. The effect was successful: 'People began to realise that indeed they were [works of art],' she observed, noting that the arrangement of the exhibition inculcated the viewers into a performance of this new mindset; it was their progress through the galleries that brought about their change of mind:

> Visitors were eased into the idea by a row of ships' figure heads and cases of other acceptable art-objects, and were brought gradually to accept comic postcards and beer labels. All through the exhibition the new and commonplace were seen near the old and safe, and by the end most people felt able to accept a talking lemon extolling Idris lemon squash and Bassetts Liquorice Allsorts isolated under a spot light.'[33]

The exhibition ended with wrappers, labels, carrier bags and advertising material, throwaway items which would blend into the material world outside the gallery and – Jones hoped – encourage visitors to take their newly calibrated aesthetic framework with them when they left. She wanted to situate her revolutionary aesthetic within the mid-century's new appreciation of how objects can become focal points in the restless onrush of history and time. Her instant classics, which she considered to be collectable as soon as they were manufactured, sped up the inevitable process by which time confers a patina of acceptability onto humble things. Like 'the great collector Pachinger' mentioned by Walter Benjamin in *The Arcades Project*, who stoops to pick up 'a misprinted streetcar ticket that had been in circulation for only a few hours' and yet has been the object of his search for weeks, Jones wants to complicate the distinction between the strange and the everyday.[34] Pachinger, according to Benjamin, eventually succumbed to a radical uncertainty about the status of ordinary things: 'He hardly knows any more how things stand in the world; explains to his visitor – alongside the most antique implements – the use of pocket handkerchiefs, hand mirrors, and the like.' Moreover, he could repurpose any object into an optical instrument, seeming 'to look through them into their distance, like an augur.'[35] Likewise, the objects in the *Black Eyes* exhibition telescope the distance between the familiar and the strange. Their full meaning exceeds their mere utility.

If many of Jones's exhibits seemed informed by a kind of perverse nostalgia for the nearly-old and the not-quite-good, the exhibition as a whole laid out a manifesto for a distinctively modern measure of quality which deliberately overturned traditional distinctions between art, design and rubbish. As she wrote in the catalogue:

The things in this exhibition are seldom found in museums and galleries. Some of them are big and bright, visible enough, but others we hang on the bedroom wall, accept in the shops and cinemas, stare at blankly on the bus and rarely consider closely.[36]

Jones was inviting her visitors to reject fastidious elitism in favour of a kind of haptic familiarity. Such objects could thus become the uncanny doubles of themselves, simultaneously inhabiting the everyday and estranged from it in the zone of aesthetic expression. A cartoon in the *Evening News* neatly expressed the radicalism of this inversion of value: it depicted a heap of canal-related bric-a-brac, from which one lowly object stands out. 'Bargepole,' reads the caption. 'Please do not touch.'[37]

'BUT HORROR STILL APPEARS': UPSTART SKIN AND *UNHEIMLICH* HYBRIDS

Yet Jones's project did not aim only to expose what lay *beyond* the surface of things, but also to bring those surfaces themselves into a more critical zone of looking. She insists that we gaze frankly at the objects 'we think ... are ugly', the 'artificial flowers, bus tickets, lino ... and Brumas hotwater bottles'.[38] The popular arts, moreover, partake in horror via their imperturbable tendency towards 'realistic representation':

> Realism is a strong vernacular urge – a little dog is nice; let us have one for our calendar, our mantelpiece, for a doorstop or a fireplace. He is made of flock paper, pottery, iron or tiles, as like as may be. He expresses the artist, of course, but not deliberately: the dog is more important than the man.[39]

Such realism might seem at odds with a gothic sensibility, but by unseating the idea that a pure essence of subjective affect must be the prime directive of aesthetic endeavour, Jones opens up the possibility that less congenial forces are at work in the act of representation. This rejection of modernist interiority was exemplified by the profusion of animals which strayed into most sections of the exhibition, from 'Agriculture' to 'Drinking', but was expressed most powerfully in the taxidermied specimens which appeared in 'Pet's Corner' in the form of a stuffed alligator, a 'hoof mounted as a souvenir' and 'two cases of birds representing "The Death and Burial of Cock Robin"'.[40] A stuffed animal may be understood as the ultimate in tautological realism: the object is fashioned out of the very thing it is called upon to represent. On the other hand, it speaks also of the horror that Jones saw as lacking in fine art: the uncanny persistence of the dead in life, the porosity of the border between presence and absence. Here, the animal gaze that meets the spectator's critical eye suggests a rival subjectivity inhabiting the deathless object which refuses to lie down.

Taxidermy could also be called on to provide a gloss on the class-stratification of cultural expression. In *The Unsophisticated Arts*, Jones notes the difference between hunting trophies in standard poses, fashioned from the 'reliable parcels' sent home by colonial safari veterans, and the sentimental souvenirs of pet-owners. 'The sorrowful,' she says, 'have ideas. They try to explain, with gestures and inadequate grey snapshots, the little ways of Rover.'[41] It is a typically wry observation, but it also implicitly challenges the vertical model of aesthetic value. Rover's preserved pelt has as much meaning stuffed into it as the hunter's masks or rugs; perhaps more, because the 'sorrowful' want to preserve the particularities of non-human subjectivity, not just make a symbolic statement about status and power. The bereaved pet-owner *requires* an object that will look back at its maker/spectator, and collaborate in the illusion that the true identity of the dead beast can be materialised by its furry cenotaph.

In taxidermy, the uncanny inevitably intrudes into such fantasies of revenance and reanimation. The reason the Victorians liked stuffed animals, Jones explains in *The Unsophisticated Arts*, is that 'many of them [were] enclosed in their accustomed cases, removed from us into their special glass world'. In contrast, modern specimens 'stand free, and come too close to us.'[42] And while she praises the anthropomorphic tableaux of Walter Potter's taxidermy museum (the source of 'The Death and Burial of Cock Robin', which she borrowed for the exhibition) as 'magnificent – stuffed Academy painting'[43] she closes the chapter on a shudder, with a description of a mermaid 'sold to gullible sailors' that is

> half baby anthropoid ape and half fish, stuffed together and embellished with breasts and a wig. Today it is old and shrivelled and deceives nobody, but its demi-semi humanity is horrible, and fills one with pleasure that the law, or some technical trouble with the skin, prevents us from having dead Auntie stuffed to hold a standard lamp.[44]

The *unheimlich* hybrid, too close to home for comfort, is central to Jones's conception of popular art as both a reservoir and release-valve for horror. The horror of death-in-life and life-in-death appears in her casual reference to the embalmed corpse of folk art and the restless transience of the popular ('most of the folk arts are dead, or self-consciously preserved by societies').[45] And it is there in her valorisation of objects that 'lean to disquiet, the baroque and sometimes horror':

> Fear is concealed by sophisticated man, and today in any case he has less of it to express, as urban amenities are driving the dark edges round the cities further and further towards the sea. But horror still appears suddenly in peaceful streets and fields, finding expression in Punch and Judy or the *Police Gazette*, in a ventriloquist's dummy, in sad wooden architecture by riversides, in the little tents that house the freaks at a fair.[46]

When tattoos appeared in Jones's exhibition (in the 'Personal Adornment' section) it was in the form of copies of an anonymous nineteenth-century painting of two female nudes 'with recent overpainting of tattooing patterns by Mr George Burchett' – perhaps the exhibition's most impertinent subversion of the expected norms of art viewership.[47] But Jones was also interested in the gothic transformation which occurs when ink is applied to flesh, and the link between tattooing and colonial exploration: 'Precise dates and origins for the introduction of tattooing into this country remain obscure,' she writes in *The Unsophisticated Arts*, 'but the Tahitian derivation of the word and the persistently oriental character of many of the designs suggest that it came back like tea and parrots with the early explorers.'[48] She notes, too, the intersection between tattooing and the life-changing physical transformations of war veterans.

> The new development of [cosmetic tattooing] was its application to plastic surgery during the Second World War: grafted skin on the lower part of the face, for instance, lacked all definition, so the tattooists were called in to draw lips and faint blue chins onto the blank flesh.[49]

The new aesthetic that Jones is announcing has been conditioned by the sensorium of war and post-war displacement, in which human affect has been blanked, while familiar objects become so defamiliarised at the point of their potential annihilation that they now seem disturbingly close to uncanny revolt. Jones's curatorial practice was a response to this gothic confusion of life and death, art and identity, subject and object. The cornucopia of grave goods, restless effigies, and buried treasures at the *Black Eyes* exhibition was not just an evocation of plenty, or an exercise in nostalgia; it was a room full of baleful witnesses, staring back at the complacent consumers who came to look at them.

'ORIENTAL FLAVOUR': POPULAR ALTERITY AND MASS ALIENATION

Yet despite its enthusiasm for sociological rule-breaking, *Black Eyes and Lemonade* also begs questions about the bourgeois orientalisation of working-class culture. The 'unsophisticated' exuberance and outlandish decoration which Jones favoured in her chosen exhibits infused indigenous British subcultures with a consolatory tang of otherness that echoed the discourses of 'primitivism' by which non-Western art was kept in its place within the structures of colonialism. The exhibition's title borrowed its evocation of an easily assembled festivity from the orientalist poet Thomas Moore: 'A Persian's heaven is easily made | Tis but – black eyes and lemonade.'[50] This quotation was chosen, according to Jones's catalogue introduction, because it 'seem[ed] to express the vigour, sparkle and colour of popular art rather better than the words "popular art" … Even the oriental flavour is valid, for English decoration is always susceptible to exotic influences.'[51]

In the context of the Festival of Britain celebrations, this was a somewhat radical suggestion. In general, the various events staged in 1951 expressed a conspicuously inward-looking national agenda, and ideas about empire, decolonisation and migration were notably absent from the main London exhibitions at the South Bank and the Science Museum. Becky Conekin has argued that this silence was due to a combination of national embarrassment about the end of the empire – understood as a 'loss of British power and prestige in a period already filled with disappointment and uncertainty' – and of a new emphasis on science, rather than foreign adventure, as the motor of British progress.[52] This was not the whole story, however. One exception to the general stony silence was an exhibition of 'Traditional Art and Sculpture from the Colonies' at the Imperial Institute, and its catalogue, written by William Fagg (then the assistant keeper of anthropology at the British Museum), provides a curious echo of Jones's in that it addresses an assumed cohort of baffled, potentially resentful (and exclusively white, middle-class) fine art enthusiasts, who must be coaxed into a recalibration of aesthetic perception:

> The European who seeks to 'understand' what is usually called 'primitive' art, to cultivate a state of mind and heart receptive to its strange forms and rhythms, must begin by divesting himself of some of the assumptions which are so fundamental in modern European thought that he is probably unconscious of the part which they play in forming his own reactions to art and to life.[53]

Post-imperial and socio-cultural self-critique might be the natural corollary of even such limited aesthetic adjustment: an uncomfortable process which the planners of the Festival largely shunned. The shocking idea that Manichean binaries like 'high' and 'low', 'primitive' and 'civilised', might not stand up to scrutiny could only be processed as a kind of cleansing conceptual fire which conveniently obliterated historical guilt. In 1948–49, the ICA's Herbert Read had staged *40,000 Years of Modern Art* in an attempt to draw comparisons between 'African art' – lumped together and understood as something eerily, almost inhumanly, timeless – and the bleeding edge of Western modernist practice. The air of self-congratulation evident in the press conference Read gave prior to its opening attests to the condescending attitude to non-Western culture which such a comparison implied:

> The art of primitive people is no longer to us merely a manifestation of the disgusting idol worship of savages and cannibals. We have discovered in it powers of invention and expression which fill us with amazement and seem to point the way to new forms of art which can combine primitive vitality and vision with modern technique and sensibility.[54]

Jones's position in relation to such colonial hauteur is interesting. Both Read and Fagg were asserting that non-Western art was so inexplicable and foreign that only viewers with an elevated level of connoisseurship would be able to access its full power. Conversely, the 'oriental' flavour that Jones found in British popular art argued that assimilation of the other into twentieth-century mass culture could be almost instantaneous. Indeed, her collection celebrated the way cultures of diaspora and displacement had already been subsumed into popular taste: she loved barge decorations, fairground attractions, circuses and ships' figureheads – the work of travelling people whose non-Anglo-Saxon heritage, long since naturalised, remained embedded in their visual style. Jones's point was that creativity is restless and unbounded; by borrowing the Moore quotation for her exhibition's title, however, she was making explicit the connection between a de-historicised, modern version of aesthetic multiculturalism and the superficial cultural appropriations of the *Arabian Nights* boom which began in 1704 and had inspired Moore's *Intercepted Letters*. As Ros Ballaster has pointed out in *Fabulous Orients*, such processes of cultural assimilation have never been straightforward:

> Stories are not simple freight; in their passage from East to West they are often radically altered to become hybrid commodities and the bearers of multiple new meanings. Thus, through their ostensible depiction of life in the eastern harem, the *Arabian Nights Entertainments* could, amongst other things, provide a window for English readers into the 'précieuse' culture of the eighteenth-century French salon.[55]

Such visual markers of so-called Oriental style had washed out, by the middle of the twentieth century, to the margins of popular culture, where Jones found them in the arabesque patterns of painted bargeware (in the exhibition's 'Transport' section) and a nutmeg grater in the shape of the Brighton Pavilion (to be found in 'Souvenirs'). Jones's intervention sought to reverse this geographical trajectory, not as a critique of colonialism, but as a critique of class; by reinstating to this hybrid style the prestige of art, she was dispelling any notion that cultural value should be fixed by a static system of taste.[56] On the contrary, Jones finds value in the unruly translations and tireless reiterations by which an archaic and exotic visual code could be transmitted into the homely material cultures she encountered, and lose their markers of internationalism completely. Instead, the intricacy of vernacular decoration comes to express only a disconnected, uncanny otherness. Like the travelling populations that preserve them, such popular arts are 'complex, unsubtle, often impermanent, they lean to disquiet'.[57] Jones's theorisation of the vernacular thing-world depended on the cultural resonance of objects in themselves, and operated via a curatorial practice that relied on chaotic contiguity of the junk shop to reveal a timeless layer of meaning.[58] She was less interested in the kind of Mass-Observation-style valorisation of the ordinary that had characterised pre-war counter-modernism, than in the elevation of a new category of the extraordinary, neither 'charming' nor sophisticated, but shouty and unselfconscious.

Yet in doing so, her curatorial practice depended on an erasure of cultural specificity at a time when an 'exotic' identity could still turn waves of scattered people into undifferentiated 'foreigners'. Post-war 'displaced persons' were still much in the news; in 1945, there were between twenty and thirty million stateless refugees in Europe, 'myriads of desperate, sick and starving people', as Lord Reading put it in a House of Lords debate.[59] A year later, this figure was estimated to be down to 500,000 and the UNO's short-lived Special Committee on Refugees and Displaced Persons was wound up.[60] By 1951 Britain had absorbed 85,429 refugees, mainly from Eastern Europe.[61] The Intergovernmental Committee for European Migration was set up that year and resettled 155,000 people in its first two years, many to America, Canada, Australia and South America, but by this time there were also significant new Polish communities in Britain, both in London and in the 'temporary' camps – some of which existed into the 1960s – which were set up in rural areas after the Soviet annexation of Eastern Poland.[62] Outside Britain, the creation of Israel in 1948, while addressing an important aspect of Europe's refugee crisis, was seen to have 'created a large and intractable problem of displaced Arabs', as a *Times* editorial put it in 1956.[63] This editorial also noted that 70,000 refugees still remained in 200 European Displaced Person camps. Meanwhile, colonial immigration was beginning to influence British urban culture sufficiently to interest the sociologist Michael Banton, whose study of Cable Street in Stepney, *The Coloured Quarter: Negro Immigrants in an English City* (published in 1955 but based on research carried out in 1950–51) set out the problems of the newly coined 'racial relations'.[64]

Banton noted that the immigration of African-Caribbean workers took place within the well-established multiculturalism of east London. In the so-called 'coloured quarter' of Stepney, he noted:

> There is a Maltese-run fish and chip shop, an Italian restaurant which opens during the daytime for a white clientele, and a Greek café. Shops at the beginning of the street are of Jewish and English ownership ... A side turning leads down to a Somali café, a Greek café, and a Pakistani café-cum-lodging house. A little farther up the street is a general store run by a French family, two hairdressers – one an Arab, the other from Trinidad – a dyer's and cleaner's run by a Guianese, and a Pakistani café with an African and West Indian clientele.[65]

Although he was broadly sympathetic to London's migrant populations and troubled by the xenophobic oppression they encountered, Banton's own research methodology in this early study had a problematic tendency to foreground white-British perspectives, including his own, at the expense of immigrant voices. This included noting that, to a white middle-class researcher, this part of London took on a distinctly gothic aspect. 'To the passer-by,' Banton writes, the area is a strange and definitely a frightening one ... To the ordinary Englishman used to a humdrum existence, this is the sort of place where anything might happen, and, if the things in the magazines do happen then they must happen here.[66]

As Banton saw it, the estrangement worked both ways: he describes his own uncanny transformation into an unwelcome alien when he enters a pub or café in the area;

> the other customers will scrutinise [me] thoroughly and there is an atmosphere so hostile that anyone but a coloured man, a seaman, or one of the poorest of the native population, will come to feel that he does not 'belong' there and that he is not wanted.[67]

He admits, however, that it is the relatively new immigrants of colour who experience the most profound sense of their own problematic visibility in their encounters with racism. 'What is little more than a category of people of similar appearance,' he writes, 'is made into a self-conscious social group by the attitudes shown towards them by the British public.'[68]

Incomers who find themselves uncomfortably objectified by their outsider status may begin to turn a critical eye on the system which has turned them into a form of spectacle. Before moving on to Sam Selvon's treatment of this problematic, it is worth considering how class and identity intersected with the idea of immigration in the wider culture of the period, via two groundbreaking film-makers who were also concerned with visibility and belonging.

'WHAT I REALLY WANTED WAS SILENCE': REFRAMING IMMIGRATION IN LORENZA MAZZETTI'S *TOGETHER*

Two of the three films screened at the National Film Theatre's *Free Cinema* programme in 1956 were by immigrant directors: *Momma Don't Allow* by Karel Reisz, and Lorenza Mazzetti's *Together*. Whereas the third film, *O Dreamland* by Lindsay Anderson, winced with fastidious disgust at the dreary mechanics of mainstream recreation, both Reisz and Mazzetti demonstrate a sharp eye for the lively contradictions and displacements of mid-century working-class culture. Reisz's observational documentary, filmed at the Wood Green Jazz Club, provides a vivid glimpse of a new generation of young, white, working-class people who find ecstatic self-affirmation by participating in a well-defined subculture of fashion, music and lindy-hop dance moves. The film's narrative impetus springs from the discomfort the regulars feel when they are visited by a group of curious, upper-class intruders – fur-clad aliens who can be tolerated only insofar as they are prepared to loosen up and blend in. The film is remarkable for its wordless evocation of a vibrant culture which, when it is not ignored by the mainstream, is patronised as an exotic oddity. Yet it is people of colour who are most conspicuous by their absence here; the African-American origins of jazz are occluded, and although the soundtrack features music by the Chris Barber jazz band, who organised the first British tours of African-American jazz artists in the 1950s, no non-white musicians are credited.[69]

If people of colour are silently erased from Reisz's account of British jazz subculture, the erasure of outsider experience is both the subject of Lorenza Mazzetti's *Together*, and encoded within its aesthetic strategy. Set in the East End of London, it tells the story of two outsiders (perhaps brothers) who fail to assimilate and blend in. They are not explicitly identified as immigrants, but they inhabit a similarly marginal social space: they work together on the docks, share a mean little room in a boarding house, and represent a symbolic kind of non-specific foreignness. The suggestive opacity of the film's narrative is made possible by the fact that they communicate with each other in sign language (they appear to be deaf), and this private discourse emphasises their self-contained isolation from the rest of society, and suggests the beguiling possibility of secret cultures which are not susceptible to mainstream interpretation. Significantly, their inner lives remain inscrutable to the audience. Whereas Reisz's camera inserts itself into the heart of the heaving dancefloor and participates in the performance of self-display, Mazzetti holds back from her characters, framing them carefully within an urban landscape of dusty bombsites, narrow streets and the river's sudden watery vistas. Two artists were cast in the lead roles: Eduardo Paolozzi – already at this point established as a member of the Independent Group – and the painter Michael Andrews, then a student at the Slade, where Mazzetti also studied. They play the men with a kind of intense stillness; they pass in silence through the uproar of the docks, the local pub, and a crowded funfair. In these public spaces they form a discrete, self-contained unit, but tension arises when they find themselves adrift on eerily empty city streets still punctuated by bombsites; a pack of feral children follow them everywhere, taunting them for their difference. It is this childish bullying that precipitates the film's tragic climax, as Andrews's character is pushed off a wall into the Thames, where he drowns.

In a 2012 interview with Christophe Dupin in *Sight & Sound*, Mazzetti explained that *Together* was an exercise in personal post-war recuperation. Both her parents had died when she was young and her aunt, who was bringing her up, was killed by the SS, along with her cousins; her uncle later committed suicide. She told Dupin:

> I had serious psychological problems because of my past, but as no one knew about it, the only way to express my anxiety was to translate it unconsciously into a film script ... I'd projected my own feeling of being different onto these characters, who were constantly followed by a group of children who shouted things they couldn't hear.[70]

Like harbingers of the future, the children haunting the streets seem to represent the superannuation of an old social order which has been atomised by the bombs, just as the buildings have been. As the film's title implies, the two men will survive only as long as they stay together; Paolozzi's character, the more withdrawn of the two, has trouble with the daily routines of washing and dressing, while Andrews's, though more competent and cheerful, is physically weak and vulnerable. It is their co-operation that allows them to function in the world, and the heart-breaking upshot of the drowning is that Paolozzi's character, absent for a few fatal minutes, returns to the baffling absence of his companion and cannot think of anything to do, except continue to wait for him.

According to her recollections in the 2012 interview, when Mazzetti first conceived it the film was originally called *The Glass Marbles* because of the fascination these objects have for Paolozzi's character. He picks them up from the street, where the children had previously been seen playing with them, and then carries them everywhere with him, taking them out of his pocket from time to time to look at them and roll them in his hands. They are solid symbols, something to hold onto in a world often reduced to inexplicable abstractions. An image of his self-containment, they also perhaps represent the camera's glass eye and its ability to create a miniature world. Jones drew a similar comparison in order to describe the limitations of human vision, describing the 'twisted spiral of filaments' which marbles contain as 'thin music translated into coloured glass, crimson with pale blue, fire with canary, emerald with rose. The similar sphere of the eye, however closely juxtaposed to the harder crystal, peers in vain through the twined colours to see the heart'.[71] Like Jones's ephemera, Paolozzi's marbles have been plucked out of the dross of the street and animated with new meaning and value, and through these glass symbols of the artistic gaze, Mazzetti is surely saying something about the concrete vision of her own semi-documentary filmic practice. The film's lack of synchronised sound (necessitated by her low budget) is used to create an oneiric counterpoint to the everyday setting and to show how the characters' watchfulness redefines their world with a supercharged visual perception. Mazzetti remembered rejecting some script additions by her then boyfriend Denis Horne, because what he had written 'had lots of dialogue, and what I really wanted was silence'.[72]

The marbles are also playthings, and gesture towards the feral uncanniness of play. If the glass eye of the artist is a kind of toy, it is one that threatens loss as well as perception. Paolozzi takes care to hold on to the marbles, but his brother slips out of his grasp. In the film's closing moments, Mazzetti includes a shot of a barge chugging away down the river, oblivious to the violent drama that has just taken place. There is no Sutton Hoo-style object-enabled resurrection here – just a man who has sunk without trace.

'THE SET-UP LOOK LIKE THE WORLD OF ART': PERFORMING ALTERITY IN *THE LONELY LONDONERS*

In the same year that *Together* and *Momma Don't Allow* were showing at the National Film Theatre, another portrait of migrant, working-class alienation and aestheticised alterity found expression in Sam Selvon's novel *The Lonely Londoners*.[73] Here, the water-borne outsiders are workers from the Caribbean, surviving racism, socio-economic exclusion and cultural rupture in a strange, cold country. This episodic, multi-vocal novel is held together by the symmetry of two contrasting viewpoints – that of Moses Alouetta, an old hand who knows all the drawbacks and pitfalls of London life, and of the eternal optimist Henry Oliver, nicknamed Sir Galahad, who is newly arrived and determined to take part in London's transactional spectacle. Selvon, in his quest to overturn – or at least satirise – the objectifying discourses of racism, proposes to harness an aesthetic reversal of value partially analogous to that which was attempted by Jones: his characters perceive and reject (white) hierarchies and refuse to be construed by them, and in doing so, they bring about new ways of seeing and understanding the structures of consumption and urban modernity. But whereas the white visitors to the *Black Eyes and Lemonade* exhibition could choose to read the unruly consumer goods on display as a blueprint for their own potential recalcitrance, many of the newly arrived people of colour, forced to experience *themselves* as objects under the spotlight of white scrutiny, might find Jones's exposé of the exoticism and alterity of commodity culture far from refreshing or empowering. Instead, Selvon's characters invert existing power relations by writing themselves into an urban aesthetic of semantically untethered, explicitly *performative* consumerism.

Galahad, unlike Moses, understands that his identity will be read as spectacle by white Londoners whether he wills it or not, and decides to make the process a conscious one. During the week, he is as dirty and scruffy as any other factory labourer exhausted by poverty wages and long-term night-working. But he hopes to escape this abject status during his leisure time. 'When you dressing, you dressing,' he observes, and on an evening date, in his sharply tailored suits ('a seam that could cut you'), carefully accessorised with a long silver watch chain and 'a plastic raincoat hanging on his arm', Galahad is 'cool as a lord' and 'walk[s] like a king'.[74] His destination is Piccadilly Circus:

> That circus have a magnet for him, that circus represent life, that circus is the beginning and the ending of the world. Every time he go there, he have the same feeling like when he see it the first night, drink coca-cola, any time is guinness time, bovril and the fireworks, a million flashing lights, gay laughter, the wide doors of theatres, the huge posters, everready batteries, rich people going into tall hotels, people going to the theatre, people sitting and standing and walking and talking and laughing and buses and cars and Galahad Esquire, in all this, standing there in the big city, in London. Oh Lord.[75]

Galahad experiences the visual cacophony of advertising and conspicuous consumption as a semiotic system into which he can insert himself – a fictive alternative to the invisibility he experiences during his working hours. Like the other African-Caribbean Londoners in the novel, he is simultaneously hyper-visible –because of his skin colour and his strangeness to white eyes – and uncannily spectral in his transactions with a mainstream culture which wants to deny his identity and agency. The freewheeling churn of the 'circus', where beginnings and endings coil around each other, makes it a revolutionary space that rotates and realigns the norms of social relations. As Mpalive-Hangson Msiska has argued, Selvon presents Galahad as a black flâneur, a figure who, like his white counterparts in the work of Baudelaire and Benjamin, 'celebrates the materialism of the city' and 'revels in being on the street' but unlike them, 'cannot walk all streets with equal freedom' so that his flânerie becomes a performance of the 'tension between his racialised metropolitan identity and his universal claim to an identity beyond his racial collectivity – as a man of the city as a whole'.[76] Galahad is a new type of Londoner, ready to take his place in the 'tall hotels' and determined not to sink into the dirt and dismay of abjection and boarding-house liminality.

Time and again in the novel, Selvon reveals and critiques the contactless encounters that occur between the vertically estranged viewpoints away from which Galahad wants to navigate. 'Old fellars,' the narrator notes,

> sometimes they walk up a street in a plush area with their cap in their hand, and sing in a high falsetto, looking up at the high windows, where the high and mighty living, and now and then a window would open and somebody would throw down threepence or a tanner.[77]

Not only is the 'old fellar' made invisible by the 'highness' which enables this anonymous exchange, but so is the unseen donor; the narrator speculates that behind the window there might be 'some woman that sleep late after a night at the Savoy or Dorchester' but 'if she have a thought at all, it never go further than to cause the window to open and the tanner to fall down'.[78] Whether her act of casual charity is caused by a 'good mood' or a mixture of insomnia and guilt, the woman remains indifferent to the particularity of the person behind 'that voice quavering in the cold':

> In fact when the woman throw the tanner from the window she didn't even look down: if a man was a mile away and he was controlling a loudspeaker in the street moving up and down, the tanner would have come the same way. Also, for the old test who singing, it ain't have no thought at all about where this tanner come from, or who throw it, man woman or child, it ain't make no difference. All he know is that a tanner fall in the road, and he had to watch it else it roll and get lost.[79]

By equating the old man with a machinic avatar in the form of the remote-controlled loudspeaker, Selvon reveals in the exchange of the coin the spectrality inherent in all rigidly codified subject–object relations, and not only in the abjection of the unruly subaltern. In contrast, Galahad's act of self-performance lifts him out of this hardscrabble gutter and makes him sharply, even dangerously, visible ('a seam that could cut you'). Yet his agency is always in danger of abrupt curtailment by the reification implied by such fetishised visibility. Several characters in the novel find themselves reduced to the status of novelty collectibles within the narrow purview of the curious white upper-class gaze; the man nicknamed Big City describes how he was plucked from the street by the driver of a 'big limousine' who 'ask me if I from the West Indies, and I say yes, and he say that Lady – want to meet a West Indian, if I would come'.[80] Moses, too, finds himself invited to perform the role of fashionable accessory at a Knightsbridge club

> where only the high and the mighty is but with all of that they feel they can't get big thrills unless they have a black man in the company and when Moses leave afterwards they push five pounds in his hand and pat him on the back and say that was a jolly good show.[81]

During the extended stream of consciousness passage which accompanies Galahad's walk through a summer evening in the city, he notes that white people

> want you to live up to the films and stories they hear about black people living primitive in the jungles of the world that is why you will see so many of them African fellars in the city with their hair high up on the head like they ain't had a trim for years and with a scar on their faces and a ferocious expression going about with some real sharp chicks the cruder you are the more they like you.[82]

He recalls an anecdote about an unnamed Jamaican man invited for one night into a woman's smart Chelsea flat

> with all sorts of surrealistic painting on the walls and contemporary furniture in the G-plan the poor fellar bewildered and asking questions to improve himself because the set-up look like the World of Art but the number not interested in passing on any knowledge she only interested in one thing and in the heat of emotion she call the Jamaican a black bastard though she didn't mean it as an insult but as a compliment under the circumstances but the Jamaican fellar get vex and he stop and say why the hell you call me a black bastard and he thump the woman and went away.[83]

The brutal turn taken by this encounter is just the most obvious manifestation of the violence Selvon sees in the perverse aesthetic strategy of racism. As Msiska notes, there is always something 'dangerous and menacing' in the essential restlessness and sensorial hunger of flânerie, and this can only be exacerbated by the sexualised stereotypes applied exclusively to the black flâneur.[84]

Yet arguably *The Lonely Londoners* also accesses an alternative mythological discourse to that of the flâneur: one which harnesses the inverted power relations of post-colonial gothic. The references to the supernatural in

Selvon's novel have not often been remarked, but his interest in the magical practices of Obeah are evident in the short stories collected in *Ways of Sunlight* (1957), published a year after *The Lonely Londoners*.[85] These include 'Obeah in the Grove', which recounts the magical revenge taken by a group of Trinidadian immigrants who have been threatened with eviction from a flat in Ladbroke Grove by landlords who wish to empty the property as a precursor to gentrification. In an interview with Michel Fabre in the 1970s, Selvon stated:

> I treat obeah and magic as a natural occurrence; to me it is not exotic. I am interested in the human point of interest, in the way people believe in it and react to it in Trinidad, for instance, but I had no anthropological intent.[86]

For Lizabeth Paravisini-Gebert, the practice of Obeah (and its linked mythology of the zombie) is the key characteristic of the post-colonial gothic of the Caribbean, and of the turn which displaces the Eurocentrism of the genre by foregrounding the eerie self-alienation of the non-white experience within the spaces of colonialism. 'With the inclusion of the colonial, a new sort of darkness – of race, landscape, erotic desire and despair – enters the Gothic genre,' she writes.[87] And whereas, for white British writers, the colonial subject might become 'the obscene cannibalistic personification of evil', for Caribbean authors, 'gothic conventions play a crucial role in unveiling the atrocities of the slave system'.[88] In Mary Prince's abolitionist autobiography *The History of Mary Prince* (1831), for instance, the enslaved and tortured body materialises its insistent visibility as a witness to atrocity. This sense of the colonised body as a locus of horror makes the figures of zombies and Obeah men, Paravisini-Gebert argues, a potent representation of 'the conflicts and ambiguities of colonial situations' and Obeah itself 'the primary conduit for an ideology of rebellion'.[89]

Such conflicts and ambiguities could make the same journey of reverse colonisation as did the cursed mummies repatriated by Egyptologists in tales of gothic antiquarianism earlier in the twentieth century, except now the power of vengeful magic is wielded by living practitioners of the occult, not reanimated museum pieces. In 'Obeah in the Grove', for instance, one of the threatened tenants, Fiji, proposes that they

> work a little zeppy on the house. Just a little thing. Nothing much. The roof might fall in. The flooring might drop out. The walls might cave in. The whole house might tumble down one night as if the vengeance of Moko hit it.[90]

To this end, he sends for certain sketchily described 'things' from Jamaica, and his landlady hears him behind closed doors, 'talking to himself or singing or chanting something'; the next morning he instructs his friends to secrete the objects – a 'green bottle', a 'big bone' – in key locations during the night.[91]

'Now you and me ain't going to argue about Obeah,' the narrator cuts in at this point. 'I have other things to do, and I only want to give you the episode how it happen.'[92] The curse appears to work perfectly: no prospective buyer will touch the house ('in fact, a week later one of them was mad').[93] Both landlord and landlady suffer injuries as parts of the house collapse, and the landlord loses his job. The house, the narrator observes, 'get a kind of look about it, people afraid to even pass near it in the street'; it stands empty to this day, we are told, ''cause that house have the vengeance of Moko on it and it might tumble down any time'.[94]

Selvon uses the idea of the curse to poke fun at white attitudes towards neighbourhoods inhabited by people of colour, but he makes a serious point about the weird agency which is ascribed to those deemed magically capable of causing such unbearable existential discomfort to white people – and even chilling the furnaces of capitalism – simply by existing. Michael Banton described this phenomenon in his Stepney study: 'A Jamaican was told by an estate agent that if he were to purchase and occupy a certain house it would lower the value of the properties on either side by £100 or more,' he records, noting the self-deluding aspect of such racism:

> To have coloured people living next door would suggest to many [white] people that they were residing in a poor class neighbourhood ... As immigrants tend to take over the least attractive neighbourhoods there is logic in this train of thought. At other times, however, a district may have been declining for many years; when coloured people move in the residents blame them for the decline though they are its result, not its cause.[95]

In Selvon's story, the house's owners hope at first to capitalise on this very effect, letting rooms to the African-Caribbean characters as a way of scaring away a group of tenacious, white, sitting tenants. When Fiji seizes control of the mysterious negative power that has been bestowed on him by white panic, he is both subverting and ironically confirming the racist narrative that has been used against him. Yet his situation is not improved by this reclamation of agency; the men are still homeless at the end of the story, and Selvon leaves hanging the question of who, in the end, has really been cursed in the course of this uncanny transaction.

The same question arises in *The Lonely Londoners*, where superstition is more complexly elaborated and elided with the physical and psychological repercussions of economic exclusion. 'It had one bitter season,' the narrator recounts

> when it look like the vengeance of Moko fall on all the boys of London. Nobody can't get any work, fellars who had work losing it, and all over the place it look like if Operation Pressure gone into execution in a big way.[96]

Living in such hardship, many of the 'boys' are condemned to live a kind of death-in-life, demonstrating an almost supernatural ability to cling on to existence in the face of starvation. 'It had a time when Bart train himself to live on tea for weeks,' the narrator comments. 'He nearly dead in that room ... But fellars like Bart, ordinary death through illness not make for them.'[97] Another man, nicknamed Captain, also seems able to cheat death:

> It have some men in this world, they don't do nothing at all, and you feel that they would dead from starvation, but day after day you meeting them and they looking hale, they laughing and they talking as if they have a million dollars, and in truth it look as if they would not only live longer than you but they would dead happier. Cap was a man like that.[98]

Nevertheless, delirious with hunger at one point, Cap hallucinates a 'white pigeon flying over his head' which he believes 'must be the spirit of my father in Nigeria', and also sees an 'angel with a harp' hovering over Moses as he sleeps.[99] Later, when he is starving, Cap hits on the idea of catching and eating the seagulls which land on his window sill, but in doing so makes his own hallucination a reality: one bird escapes from his snare and flaps around his ceiling, the ironic concretisation of his supposedly magical visitation.[100]

Characteristically, Galahad takes matters into his own hands during this period of famine, and sets out to trap one of the pigeons in Kensington Gardens. In doing so, however, he becomes even more of a gothic oddity in the eyes of the 'Nordics' (Selvon's term for white people) who already consider him a 'witchdoctor' for his apparent imperviousness to cold; a passing dog-walker accuses him of being 'a cruel, cruel beast' a 'monster', and a 'killer', and when he brings the pigeon home, he can barely bring himself to eat it.[101] Galahad's attempts to perform and reclaim his own otherness may allow him to shake off the most superstitious assumptions of his white interpreters, but he cannot escape a more profound sense of uncanny fracture brought about by racism. In perhaps the novel's most famous passage, he experiences a radical dissociation from his own skin:

> Galahad watch the colour of this hand, and talk to it, saying, 'Colour, is you that causing all this, you know. Why the hell you can't be blue, or red or green, if you can't be white? You know is you that cause a lot of misery in the world. Is not me, you know, is you! I ain't do anything to infuriate the people and them, is you! Look at you, you so black and innocent, and this time so you causing misery all over the world!'[102]

Galahad is addressing his skin as the troubling relic of his vestigial colonial identity, and of himself as the failed simulacrum of a hegemonic norm of whiteness. As Homi Bhabha describes it, this assumption that people of colour should mimic white habits and behaviours – the concept of an otherness that is 'almost the same, *but not quite*' – is as essentially gothic in its expression as Barbara Jones's collection of unnerving human simulacra at the *Black Eyes and Lemonade* exhibition: it makes visible a region of repressed horror which would otherwise remain hidden.[103] 'Black skin splits under the racist gaze,' Bhabha notes, 'displaced into signs of bestiality, genitalia, grotesquerie, which reveals the phobic myth of the undifferentiated whole white body.'[104] The reification and dehumanisation of the immigrant body as a spectacular object is thus implicated in the idea of skin-pigment having a malignant agency ascribed to it, from which the man who bears it may long to be dissociated. In Selvon's novel, this longing for dissociation makes Galahad's own body uncanny to him.

Describing the 'museum gothic', Roger Luckhurst notes that the collection and exhibition of dislocated objects 'comes with a glimmer of a superstitious thought that these things might slip from commodity fetishes back into roles as genuine magical fetishes'.[105] *The Lonely Londoners* can be read as a gothic novel within the specifically mid-century iteration which this book seeks to delineate: its uncanny elements are firmly imbricated in social relations and the fetishes of commodity culture. Its haunted locations are not gothic ruins, nor even imperial museums, but the dirty, damaged streetscapes of the everyday, and the upstart objects which wash up there, trailing uncomfortable histories.

'SO DIFFERENT, SO APPEALING': THE INDEPENDENT GROUP AND THE WEIRDNESS OF THE EVERYDAY

Economic necessity caused African-Caribbean migrants to transform the visual culture of their neighbourhoods in specific ways, which often remained unacknowledged. Michael Banton was struck by the peculiar effects created when tenants, informally but firmly segregated into the least desirable residential areas available, attempted to make their homes more comfortable:

> It would seem that at one time the surplus ex-army goods sold in the neighbourhood included a supply of fire control panorama: these are large oblong stylised pictures of town and country scenes on thick paper which are used for teaching soldiers how to indicate targets when giving fire control orders. These papers were bought by some people and used for papering the walls of their rooms, creating an extraordinarily bizarre effect, matched only by a basement room which had been papered entirely with pictures cut from magazines.[106]

A remarkably similar ad-hoc approach to decoration would be harnessed by the Independent Group in the name of pop art; Eduardo Paolozzi, in particular, had been collecting American magazine illustrations since the 1940s, and reimagining them for collages about restless consumer desire, such as *Dr Pepper* (1948). Indeed, when he presided over the first meeting of the Independent Group in 1952, he projected a series of such images on the wall via an epidiascope, and called the resulting collection *Bunk!*[107] For the Independent Group, inspired by André Malraux's concept of the 'musée imaginaire', any object or image could make the transition into art, resulting in another radical disturbance of aesthetic categorisation. Malraux had conceived his new aesthetic in terms of exposure to exotic and uncanny new sights which glibly reinforced old hierarchies; he wanted to open the eyes of art students not only to great paintings but to 'a host of second-rank pictures, archaic arts, Indian, Chinese and Pre-Columbian sculpture of the best periods, Romanesque frescoes, Negro and "folk art", a fair quantity of Byzantine art'.[108] Nigel Henderson also looked to imagery from ethnography and anthropology to find echoes of the modern vernacular and a justifying aesthetic which might reconcile them, but whereas Malraux – like Herbert Read in *40,000 Years of Modern Art* – had requisitioned non-Western art as theoretical cover for transgressions against classicism, the Independent Group, and Henderson in particular, introduced the idea of creative alterity into practices much closer to home.

From 1948 to 1952, Henderson lived and worked in Bethnal Green, where his wife Judith, a sociologist, was studying working-class social rituals on Chisenhall Road – and in particular, those of the family next door, the Samuels, whom Henderson also photographed extensively:

> Judith's job was to take responsibility for a course called 'Discover Your Neighbour' ... with the object of putting before professional people such as doctors, lawyers, probation officers, priests etc. ... an analysis of the historical conditioning forces acting on a community and bringing, over time, a cohesive system of attitudes, sympathies, prejudices – what you like – which would in some measure represent such a community.[109]

His Bethnal Green photographs often feature the marks and scratches made by non-artists on the walls and pavements of the streetscape, such as graffiti and hopscotch – just as Jones had curated billboards, shop signs and a live pavement artist called Mr McErnean working on the gallery floor.[110] Like the muralists and ruin-dwellers in the previous chapter, Henderson's eye was informed by the strangeness of war-damaged buildings:

> Houses chopped by bombs while ladies were still sitting on the lavatory, the rest of the house gone but the wallpaper and the fires still burning in the grate. Who can hold a candle to that kind of real life Surrealism?[111]

His response to this question, and to the ongoing mid-century project of dismantling the boundaries that separate art from the everyday, was *Parallel of Life and Art* (1953), which presented visitors with an overwhelmingly immersive walk-through experience, suspending images from the ceiling and at all angles so that the viewer's eye was flooded with competing perspectives. This style of installation amounted to a rejection of the haptic and auratic properties of things and artworks. Originals by Henderson and Paolozzi were presented as photographs of themselves, while the work of Jackson Pollock appeared in the form of a candid shot of him painting in his studio, photographed by Hans

Namuth and published in *Life* magazine. Photography disrupted the authorial subject's claim to self-expression while at the same time allowing for the autonomy of the thing being observed. Reviewing the show in *Art News and Review*, Bryan Robertson of the Whitechapel Gallery noted: 'The exhibition ... leaves the spectator with the feeling that the barriers between the artist, the scientist and the technician are dissolving in a singularly potent way.'[112] Other barriers were broken down as well: the juxtaposition of photomicrographs, aerial views and x-rays, alongside images from newspapers and books, dismantled assumptions about scale and spatiality. Time, too, was disrupted and flattened, with ancient artefacts, modern art and timeless natural forms placed together. As Ben Highmore has pointed out, when Henderson photographed the installation he placed his own young daughter Justin into shot beneath a photograph of the remains of a dead child excavated at Pompeii;[113] it is as if the Roman child, who was transformed into a thing first by the hot volcanic ash which encased its corpse, and then by the actions of archaeologists who unearthed it and turned it into a museum exhibit, has been uncannily resurrected within the suggestively open, dialogical and anachronic installation.

But by the time he was working on 'Patio and Pavilion' in 1956, Henderson was confident enough of the articulacy of objects themselves to remove the frame of photography and rely on installation alone to mediate them. Members of the Independent Group made up twelve of the thirty-six participants in the group show *This is Tomorrow* at the Whitechapel Gallery, which was conceived as a series of individual environments grappling with ideas about design and spatial habitats. 'Patio and Pavilion' was part of their joint contribution. This shed-like space, created by Henderson, Paolozzi, and Alison and Peter Smithson, was filled with artfully arranged junk and debris, much of it retrieved from bombsites. Some of them were simply placed on the floor or arranged on tables, others were placed on the translucent corrugated plastic of the pavilion's roof, so that their ghostly forms were visible from within the structure, like a kind of three-dimensional photogram. There was no explicit reference to Barbara Jones's exhibition, which had filled the same space five years earlier, but *This is Tomorrow* was surely the logical culmination of her critique of bourgeois connoisseurship. It was described by Lawrence Alloway in the catalogue's introduction as 'a lesson in spectatorship':

> [It] cuts across the learned responses of conventional perception. In *This Is Tomorrow* the visitor is exposed to space effects, play with signs, a wide range of materials and structures, which, taken together, make of art and architecture a many-channelled activity, as factual and far from ideal standards as the street outside.[114]

'Patio and Pavilion' took this definition to its most abstract extreme. As the Smithsons explained in a BBC radio programme about the exhibition:

> We worked on a kind of symbolic habitat in which are found responses, in some form or other, to the basic human needs ... The actual form is very simple, a 'patio' or enclosed space, in which sits a 'pavilion'. The patio and pavilion are furnished with objects which are symbols for the things we need: for example, a wheel image for movement and for machines.[115]

Presided over by Henderson's large photocollage of a head (glossed in the catalogue as 'for man himself – his brain & his machines') and reverently displayed in a roped-off zone, the curated bombsite fragments resembled the precious relics retrieved from an archaeological dig. Robert Melville's response in the *Architectural Review* found homeliness in the collection, commenting that the installation 'returned us safely to the bicycle shed at the bottom of the garden in a singular tribute to the pottering man'.[116] Yet Reyner Banham instead described the mesmeric accumulation of 'objects, images, shards of real and imaginary civilisations dredged up from the subconscious of Eduardo Paolozzi, Nigel Henderson ... a kind of personal archaeology which you just had to stand and look at'.[117]

The most famous image from *This is Tomorrow*, however, is Richard Hamilton's epoch-defining collage, *Just what is it that makes today's homes so different, so appealing?*, which evokes a different kind of visual articulacy: the mythopoeic aesthetic of consumer desire as expressed in American advertising imagery. In Hamilton's collage – which was printed in the catalogue but not exhibited in the gallery – the walls of 'today's homes' are unpunctured by bombs and unravaged by time, and seem determined to stand firm in their uninflected modernity. Yet the influx of American mass-cultural signifiers nevertheless testifies to an ongoing porosity: the domestic scene here is no more private than it was for the lady sitting on the toilet of her blitzed house. The human nude, represented in the foreground by a found image of the bodybuilder Irwin 'Zabo' Koszewski, is as commoditised and rectified as the utilitarian label on the can of tinned ham prominently displayed on the coffee table.[118] Outside the window, a cinema marquee is advertising *The Jazz Singer*, a film about Jewish-American identity and assimilation in which the lead character is an emotionally conflicted performer trying to reconcile his secular ambitions with his heritage as a cantor's son. Problematically, he uses blackface to erase his ethnic identity – while (like the clubbers in *Momma Don't Allow*) simultaneously erasing the African-American jazz artists who invented the form that he has appropriated.[119] In Hamilton's collage, Al Jolson's face is not visible – only his white gloves evoke his 'minstrel' costume – but his presence underlines the themes of doubling, estrangement and contested skin which link Hamilton's poster to Jones's exhibition and Selvon's fiction. This is collage as a taxidermied approximation of the materiality of real life, horrific in its banality.

Marshall McLuhan called advertising 'the folklore of industrial man', connecting the domesticated desire for exotic plenitude with the ancient myth-making of communal oral tradition.[120] Hamilton's picture seizes on American visual culture to solicit the same dialectic of otherness and familiarity implicated in Jones's decision to follow the traces of 'Oriental' decoration from the street fairs and canal barges into the art gallery. Past, present, *heimlich* and *unheimlich* all threaten to occupy identical space-time in the uncannily shifting sands of post-war culture. The Sutton Hoo chieftain's missing body has been replaced by a parodically priapic body builder, a place-holder for the subject's ultra-presence in advertising's rhetoric of elusive identity. Confronted by objects and spaces which no longer frame experience in an easily interpretable way, material culture comes to be haunted by the idea of human subjectivity. As Jones puts it:

> A human figure stands perpetually behind each of us, and in solitude or darkness moves into the margin of focus, but never stands square in sight. Those of us who are most afraid seek to exorcise this figure by making its portrait, the horrid simulacra of man.[121]

In the next chapter, the materiality of the body itself comes into focus as visual technologies enable new kinds of simulacra to stand in for the human subject. If the gaze was a vector of ideological conflict in the mid-century performance of identity, the invention of television, and the spectrality of its images, would open up further questions about visibility, autonomy and power.

NOTES

1. See Angela Care Evans, *The Sutton Hoo Ship Burial* (London: British Museum, 1986), pp. 19–22 for a full account of the excavation.
2. 'Anglo-Saxon burial ship: treasures found in excavation on Suffolk estate', *Manchester Guardian*, 31 July 1939, p. 13; 'Ship burial in Suffolk: jury's finding on gold and silver, not "treasure trove"', *The Times*, 15 August 1939, p. 9.
3. 'A mystery burial ship: treasures without a body', *The Times*, 23 February 1940, p. 6.
4. C.W. Phillips, 'The Excavation of the Sutton Hoo Ship-Burial', in R.L.S. Bruce-Mitford, ed., *Recent Archaeological Excavations in Britain* (London: Routledge & Kegan Paul, 1956), pp. 159–60.
5. Phillips, 'Excavation of the Sutton Hoo Ship-Burial', p. 161.
6. Phillips, 'Excavation of the Sutton Hoo Ship-Burial', p. 161.
7. R.L.S. Bruce-Mitford, 'The Sutton Hoo Ship-Burial', *Scientific American*, 184:4 (April 1951), 24–30 (p. 24).
8. 'London's museums renewed and rising popular demand: the aftermath of war', *The Times*, 7 June 1946, p. 7.
9. Waugh, *Brideshead Revisited*, p. 5.
10. See Care Evans, *Sutton Hoo Ship Burial*, pp. 59–62 for a dismissal of the theory that some items suggest a Christian sensibility.
11. *South Bank Exhibition London*, p. 63.
12. *South Bank Exhibition London*, p. 65.
13. 'Discoveries at Sutton Hoo: Anglo-Saxon art', *Manchester Guardian*, 27 September 1939, p. 6.

14 Roger Luckhurst, *The Mummy's Curse: The True History of a Dark Fantasy* (Oxford: Oxford University Press, 2014), p. 166.
15 Lizbeth Paravisini-Gebert, 'Colonial and Post-Colonial Gothic: The Caribbean', in Jerrold E. Hogle, ed., *The Cambridge Companion to Gothic Fiction* (Cambridge: Cambridge University Press, 2002), pp. 232–33.
16 Paravisini-Gebert, 'Colonial and Post-Colonial Gothic', p. 233.
17 Sam Selvon, *The Lonely Londoners* (London: Penguin, 2006).
18 Noel Carrington and Clarke Hutton, *Popular Art in Britain* (London: Penguin, 1945); thus on the title page; the cover gives the title as *Popular English Art*.
19 Carrington and Hutton, *Popular Art*, p. 11.
20 Barbara Jones, 'Introduction', *Black Eyes and Lemonade*, exhibition catalogue (London: Whitechapel Gallery, 1951) p. 6.
21 Barbara Jones, *The Unsophisticated Arts* (London: Architectural Press, 1951) p. 123.
22 The two waxworks were Queen Caroline and the late Chief Rabbi Joseph Hertz, although these specimens were chosen for their availability rather than for any thematic relevance.
23 Jones, *The Unsophisticated Arts*, p. 126; p. 132.
24 Gillian Whiteley, 'Kitsch as Cultural Capital: Black Eyes and Lemonade and Populist aesthetics in Fifties Britain', in Monica Kjellman-Chapin, ed., *Kitsch: History, Theory, Practice* (Newcastle Upon Tyne: Cambridge Scholars, 2013), pp. 40–57.
25 Letters and notes from the SEA dated June 1950, in private Barbara Jones papers, quoted in Whiteley, 'Kitsch as Cultural Capital', p. 49.
26 SEA document, dated 27 March 1951, Barbara Jones papers, quoted in Whiteley, 'Kitsch as Cultural Capital', p. 49.
27 Jones, 'Introduction', p. 6.
28 Visitor numbers from minutes in the Whitechapel archive.
29 Barbara Jones, 'Introduction', p. 6.
30 Barbara Jones, 'Popular Arts', in Banham and Hillier, *Tonic*, pp. 129–32 (p. 132).
31 Jones, 'Introduction', p. 7.
32 Jones, 'Introduction', p. 5.
33 Jones, 'Popular Arts', p. 131.
34 Walter Benjamin, *The Arcades Project*, trans. Howard Eiland and Kevin McLaughlin (Cambridge, MA: Harvard University Press, 1999), p. 207.
35 Benjamin, *The Arcades Project*, p. 207.
36 Jones, 'Introduction', p. 5.
37 'Bargepole – please do not touch', cartoon caption, *Evening News*, 8 September 1951, p. 13.
38 Jones, 'Introduction', p. 7. Brumas was the name of a polar bear cub born, to much public interest, at London Zoo in 1949.
39 Jones, 'Introduction', p. 7.
40 Jones, 'Introduction', p. 15.
41 Jones, *The Unsophisticated Arts*, p. 19.
42 Jones, *The Unsophisticated Arts*, p. 20.
43 Jones, *The Unsophisticated Arts*, p. 21.
44 Jones, *The Unsophisticated Arts*, p. 21.
45 Jones, *The Unsophisticated Arts*, p. 9.
46 Jones, *The Unsophisticated Arts*, p. 10.

47 Jones, 'Introduction', p. 41.
48 Jones, *The Unsophisticated Arts*, p. 109.
49 Jones, *The Unsophisticated Arts*, p. 109.
50 Thomas Moore, Letter 6, *Intercepted Letters; or, The Two-Penny Postbag* (London, 1813) (facsimile edition printed by Bibliobazaar, 2010), unpaginated.
51 Jones, 'Introduction', p. 5.
52 Becky E. Conekin, *'The Autobiography of a Nation': The 1951 Festival of Britain* (Manchester: Manchester University Press, 2003), p. 184.
53 William Fagg, *Traditional Sculpture from the Colonies* (London: Colonial Office, 1951), p. 3.
54 Unpublished transcript of Herbert Read's press conference speech, undated, p. 2, ICA Archives. Quoted in Anne Massey, *The Independent Group: Modernism and Mass Culture in Britain, 1945–59* (Manchester: Manchester University Press, 1995), p. 25
55 Ros Ballaster, *Fabulous Orients: Fictions of the East in England 1662–1785* (Oxford: Oxford University Press, 2005), p. 4.
56 See for instance, T.S. Eliot's argument in *Culture*.
57 Jones, *The Unsophisticated Arts*, p. 10.
58 The junk shop analogy was noted at the time in a review by G.S. Whittet, 'London commentary', *Studio International*, November 1951, p. 154.
59 'Adrift in Europe', *The Times*, 8 February 1945, p. 5. For a full account of international efforts to solve the refugee problem after the Second World War, see also Gerard Daniel Cohen, *In War's Wake: Europe's Displaced Persons in the Postwar Order* (Oxford: Oxford University Press, 2012), pp. 13–34.
60 'Homeless people of Europe: UNO committee's work ending', *The Times*, 1 June 1946, p. 4.
61 'Displaced persons for England: women of Baltic States', *The Times*, 24 July 1946, p. 4; 'New homes for 893,000 refugees', *The Times*, 28 March 1951, p. 3.
62 'Surplus population of Europe: help for migrants', *The Times*, 7 December 1953, p. 6; 'Exiles in Britain: flourishing Slav settlements in our midst', *The Times*, 20 June 1953, p. 7.
63 'Those who are left', *The Times*, 8 March 1956, p. 11.
64 Michael Banton, *The Coloured Quarter: Negro Immigrants in an English City* (London: Cape, 1955).
65 Banton, *The Coloured Quarter*, p. 93.
66 Banton, *The Coloured Quarter*, p. 92.
67 Banton, *The Coloured Quarter*, p. 92.
68 Banton, *The Coloured Quarter*, p. 88.
69 Artists whose British tours were organised by Chris Barber at this time included Big Bill Broonzy in 1954 and Muddy Waters in 1958. See 'Blues History' an interview with Chris Barber in *fROOTS Magazine*, August/September 2005, www.chrisbarber.net/archives/froots/froots.htm [accessed 28 January 2018]. See also *Later with Jools Holland* (Episode 31.5, BBC, 2008), www.youtube.com/watch?v=zFWHudQQ82A [accessed 28 January 2018].
70 Bryony Dixon and Christophe Dupin, 'Soup dreams', *Sight & Sound*, March 2001, pp. 28–30 (p. 29).
71 Jones, *The Unsophisticated Arts*, p. 145.

72 Dixon and Dupin, 'Soup dreams', p. 29.
73 Selvon, *The Lonely Londoners*.
74 Selvon, *The Lonely Londoners*, pp. 74–75. For more on the semantics of the plastic raincoat in the mid-century, see Chapter 5.
75 Selvon, *The Lonely Londoners*, p. 79.
76 Mpalive-Hangson Msiska, 'Sam Selvon's *The Lonely Londoners* and the Structure of Black Metropolitan Life', *African and Black Diaspora: An International Journal*, 2:1 (January 2009), 5–27. pp. 8–9.
77 Selvon, *The Lonely Londoners*, p. 61.
78 Selvon, *The Lonely Londoners*, p. 61.
79 Selvon, *The Lonely Londoners*, p. 61.
80 Selvon, *The Lonely Londoners*, p. 92.
81 Selvon, *The Lonely Londoners*, p. 101.
82 Selvon, *The Lonely Londoners*, p. 100.
83 Selvon, *The Lonely Londoners*, p. 101.
84 Msiska, 'Sam Selvon's *The Lonely Londoners*', p. 10.
85 Sam Selvon, *Ways of Sunlight* (London: Hodder Education, 2015).
86 Michel Fabre, 'Samuel Selvon: Interviews and Conversations', in Susheila Nasta, ed., *Critical Perspectives on Sam Selvon* (Washington DC: Three Continents Press, 1988), p. 65.
87 Paravisini-Gebert, 'Colonial and Post-Colonial Gothic', p. 229.
88 Paravisini-Gebert, 'Colonial and Post-Colonial Gothic', pp. 231–32.
89 Paravisini-Gebert, 'Colonial and Post-Colonial Gothic', p. 233; p. 235.
90 Selvon, *Ways of Sunlight*, p. 159. 'The vengeance of Moko' is a Trinidadian expression referring to 'unrelenting punitive force', according to Maureen Warner Lewis in *Guinea's Other Suns: The African Dynamic in Trinidad Culture* (Dover, MA: Majority Press, 1991) p. 16. She compares the expression with the name 'moko-jumbi' given to a stiltwaker in Trinidadian masquerade who represents a watchful god or spirit, and speculates that the name may refer to a tribe called Moko from Calabar, near the Niger Delta, members of which were among those forcibly taken as slaves to Trinidad.
91 Selvon, *Ways of Sunlight*, p. 161; p. 153.
92 Selvon, *Ways of Sunlight*, p. 161.
93 Selvon, *Ways of Sunlight*, p. 162.
94 Selvon, *Ways of Sunlight*, p. 162.
95 Banton, *The Coloured Quarter*, p. 71.
96 Selvon, *The Lonely Londoners*, p. 116.
97 Selvon, *The Lonely Londoners*, pp. 49–50.
98 Selvon, *The Lonely Londoners*, p. 31.
99 Selvon, *The Lonely Londoners*, p. 32.
100 Selvon, *The Lonely Londoners*, pp. 132–33.
101 Selvon, *The Lonely Londoners*, p. 117; p. 119.
102 Selvon, *The Lonely Londoners*, p. 77.
103 Homi Bhabha, 'Of Mimicry and Man: The Ambivalence of Colonial Discourse', *October*, 28 (Spring 1984), 125–33 (p. 127), emphasis in the original.
104 Bhabha, 'Of Mimicry and Man', pp. 132–33.
105 Luckhurst, *The Mummy's Curse*, p. 175.

106 Banton, *The Coloured Quarter*, p. 109.
107 See Massey, *The Independent Group*, p. 46.
108 André Malraux, *The Voices of Silence*, trans. Stuart Gilbert (London: Secker & Warburg, 1956), p. 16.
109 *Nigel Henderson: Photographs of Bethnal Green 1949–1952*, exhibition catalogue (Nottingham: Midland Group, 1978), p. 3.
110 See Ben Highmore, 'Hopscotch Modernism: On Everyday Life and Blurring of Art and Social Science', *Modernist Cultures*, 2:1 (Summer 2006), 70–79.
111 Henderson, interviewed by David Mellor in 'Mass-Observation: The Intellectual Climate', *Camerawork*, 11 (September 1978), 4–5.
112 Bryan Robertson, 'Parallel of life and art', *Art News and Review*, 19 September 1953, p. 6.
113 Ben Highmore 'Something out of nothing: concretising the immaterial in Brutalism', plenary at 'Objects of Modernity', 23–24 June 2014, University of Birmingham.
114 Lawrence Alloway, 'Design as Human Activity', in *This Is Tomorrow*, exhibition catalogue (Whitechapel Gallery, 1956), unpaginated.
115 Alison and Peter Smithson, *Changing the Art of Inhabitation* (London: Ellipsis, 1994), p. 109.
116 Robert Melville, 'Exhibitions', *Architectural Review*, 120 (November 1956), 332–34 (p. 334).
117 Banham, recorded in 1976 as part of the Arts Council Film *Fathers of Pop*, but not used. Quoted in Victoria Walsh, *Nigel Henderson: Parallel of Life and Art* (London: Thames & Hudson, 2001), p. 117.
118 For a fascinating account of the origins of the images used in the collage, see John-Paul Stonard, 'Pop in the Age of Boom: Richard Hamilton's "Just What is it That Makes Today's Homes So Different, So Appealing?"', *Burlington Magazine* (September 2007) 607–20.
119 *The Jazz Singer*, dir. Alan Crosland, 1927. For a detailed analysis of the use of black-face in the film, see Corin Willis, 'Meaning and value in *The Jazz Singer*' in John Gibbs and Douglas Pye, eds., *Style and Meaning: Studies in the Detailed Analysis of Film* (Manchester: Manchester University Press, 2005), pp. 127–40.
120 Marshall McLuhan, *The Mechanical Bride: Folklore of Industrial Man* (New York: Vanguard, 1951).
121 Jones, *The Unsophisticated Arts*, p. 117.

3

MACHINES AND SPECTRALITY: THE GOTHIC POTENTIAL OF TECHNOLOGY

'You need not be there.' An strapline for an advertisement for Pye television sets published in 1949 struck a surprisingly diffident, even negative note, given that it was promoting a new technological wonder. Television, still in its infancy, had yet to prove it had something to offer beyond an off-putting uncanniness: this was an apparatus that seemed to make concepts such as presence and absence suddenly complicated or even paradoxical; when things could be materialised out of thin air inside something as bafflingly high-tech as a cathode-ray tube, what might be made to *disappear* by similarly inexplicable means? To compensate for any resistance this unease might cause in the buying public, Pye promoted its product as a way of dispensing with the nuisance of mere humdrum physical presence in favour of a superior ability to oversee and master the world. The illustration accompanying the advertisement presented the undesirable, outmoded alternative to televisually mediated experience: a small, clownish cartoon figure is trying to view an unspecified spectacle, but is dwarfed by a solid wall of blank backs belonging to taller, more modern and – it is implied – more capable and assertive men. 'Bert always likes to be there, but personally we prefer to see it, and we're sure you do too,' runs the caption. 'There is no better way of doing this than by a Pye.'[1]

The implied binary stand-off between vision and presence – 'being there' versus 'seeing it' – meant that the rise of television intersected neatly with philosophical debates current at the time, in which the status of human consciousness, as a material, neurobiological phenomenon on the one hand, or as an immaterial manifestation of selfhood on the other, was being contested. New technologies seemed to offer novel insights into the ontology of the mind and of apprehension itself. Of course, machines – always a special category of object – had been susceptible to such metaphorical appropriation since the Enlightenment, when Descartes compared certain aspects of the human mind to a clockwork mechanism.[2] Later, photography and cinema enlarged the scopic capabilities of the culture on a diachronic plane by carrying visual imprints of the past into the present; but now, in the mid-century, live television was promising to telescope space within a synchronic instant, bringing the spectacle into the home or – as in the Pye advertisement – carrying the home viewer into the spectacle as it happened. Thus the viewer would be implicated in the process of dematerialisation and rematerialisation which the apparatus achieves; like the picture on the screen, he or she is 'there' and 'not-there' simultaneously. Arguably, the meeting point of viewer and spectacle is experienced as a third, middle zone, inside the medium itself. The idea of being 'present' escapes both time and space.

This technological enhancement of human vision coincided with new ideas about human consciousness to contribute to a distinctive cultural turn. In this chapter, I will argue that one of the mid-century's cultural responses to this prevailing atmosphere of innovation and uncertainty informed a new iteration of the gothic, which created its own kind of ludic 'third space' in which the uncanny resonances of modernity – its revenant truths and haunting perspectives, its other worlds and alternative life-forms – could be materialised, examined and confronted.[3] Reading Orwell's *Nineteen Eighty-Four* as a mid-century gothic text, it is possible to see how the age of television could transform a real, solid thing like an antique glass paperweight, with an apparently immutable adhesion to the linearity of time and the geometry of space, into a historical anchor for, and sometimes a hostile witness to, human mutability. Conversely, new objects such as televisions, radar screens, and early computers seemed capable of enabling the disruption of linearity and geometry, and of assuming a quasi-lifelike power over time and space. As we shall see later in the chapter, the gothic turn is clearly discernible in the writings of mid-century scientists investigating human thought, such as William Grey Walter and Alan Turing. Philosophical, neurological and cybernetic enquiry raised questions about the exact relationship between abstract thought and brain activity, and the cathode-ray screen was where these concerns shimmered into view. Technological metaphors for human consciousness were revisited and redrawn to take account of new types of machine. Lacan's mid-century development of Freud's ideas depended on the age's new technologies of presence and vision, while the novel images that came into being on these new screens overturned old ideas about what images themselves might be capable of.

In the two previous chapters, I have examined what happened to the idea of art when everyday objects erupted into the realm of aesthetics; this chapter explores what happened to the idea of objects when images (mediated by technology) began to intervene in the territory of things. The analogy between images and objects – or images *as* objects – is itself essentially a gothic one; the blurring of boundaries between categories, coupled with unease about the disruption of proper spatial and temporal order, produces an uncanny effect and supercharges the objects and images with meaning – meaning which often buckles and flexes under such semantic pressure. This idea has informed the post-modern theory of uncanny visual culture expounded by W.T.J. Mitchell in *What Do Pictures Want?*, in which he proposes to

> shift the question from what pictures *do* to what they *want*, from power to desire, from the model of the dominant power to be opposed, to the model of the subaltern to be interrogated or (better) to be invited to speak.[4]

Indeed arguably, Mitchell attributes to picture-things not just an interrogation of the subject/object dialectic but an agglomeration of qualities ('animation... vitality... agency, motivation, autonomy, aura, fecundity') that suggest that 'pictures are something like life-forms'.[5] The new televisual images of the post-war period seemed to contemporary audience to possess just this quality of lifelikeness. Such images, according to Mitchell, become tropic figures, like dream-objects, which reflect the consciousness of the human subject. Art, and by extension all media, create the essential context in which pictures manifest themselves as autonomous agents: 'If images are life-forms, and objects are the bodies they animate, then media are the habitats or ecosystems in which pictures come alive.'[6] But as thresholds or conduits for meaning, media are in a constant state of crisis, sucking in and spewing forth interchangeable subjects and objects:

> Perhaps this is the fundamental paradox built into the concept of media as such. A medium just is a 'middle', an in-between or go-between, a space or pathway or messenger that connects two things. ... The problem arises when we try to determine the boundaries of the medium. ... If media are middles, they are ever-elastic middles that expand to include what look at first like their outer boundaries. The medium does not lie between sender and receiver; it includes and constitutes them.[7]

Jeffrey Sconce has argued, from a similarly post-modern position, that television instantiates a 'flowing metatextual empire'[8] in which viewers 'like ghosts and psychotics ... wander through a hallucinatory world of eternal simulation'.[9] His history of *Haunted Media* describes American cultural responses to technological telepresence in terms of a repeated return to the gothic mood. His analysis identifies three recurring fictions – 'disembodiment, teleportation and anthropomorphisation' – which respond to telecommunication's 'power to atomise and disperse both body and consciousness across the vast expanses of the universe'.[10] He is less interested, however, in the dialectical relationship between this atomisation and the world of solid objects which, I will argue in this chapter, defines the mid-century in British culture generally, and in cathode-ray-enabled culture in particular.

VISIONS OF THE UNCANNY: CATHODE-RAY TUBES, TELEPRESENCE AND THE MEDIATED SUBJECT

When the BBC television service launched in London in 1936, it had its own theme tune, sung by Adele Dixon. Intercut with exciting shots of hulking cameras and lab-coated technicians sitting in front of banks of switches, the song referred to television's 'new enchantment' and included the lines

> A mighty maze of mystic, magic rays
> Is all about us in the blue,
> And in sight and sound they trace
> Living pictures out of space
> To bring a new wonder to you.[11]

This veneer of mysticality is striking but it was not unusual. All along, the technology that made television possible had been presented to the public as an uncanny phenomenon. An early US newspaper report about the invention of the Coolidge vacuum tube – a forerunner of both x-ray and cathode-ray tubes – describes the apparatus as 'an alchemist that changes solids into liquids and liquids into solids'.[12] Its tone is a mixture of awe and disquiet and its sub-headline, 'what will it do for Humanity?', hints at the related but less comfortable question: what will it do *to* humanity? A *Scientific Monthly* article in 1926 continued the theme of the disquieting agency of cathode rays, remarking on various miraculous phenomena associated with the passage of electrons through a sealed glass tube, including a haze of light in the air, the materialisation of a new yellow compound, and the observation of long- and short-lived luminescence in various substances.[13] By the time the CRT was developed into a screen by devising a way to control the luminescence with electro-magnetic fields, these hand-blown pieces of heavy glass were firmly understood as a kind of crystal ball, where messages materialised out of the ether. Viewers peering into one of the early television sets, which reflected the boxed-in screen onto a mirror lid set at an angle above it, were invited to perceive themselves not only as cutting-edge early adopters, but also as soothsayers interpreting strange signs from another realm. From a scientific point of view, the discovery of cathode rays provided proof of the existence of subatomic particles and inaugurated the development of electronics. But the CRT also promised to redefine materiality. Whereas x-rays enabled human vision to access the inner structures of familiar things and human bodies, cathode rays seemed able to conjure new things into existence, and to access the inner life of the human mind.

The BBC song about 'magic mystic rays' flying around in the air was based on the misconception that cathode rays themselves – rather than the less exotic radio waves – are transmitted through the ether; the cathode rays have leaked out, so to speak, from the core of the television set and into the human realm. This sense that cathode rays were 'all about us', an enveloping cloud out of which wonders would materialise, demonstrates how these new viewers became conceptually imbricated with the technology; the human subject was no longer merely a receiver of signs, but was understood as making an essential contribution to the picture. Freud's essay on *The Uncanny* is much concerned with reading and writing, and the double or ambiguous meanings which create an uncanny effect by allowing us to glimpse the traces of the unconscious: the *Unheimlich*, he wrote,

> arises when the boundary between fantasy and reality is blurred, when we are faced with the reality of something that we have until now considered imaginary, when a symbol takes on the full function and significance of what it symbolises.[14]

The cathode-ray screen similarly performs and makes apparent the process of interpretation and inscription: it operates as an autonomous reader and writer, reading an electronic code and reinscribing it in a palimpsest of pixelated lines, their outputs operating independently of any human agenda. The cathode-ray tube might be described as an uncanniness machine, not only generating uncertainty about reality, but also exposing and dramatising the machinery of semiotic response. Sigmund Freud's chosen exemplar of *unheimlich* storytelling, Hoffmann's 'The Sandman', itself dramatises this process via the agency of a piece of scientific apparatus, in repeated encounters between a flawed reader, the neurotic Nathaniel, and the Sandman himself, who appears first as the alchemist Coppelius who threatens to burn out the young Nathaniel's eyes, and later as the technician – Freud calls him an optician ('Optiker') – who peddles barometers, telescopes and other scientific prosthetics for human vision. Nathaniel comes to fear all such technological objects which access the real, mediate it and then output it in the flickering, immaterial realm of the symbolic, and his neurosis eventually leads to his suicide. For Freud, Hoffman's emphasis on eyes was proof that the uncanny was connected with the post-Oedipal castration complex, but it is notable that his formulation of the *Unheimlich* depends on concepts which themselves uncannily duplicate the potentiality of cathode-ray tubes: not only the prioritisation of ocularity and the gaze, but the relationship between perception and deception, and the temporal and spatial displacement of objects which appear in the 'wrong' place.

The crucial difference between television and earlier visual media like film lies in the way it visualises and interprets time and space. For Walter Benjamin, writing in the 1930s, film defined modernity; the immersive experience of the cinema seemed to him to be of a piece with modernism in its alertness to cutting and fragmentation and its unflinching surgical gaze. The CRT screen, in contrast, was arguably the first *post*-modernist object, revealing the strange intimacy of subject and object and eliding completely the difference between artwork and audience. The television-viewing subject cannot partake of the powerful gaze described, for instance, in Laura Mulvey's analysis of film as a constructed representation of desire.[15] Cinema's sense of occasion, its dark spaces and gigantic representation, invite complete absorption, whereas the flickering CRT image, around which the subject hunches and squints, cannot flatter the ego in this way. Because of the simultaneity of the image, the viewer perceives her- or himself as projected through time and space, into the scene he or she is observing: he or she becomes another apparition, encountering the image in a middle zone, inside the medium itself. The idea of being 'present' shifts and curdles into telepresence.

Freud's attribution of the *Unheimlich* to the return of superannuated emotions which have been repressed similarly describes a time- and space-shifted notion of presence; the uncanny effect is the ripple of recognition we experience when confronted with something which is both repressed and visible, both present and not-present. Telepresence produces this troubling psychic reverberation because we want to understand images as asynchronic, as pieces of congealed time, like paintings and photographs. Live television, instead, like a mirror, presents the present, and then erases it. But unlike a mirror, it has no indexical relationship with reality. Freud's definition of the uncanny describes a conflation of the familiar with the enigmatic, and the same nearness/strangeness binary is disrupted by telepresence and television. The images appearing on cathode screens slip between categories: they are mirrors and maps, they are pictures and they are codes. They operate in the Symbolic realm of Lacanian theory, the realm of mediation, of language and signification; and whereas – as in the Lacanian Mirror Stage – the mirror provides a glimpse of the imaginary wholeness of the ego, these uncanny television images withhold this wholeness and elide the ego and the mirror into a cyborgian hybrid.

Hoffmann's tale is concerned with an analogous piece of visual trickery: the telescope that Coppola sells to Nathaniel perverts his perception, allowing him to see the mechanical doll Olimpia as a real woman, and making his real fiancée Clara appear to be a false contraption. Freud writes: 'It becomes clear that the author wants us too to look through the spectacles or the spyglass of the demon optician, and even, perhaps, that he has looked through such an instrument himself.'[16] For Freud, Coppola's apparatus enables Nathanial to spy on Olimpia; to broadcast himself across the space, as it were, between his room and her window in the opposite house, to bridge the gap between inalienable categories of signification, and thus to access the world of fiction and symbolism. But it also initiates an operation where the mediation and remediation of the Real causes devastating consequences for the imaginary ego. It reifies the human as well as animating and vivifying the fictional. At the end of the story, when Nathaniel stands at the top of a tower and tries, like a human transmitter, physically to throw himself into the rift of his mediated vision, he plunges to his death.

'INVOLUNTARY AND COMPULSIVE TRANSMITTERS': RADAR AND THE GHOSTS OF WAR

Michael Powell and Emeric Pressburger made a film version of Jacques Offenbach's opera *The Tales of Hoffmann* in 1951, but one of their earlier films, *A Matter of Life and Death* (1946) provides a clearer instance of the intersection of broadcast media and the gothic.[17] The film's ghost is the fighter pilot Peter Carter, who cheats death, falls in love, and then must fight to evade induction into the afterlife. His situation is initially presented as a technological glitch; Peter avoids annihilation when he bails out of his plane without a parachute, because his spirit has become tethered, via his final radio broadcast, to a radio operator called June. This tethering is personal and particular: believing he is on the brink of death, he attempts to use June as a kind of human recorder, insisting that she hears the details of his life, first in a parody of bureaucratic form-filling – 'Age: 27, 27 do you get that, that's important. Education: interrupted, violently interrupted. Religion: Church of England. Politics: conservative by nature, Labour by experience' – and then, more desperately, by way of quotations from his favourite poetry.[18]

The necessity of focusing tightly on the essence of subjectivity and identity has already been established in the introduction to the film. It opens in deep space, with an intergalactic tour-guide pointing out the globular clusters and supernovas which punctuate its vastness. Gradually, the camera zooms in on earth, which seems to be enfolded in a cacophony of radio voices. 'Listen!' the voice commands as finally, Peter's voice is picked out and we follow it into the wrecked and burning aircraft where he straddles the threshold of life and death and is in the process of delivering his desperate testimony to June. Somehow, the signals are scrambled: by transmitting his spirit into the ether along with his voice, he manages to rematerialise, unharmed, on earth, and begins his fight to stay there. His metaphysical mediation is brought into question both by the spirit world, represented by a dandyish 'conductor' who is sent from Heaven to collect him, and by science. Both June and the local medic Dr Reeves believe the whole episode to be a hallucination brought about by a 'neurological blockage'. This elision of psychopathology and poetic fancy could not be more explicit: the opening caption of the film reads: 'This is the story of two worlds, the one we know, and another which exists only in the mind of a young airman whose life and imagination have been violently shaped by war.'

When Peter is recalled to heaven, he lodges a legal appeal against his death on the basis that he has fallen in love with June. But at his court case, his only witness is a material object – June's fallen tear caught on a pink rose and solidified into glass in the timeless realm of the heavenly court. This object-witness helps to entrench the film within the gothic tradition, however firmly Peter's ghostliness is excised by the surgeon's knife as he undergoes brain surgery. Moreover, the idea that Peter's supernatural revenance is as much technological as medical is supported by the 'important' fact of his age, which was the first thing he wanted June to know when he was talking to her from the burning plane; since the film is set in May 1945, Peter must have been born in 1918, at the end of First World War, and the beginning of the radio era. As a child of the medium, he can exist in it as his natural element – a facility which, as we will see later in this chapter, contrasts sharply with the fate of George Orwell's Winston Smith in *Nineteen Eighty-Four*, born in '1944 or 1945'.[19] Winston was also born at the end of a war and the start of a new medium; but as we will see later in the chapter, this will condemn, rather than reprieve, him.

It was the Second World War that precipitated the superannuation of radio telecommunication by the development of visual media. By 1944, the invention of television's secret military doppelgänger, radar, had started to be reported obliquely in the press. In November *The Times* mentioned the existence of a 'complex mechanism ... known to RAF crews as the "gen-box" and to Americans as "mickey"' which 'enables bombs to be aimed with uncanny accuracy through cloud, smoke, haze, or darkness'.[20] A month later, the *Illustrated London News* carried a full-page article featuring an artist's impression of the technology and a more detailed explanation of how 'the transmitter sends a downward signal at 186,000 miles per second, this hitting the earth beneath and bouncing upwards again at the same speed to the aircraft'.[21] Known as the 'gen-box' or 'black-box', the apparatus 'receiving the echoed signals, translates them by an electronic system, employing the television principle, into a reproduction of the landscape in shadow-tone outlines on a fluorescent screen'.[22]

In *Optical Media*, the technology theorist Friedrich Kittler asserts that television 'would not have risen to world power without World War II', and adds (borrowing from Paul Virilio's *War and Cinema*) that its military forerunner did not simply enable but had the power to command perception: 'Radar is an invisible weapon that makes things visible ... because it converts objects or enemies that do not want to be seen or measured at all into involuntary and compulsive transmitters'.[23] As the war progressed, this power extended, so that what had started as a defensive technology assumed an attacking role: radar stations were initially 'connected by radio throughout all of southern England, and they could report attacking Messerschmitts or Heinkels of the German Luftwaffe even while the approaching planes were still invisible'.[24] Later, 'airborne radar first made their blind enemies on the Luftwaffe's side visible, but after 1943 it also made the rivers, streets, and cities of the empire visible, which were destroyed by the carpet bombing of fighter-supported long-range bombers'.[25] Finally, when television was used to guide German V2 rockets, the war 'produced the first self-guided weapons systems, which have since made people, the subject of all modern philosophies, simply superfluous. With the end of the subject, a television audience became possible in the post-war period'.[26] This is a provocative cancellation of the generally accepted equivalence of audience and subject – in Kittler's analysis, an electronic prosthesis for subjective human vision ends by displacing the autonomy of the subject entirely. But his point of view finds an echo in the first major imaginative response to television culture to be published in Britain, George Orwell's *Nineteen Eighty-Four*.

'A TINY WORLD WITH ITS ATMOSPHERE COMPLETE': THE TELESCREEN AND THE GLASS PAPERWEIGHT IN ORWELL'S *NINETEEN EIGHTY-FOUR*

In the militarised dystopia of Oceania, television is primarily a technology of surveillance; the enhanced eye belongs to the Thought Police, and its object – the 'involuntary and compulsive transmitter' – is the citizen. The wall-mounted domestic telescreens, which cannot be turned off, do not offer entertainment but a stream of propaganda; they telescope space, not by transporting the viewer to a distant event, but by allowing the state to enter the private spaces of the individual.

Despite (or because of) the fact that he worked for BBC radio from 1941 to 1943, Orwell wrote a wartime essay, 'Poetry and the Microphone', in which he deplored the 'totalitarianisation' of state-controlled media:

> Few people are able to imagine the radio being used for the dissemination of anything except tripe. ... Indeed the very word 'wireless' calls up a picture either of roaring dictators or of genteel throaty voices announcing that three of our aircraft have failed to return.[27]

As a similar mechanism for the output of tripe, the telescreen is relatively easy for Winston to ignore or dismiss; compared to the visceral immersivity of the communal Two Minutes Hate, which is more analogous to a cinema screening or a political rally, the screen 'babbling away about pig-iron' in Winston's flat has little impact as a form of psychological manipulation.[28] The real control comes from the paranoia of being continuously present to the eyes of Big Brother:

> Always the eyes watching you and the voice enveloping you. Asleep or awake, working or eating, indoors or out of doors, in the bath or in bed – no escape. Nothing was your own except the few cubic centimetres inside your skull.[29]

Being both spatially and temporally 'present' is the key to survival for the general ranks of Outer Party Oceanians. The prohibition against attempts to escape the eye of the state is matched by the impossibility of escape into the private perspective of individual memory. As the book opens, Winston is attempting to 'squeeze out some childhood memory that should tell him whether London had always been quite like this'.[30] Later he tries to collect memories of the past from an old man in a pub, but 'the old man's memory was nothing but a rubbish-heap of details':[31]

> The few scattered survivors from the ancient world were incapable of comparing one age with another. They remembered a million useless things, a quarrel with a workmate, a hunt for a lost bicycle pump, the expression on a long-dead sister's face, the swirls of dust on a windy morning seventy years ago: but all the relevant facts were outside the range of their vision.[32]

The irony is that such individual memories are exactly what gives the past its human dimension, but Winston, hungry for a countervailing system to challenge the Party's hegemonic dominance, can no longer interpret such scraps of individuality as historically valid. If Winston's own vision wasn't so faulty, he might see that these junk memories tell him what he needs to know, which is that intellectual freedom and autonomy will not come by accessing an impossibly lucid, premasticated historical account, but from a collage of idiosyncratic observations and priorities, individual to each subject. A child of his times, Winston can only conceive of the failure of individual memory as an optical limitation: the past no longer exists, because it is outside the reach of technologically unboosted human perception. For Orwell, the real political importance of the new medium is in its resonance with a more general obliteration of individual vision, which can leave no mark in a culture that has stamped out history and time, and within which Party-sanctioned things bear the standardised branding of the Big Brother portrait, watching its human objects 'on coins, on stamps, on the covers of books, on banners, on posters, and on the wrappings of the cigarette packet – everywhere'.[33]

For contemporary audiences, the fact that television had no memory – was unrecorded and unrecordable – was its primary selling point. The *Daily Mail Television Handbook* makes much of the charms of 'liveness':

> The fact that actors are acting at the very moment that you are looking at them – and may faint or fluff or forget their lines – gives television a sense of immediacy and excitement which is unknown in the cinema ... The fact that personalities of every description are brought visually into your own sitting-room or lounge at the very moment in which they are engaged in interesting and intriguing activities, alone introduces a completely new element into home entertainment.[34]

But the same quality of existing in an eternal present, unable to be recorded or fixed, makes television the ideal medium for Oceania. Paper records have to be continually rewritten and 'rectified' by Winston and his co-workers at the Ministry of Truth, to make them conform with the present version of reality; he clings desperately to the memory of once holding a photograph which contradicted the Party's sanctioned version of events, even though he unhesitatingly destroyed it moments after it fell into his hands.[35] Television needs no rectification: what is broadcast one day can be contradicted the next without any historical friction. In such a culture, even when he is in possession of contraband paper and pen, Winston feels powerless:

> In front of him there lay not death but annihilation. The diary would be reduced to ashes and himself to vapour ... How could you make appeal to the future when not a trace of you, not even an anonymous word scribbled on a piece of paper, could physically survive?[36]

By writing a diary, Winston is trying to create a personal text to counteract the Party's totalising rhetoric, just as Peter Carter attempted to record the essence of his personhood via his final radio transmission. However, Winston abandons his attempt in despair when he finds himself scrawling an uncontrolled stream-of-consciousness account of his most grubby desires. It is not just the inanity of his personal record that makes Winston feel powerless, but the fragility of the paper medium itself, which he takes as a portent of his own utter deniability. Later he thinks he has found the text he needs in the illicit 'Goldstein book' passed to him by the man he takes for a rebel leader, O'Brien. In fact, like the forbidden notebook and pen, this book is a plant, a trap to provoke him into criminal activity. The only accurate records are those held by the Thought Police, as O'Brien proves when he confronts Winston with the meticulously stacked-up evidence of his thoughtcrimes. Record-making and record-keeping are the province of the state, not the individual. 'Who controls the past controls the future,' runs the Party slogan, 'and who controls the present controls the past.'[37]

Eventually Winston attempts to find an anchor, not in words or human memories, but in an inanimate object which has survived from the past and thus bears witness to the passage of time. Here is a properly mid-century solution to the problem of self-containment: he decants his longed-for identity as a complete man, a lover and a thinker, wholesale into an old glass paperweight with a tiny piece of coral inside:

> It was as though the surface of the glass had been the arch of the sky, enclosing a tiny world with its atmosphere complete. He had the feeling that he could get inside it, and that in fact he was inside it, along with the mahogany bed and the gateleg table, and the clock and the steel engraving and the paperweight itself. The paperweight was the room he was in, and the coral was Julia's life and his own, fixed in a sort of eternity at the heart of the crystal.[38]

The glass dome contains not only Winston's sense of autonomous self-hood, but also paradoxically seems to contain the room in which he places it. This is the upstairs room of the junk shop where he bought it, a love nest offered to him and his illicit girlfriend Julia by the shopkeeper, Mr Charrington. The room is a museum of pre-Party life; apart from is antique furniture, it appears to have no telescreen, and thus promises a haven in which Winston and Julia can meet for awkward trysts and shared readings of the Goldstein book.

W.T.J. Mitchell's analysis of found objects and readymades – objects which take on the properties of images when they are redescribed as art – speaks to the mid-century 'junk shop mythos' which informs not only the nostalgia trap of *Nineteen Eighty-Four*, but also Barbara Jones's curatorial practice, and the gentrification aesthetic of Marghanita Laski's *The Victorian Chaise-Longue* (discussed in the next chapter). Mitchell highlights the importance of a remediating process in the uncanny doubling of trash and treasure; referencing Lacan's anecdote about an empty sardine can bobbing in the sea, he writes:

> Everyone knows that there are just two criteria for a found object: (1) it must be ordinary, unimportant, neglected, and (until its finding) overlooked; ... and (2) its finding must be accidental, not deliberate or planned. One doesn't seek the found object ... One *finds* it. Even better: it finds you, looking back at you like Lacan's sardine can.[39]

Lacan's anecdote describes a trip in a fishing boat, during which a boy points out a floating sardine can with the words 'You see that sardine can? Do you see it? Well it doesn't see you!'[40] Lacan uses this to introduce an analysis of the gaze and the potential or actual interchange between observer and observed: the can may not 'see' Lacan but it nevertheless occupies a point in space and time which implies his visibility. The agency of the found object described by Mitchell relies on a kind of suggestively porous and even creative intersubjectivity between human consciousness and the thing-world, but it also creates the disquieting suggestion of non-human surveillance of the subject. Once the object finds you, a moment of remediation occurs: 'It may undergo an apotheosis,' Mitchell writes, 'a transfiguration of the commonplace, a redemption by art.' All the same, we may have 'a sneaking suspicion that the transfiguration was a trick.'[41] Mitchell's sense of being tricked recalls Freud's feeling of dissatisfaction on reading a gothic text that 'tricks us by promising everyday reality and then going beyond it';[42] the uncanny object, once it finds the subject, stakes a claim to a rival subjectivity and is endowed with a potential for malevolent mischief.[43] Yet whereas the found *art*-object may be redeemed by the aesthetic context in which it is understood, the charisma of the junk-shop object depends on its attendant narrative. What I refer to as the 'junk shop mythos' relies on certain key signifiers, which can be traced back at least as far as Balzac's *La peau de chagrin* (1831).[44] The powerful object around which desire coalesces is usually found in a shop which seems to appear out of nowhere to a protagonist who has lost his way. The shop is full to the point of excess, piled up with rubbish, yet despite this the person who is destined to encounter the object will spot its potential immediately, displaying an instinctive connoisseurship which attaches him to the object and makes him determined to have it. Here he encounters another crucial element of the paradigm: the reluctant shopkeeper who tries to distract him with other, worthless goods which he insists will suit his needs better. Often, this reluctance to sell – the very opposite of functional capitalism – comes along with a warning that the desired object is haunted, cursed, or otherwise undesirable. Once pulled out of the dark corner and rubbed like Aladdin's lamp, the abject object suddenly blossoms into treasure, but also threatens to exact a great price from the buyer who has performed this transformation. Winston's encounter with Mr Charrington and the paperweight follows this paradigm closely, although Winston, cut off from cultural memory, cannot possibly read the danger signs; Orwell is placing him inside a 'junked' mythos which has the same museal quality as the staged anachronism of the little room with its steel engraving and gateleg table; Winston thinks of it as an 'inviolate' world, a relic from the pre-revolutionary era like 'a pocket of the past where extinct animals could walk'.[45] The junk shop represents a form of materialised memory, but the gothic narrative it references, which Winston cannot access, contains a warning he cannot read.

In 1946, Orwell wrote an article for the *Evening Standard* in which he described his ideal junk shop, complete with a proprietor 'usually asleep in a small back room, [who] displays no eagerness to make a sale'.[46] Here, he hopes to find treasures such as agate lockets, Victorian scrap screens or 'paperweights ... that have a piece of coral enclosed in the glass, but these are always fantastically expensive'.[47] The romance of the junk shop was a popular theme in the mid-century, although it was often framed in terms of a sense of unease. 'To those whose heads are turned firmly backwards every junk shop is a menace and every cathedral town a snare,' wrote Alan Shadwick in the *Manchester Guardian* in 1948. 'Half concealed in the dim, religious light of those interiors, the antique dealers lurk, affecting an indifference that deceives nobody'.[48] His sense of entrapment derives as much from his own addiction to the past as to the wiles of the shopkeeper, however; merely reading an old book from his collection invariably triggers dissatisfaction with the present:

> Who shall blame the modern reader ... if his brooding gaze should stray from the printed page to dwell dangerously upon the 1935 table, with its twisted legs like four sticks of barley-sugar the whole carried out in fumed oak? ... And so once more into the antique shop, where, with a sinking heart, one learns that they have the very thing in the warehouse across the yard.[49]

The phenomenon was at a turning point, however. In 1952, *The Times* published a feature piece called 'Decline of the Junk Shop' in which the writer decried the new breed of shop presided over by 'young men in flashy ties and well-oiled hair and brassy young women in trousers and beads'.[50] Here, electric light illuminated once excitingly dingy corners, and the stock was all 'badly made bric a brac of a period that delighted in pretentious impedimenta'; in other words the Victorian and Edwardian decades. This is a consequence of the 'modern vogue for antiques':

> Commercialism has penetrated even to those ancient dusty shops where, unmolested by 'sales technique', we could while away an hour or two turning over forgotten relics of past ages and come away the richer for finding something that took our fancy.

In the mid-century, the prize find was not necessarily a high-quality (and preferably ludicrously underpriced) antique, but was perhaps something whose value depended on the quirk of individual taste – as we will see in the next chapter, this might even be a piece of kitsch Victoriana that could be made 'charming' by being placed within a fashionable middle-class decorative scheme. And so the gothic potential of the found object changed too – it became not so much an uncanny amulet through which the past erupts with the all-purpose destructive energy of a curse, but a heterotopian portal into an alternative time and space which addressed the individuality of the finder. The paperweight's auratic presence in *Nineteen Eighty-Four* as a kind of solid metaphor helps to focus the book's delineation of the power of images and the relation between the symbolic and the real, and can usefully be compared to Mitchell's stipulation that found objects must be '*objectionable* objects, object lessons, or even *abject* objects that have been disgraced, and discarded'.[51] Like a multi-stable gestalt image such as Wittgenstein's Duck-Rabbit, the found object doubles time and space by being two different things at once: both trash and treasure. The paperweight's very materiality, its thingliness, marks it out as an abject object, a thoughtcrime in material form ('It was a queer thing, even a compromising thing, for a Party member to have in his pocket') because its symbolic freight, as an emblem of interiority and as a portal to the past, cannot be burnt, vaporised or edited out of existence.[52] Yet its 'found' meaning turns out to be a trick, just as the art-mediated readymades were to Mitchell: the paperweight has been planted in the junk shop as a lure, and like the hidden room that it both contains and is contained by, it has deceptively magnified Winston's sense of individuality and freedom. He discovers this at the point when both the illusion and the paperweight are destroyed by the dawn raid of the Thought Police:

> Someone had picked up the glass paperweight from the table and smashed it to pieces on the hearth-stone. The fragment of coral, a tiny crinkle of pink like a sugar rosebud from a cake, rolled across the mat. How small, thought Winston, how small it always was![53]

Winston's paperweight, which he thinks is simply bearing witness to the past, has acted as a mendacious magnifying lens which enables an illusory prosthetic perception, just as the glass screen of the television set makes distant objects visible without putting them within tangible reach. Its final metaphorical flourish, delivered at the point of its destruction, finally emerges from the mediating glass to enable Winston to access a gustatory sensation from a distant past that he supposedly has found impossible to remember – a pink sugar rosebud decorating a pre-Oceanian cake. That this image seems to reference both Orson Welles's *Citizen Kane* and the Proustian madeleine of *A la recherche du temps perdu* (and echoes, perhaps, the pink rose holding June's tear in *A Matter of Life and Death*) emphasises the object's former promise as a nexus of memory and narrative, and the hopelessness of Winston as he contemplates the impossibility of such a thing continuing to exist.[54]

The idea of glass itself as a medium has been explored by Isobel Armstrong in *Victorian Glassworlds*, in which she traces the impact of glass technology on the mid-nineteenth-century imaginary. In this period,

> a glass dialectic marked contradiction, a subject in difficulties, rather than smooth transitivity. Transparency posited an oppositional world, not invisible mediation but marks on the surface, scratches, fingerprints. Minuscule impurities and bubbles of air, internal impediments to vision, signified and created internal contradictions.[55]

It is the physicality of the glass and its origin in the body of the glassblower that makes it a medium rather than a frictionless conduit of light:

> Transparency is something that eliminates itself in the process of vision. It does away with obstruction by not declaring itself as a presence. But the paradox of this self-obliterating state is that we would not call it transparent but for the presence of physical matter, however invisible – its visible invisibility is what is important about transparency. It must be both barrier and medium.[56]

A century after the period Armstrong is examining, and with vast expanses of flawless industrial plate-glass no longer providing such signifiers of subject/object mediation, another form of high-tech glass offered a different problematic of transparency. The thick glass of a television screen frames the same dialectic but in a very different way: it is understood to be transparent, since images can be seen through it; yet what is seen is not there, and what is there – the inside of the box – is not seen. Unlike the window or the mirror, the screen obliterates itself without becoming invisible. And when the apparatus is switched off, it reverts to solid, uniform opacity. Armstrong goes on to point out that when Merleau-Ponty uses the metaphor of transparency to critique the 'classical' Cartesian subject, he refers to the 'self-transparent thought, absolutely present to itself' which ignores a 'natal pact between our body and the world, between ourselves and the body'.[57] By inserting a mediating third term between subject and object, a 'moment of difficulty', experience is rescued from the purity of abstraction and aestheticisation.[58]

In the telescreen's ocular reversal, Big Brother is the viewer and the citizenry are the spectral presences flickering into and out of existence at the viewer's whim. Thus it is their sheer corporeality that Winston and Julia are trying to assert in their secret junk-shop trysts, and it is by physical pain that the Party enforcer O'Brien finally succeeds in breaking through Winston's resistance to the looking-glass logic of doublethink, which demands that individual consciousness rewrites itself reflexively to conform to a communal lie, and then forgets not just the act, but even the concept of forgetting. This requires a complete semantic breakdown, a severance of the link between real and symbolic, as exemplified by the annihilation of the unambiguous arithmetical notation of Winston's mental touchstone, 2 + 2 = 4. It is this act of untethering that puts

Nineteen Eighty-Four within the genre of mid-century gothic, which brings together cultural artefacts which tend to perform and problematise semantic unreliability of the kind that Freud used in his definition of 'uncanny'. O'Brien completes his remediation of Winston by confronting him with the disconnect between his body and his mind: first, after weeks of torture, he stands his broken form in front of a triple mirror so that Winston can experience a total alienation from his reflected self; and then he demonstrates the potency of the Party's mind-control by confronting him with his worst fear in Room 101. Winston relinquishes any hope that his physical persistence in time and space will help him to remember his individual identity. He is only the flickering apparition visible on a television screen; he is the ghost in the Party machine.

GHOSTS, MACHINES AND 'THE THING IN THE HEAD': REFLECTION AND SPECULATION IN THE HUMAN BRAIN

For Gilbert Ryle, who coined the phrase 'the ghost in the machine', this ghost was a myth, the impossible spectre of a consciousness untethered to the material fact of the body. Published the same year as *Nineteen Eighty-Four*, Ryle's *The Concept of Mind* (1949) is concerned with many of the same questions that Orwell's novel asked about subjective identity.[59] As we will see, Ryle's ideas were largely superseded by the inauguration of cognitive science triggered by neurological advances and the dawning of the computer age, but his theory illuminates the definition of consciousness within which Orwell was staging his thought-experiment. Starting from a critique of Descartes's prioritisation of abstract thought, Ryle sets out to dismantle the notion that the mind is 'a second theatre', entirely separate from the theatre of sensory evidence, and 'that its consciousness and introspection discover the scenes enacted in it'.[60] Drawing a line from phenomenological philosophical enquiry to behaviourist psychology, he argues that, rather than needing a mysterious 'Privileged Access' to subjective awareness, 'the sorts of things that I can find out about myself are the same as the sorts of things I can find out about other people, and the methods of finding them out are much the same'.[61] In Orwell's Oceania, the abolition of the ghostly theatre of the mind was achieved by flushing out 'the few cubic centimetres inside your skull' through technological supervision.[62] The logical behaviourists of the Thought Police – despite their intrusive cognitive interventions – could deduce thoughtcrimes from the words and actions of their targets. They simply decreed that anyone who claimed to possess a discrete consciousness, a 'tiny world with its atmosphere complete', inaccessible to Big Brother's disciplinary optics, must *ipso facto* be a criminal, since this self-reflective and self-illuminating cranial space could not exist inside an obedient party member. The result for Winston, and the other citizens of Oceania, was not the kind of rescue from immateriality that Ryle aspired to, but rather a total retreat from embodied personhood into a state of unthinking abstraction. Without his own theatre of the mind to act as a buffer, he was subsumed within the stream of insubstantial and endlessly rewritten doublethink emitting from the telescreens.

Indeed, the technology of television might almost have been designed to refute Ryle's radical empiricism. Along with his metaphor of the theatre, he employs the idea of phosphorescence to explain the impossibility of consciousness; he uses the simile of 'tropical sea-water, which makes itself visible by the light which it itself emits.'[63] For Galileo and Descartes, he writes, 'consciousness' was imported to play in the mental world the part played by light in the mechanical world. In this metaphorical sense the contents of the mental world were thought of as being self-luminous or refulgent,' Locke, meanwhile,

> called this supposed inner perception 'reflection' (our 'introspection'), borrowing the word 'reflection' from the familiar optical phenomenon of the reflections of faces in mirrors. The mind can 'see' or 'look at' its own operations in the 'light' given off by themselves. The myth of consciousness is a piece of para-optics.[64]

Ryle treats this as an impossibility, but the cathode-ray screen offers a concrete example of just such a self-luminous optical instrument, revealing a 'theatre' in which insubstantial subatomic particles are transformed into real sensory perceptions. Ryle's refutation of ghosts, by which he wanted to expose such gothic ideas as irrational fictions, was being rapidly overtaken by the inherent gothicism of an apparatus which could make phantoms appear in empirical time and space. And indeed, one scientist, William Grey Walter, was already attempting to make the 'theatre' of the mind literally visible, on a television screen.

Grey Walter is remembered as a pioneer of cybernetics, but his experiments in robotics grew out of his neurological research at the Burden Institute in Bristol, which tackled the question of how far, if at all, human consciousness could be considered identical to its corporeal medium, the brain. He approached the question from the opposite direction to Ryle's, proving, for instance, that the brain could physically react to stimuli before any conscious awareness was experienced. To do this, he first needed to refine the process of electroencephalography, or EEG, into a medium through which 'brainwaves' could be manifested in the outside world; only then could he attempt to understand the brain from the inside out, by building mechanical models of neurological feedback systems which could be set the task of contemplating themselves.

His final EEG breakthrough, described in his 1953 popular science book *The Living Brain*, depended on the cathode-ray tube as a means of visualising the 'moving panorama' of the brain's electrical activity.[65] It built on the strides taken in the 1930s by Hans Berger, who had brought an investigation of electrical brain activity out of the séance room and into the laboratory, but had depended on superannuated technology as its output-medium. Berger's method involved inserting silver wires under the subject's scalp and recording the brain's electrical pulses in the form of a wavy line on a photographic plate. By the 1950s, this had already been widely replaced by the ink-writing oscillograph, which moved a set of pens across a roll of constantly moving paper, and resulted in images of thickly scribbled wobbly lines. For Grey Walter, this had the disadvantage of unravelling the picture of the brain across time and space, so that its message was accessible only through a laborious act of readerly reconstruction: 'EEG records may be considered,' he wrote, 'as the bits and pieces of a mirror for the brain, itself *speculum speculorum* [a mirror of mirrors]. They must be carefully sorted before even trying to fit them together.'[66]

Grey Walter's need for an alternative method for recording, expressing and conceptualising the brain's electrical signals led him naturally to the cathode-ray tube, which could turn any electric signal into an integrated visual image. Like the strings of wavy marks on paper, this involved fragmenting the image of the brain to make it visible, but the technology also included a mechanised process of reading, which reintegrated and interpreted the pixelated information by streaming it onto the screen in the form of rapidly written and rewritten lines. It was a kind of mechanical version of the self-legibility that Gilbert Ryle had argued was impossible.

For Grey Walter, however, the key advantage of a CRT output was that it enabled him to untether brainwaves from the materiality of photography or pen and paper (both technologies which had failed Winston Smith as reliable receptacles for memory). By translating them from one medium of flow (the brain) into another (the CRT screen), he could endow them with a perceptible presence in a virtual space-time, mapping them onto a two-dimensional representation of the brain which he likened to the cartographer's Mercator Projection. His cathode-ray EEG anticipated much later breakthroughs such as CT scans and fMRI by drawing a map of a mind in the act of thinking. Thus, brainwaves, which had first been studied by spiritualistically inclined psychologists as an argument for the possibility of telepathy and life after death, promised for Grey Walter to lead to a new type of optics on a par with diagnostic x-ray, electron microscopy and radar. He could see that EEG would enable scientists to look inside the black box of the brain and see what was happening without having to open the skull or dissect neural fibres, which had hitherto been the limit of neurophysiological methodology. This meant, in effect, that the human mind could begin to contemplate itself.

Grey Walter's chapter on EEG, entitled 'A Mirror for the Brain', opens with a quotation from Lewis Carroll's *Through the Looking-Glass* which emphasises his intuition that cathode-ray technology could undergo a transformation from mirror into threshold:

> Let's pretend there's a way of getting through it somehow, Kitty. Let's pretend the glass has got all soft like gauze, so that we can get through. Why it's turning into a sort of mist now, I declare! It'll be easy to get through.[67]

Crucially, he contrasts this fairy-tale suggestion with a phenomenological theory of mind limited by an empirical adherence to the materiality of flesh: 'The Greeks had no word for it,' he begins; 'To them the brain was merely "the thing in the head".'[68] He goes on:

> More curious still is Greek negligence of the brain, considering their famous oracular behest, 'Know thyself'. Here indeed was speculation, the demand for a mirror, insistence upon a mirror. But for whom, for what? Was there, among the mysteries behind the altar, concealed perhaps in the Minerva myth, a suspicion of something more in the head than a thing, and that the organ which had to do the knowing of itself must be an organ of reflection?[69]

Ryle's logical objection to consciousness and introspection rested on what he saw as the fallacy of self-reflection, and the insistence that the mind, insofar as the term was meaningful, was identical to the brain. But for Grey Walter it was the brain's 'insistence upon a mirror' which defined the difference between brain and consciousness, since speculation could only take place in a conceptual realm which was enabled, but not confined, by 'the thing in the head'. By mapping consciousness onto empirical neuroscience, Grey Walter hoped to locate the intersection between the two.

For Jacques Lacan, the distinction between mind and body was most starkly dramatised during the infant Mirror Stage, but the mirror metaphor is not the only scopic analogue he employed to explain his reading of consciousness. In his Second Seminar, he refers to early computers as a Symbolic medium, operating linguistically through codes.[70] Television's primitive precursor, the triode lamp, is also dragooned into his metaphorical system to explain how the Imaginary intervenes in the coded outputs of language and symbols.[71] For Lacan, technological image-making demonstrated the interdependence of the Symbolic and the Imaginary, since his triode lamp needed both in order to produce its effect. Likewise, the cathode tube provides a material analogy for the fragmentary subject: it produces itself autonomously through a process that is fluid, conflicted, and 'at best … contradicts itself, cuts itself off, grinds itself up'.[72]

Television's self-legible autonomy helps to explain its uncanniness to its early users, and in fact, even in their mid-century infancy, cybernetics and computing were already starting to instigate new questions about the relationship between reality, consciousness and codes of meaning, and complicate the definition of human subjectivity, and – in the case of Grey Walter's uncannily lifelike robots – human psychopathology.

'JIGGING LIKE A CLUMSY NARCISSUS': WILLIAM GREY WALTER'S NEUROTIC ROBOTS

Grey Walter's neurological research inspired him to attempt to create a mechanical model which could mimic the brain's ability to process sensory input and use the object-world to feed back information about itself. This project was to make him famous when he unveiled his 'tortoise' robots at the Festival of Britain Exhibition of Science, staged at the South Kensington Museum in 1951. The simple robots, which he called *machina speculatrix*, were 'designed to illustrate ... the uncertainty, randomness, free will or independence so strikingly absent in most well-designed machines'.[73] Their apparent independence – they would move towards light, avoid objects in their path, and return to their 'hutches' to recharge when necessary – was the result of an electronic feedback system involving a light source, a light-sensor, and a simple circuit which specified how various inputs should be acted upon.

In his 1976 recollection of visiting the Festival, Brian Aldiss remembered his sense of anticipation about seeing these revolutionary machines which 'did something that no mechanical had done hitherto: they pottered about their cage and, when they were feeling hungry, returned to their power source and replenished their batteries of their own accord'.[74] The reality of the encounter, however, was far from magical:

> Although I understood how the metal tortoises worked, I wanted to see them for myself – to feast my eyes on them, in that expressive phrase. So I did. Squat, unlovely, but full of significance, they sat in their unlit tank, unmoving, gathering dust. A notice on the exhibit said 'out of order'.[75]

The machines' frequent breakdowns helped to quell any suggestion that science had created a rival to human thought and subjectivity. The official Festival book was at pains to stress the limitations of these lumbering but endearing quasi-animals with 'very simple "brains" ... Simple as they are, they copy certain patterns of man's behaviour and help us with human problems'.[76] Similarly, a newsreel which featured Grey Walter's research described them as 'pets' named Elsie and Elmer and showed their inventor and his wife smiling fondly as he teased them by pushing objects into their path.[77] The guide-catalogue for the Science Exhibition, meanwhile, almost ignored the robots, with the guide's writer Jacob Bronowski limiting himself to a terse parenthetical mention of the tortoises within a detailed description of the nervous system:

> The senses send their findings rather like electric signals along the nerves. Such a signal may set off an automatic or reflex action; this is how a shadow across the eye makes us blink, or an insect moves towards the light. A mechanical 'animal' can be constructed to steer itself towards the light in this automatic way.[78]

For Grey Walter himself, however – as his 1953 account shows – the real value of his robots lay not in their power to amuse the public but to demonstrate a neurological basis for consciousness. He felt he was able to demonstrate the appearance of sentience by introducing a mirror and attaching headlamps to the tortoises, so that the light-seeking feedback system induced the machines to move towards their own reflected light. The increased light level as they got closer to the mirror then caused their light to switch off; but once the reflected light had disappeared, the machine was programmed to switch its own headlamp on again – a process repeated *ad infinitum*:

> The creature therefore lingers before a mirror, flickering, twittering, and jigging like a clumsy Narcissus. The behaviour of a creature thus engaged with its own reflection is quite specific, and on a purely empirical basis, if it were observed in an animal, might be accepted as evidence of some degree of self-awareness.[79]

The importance of this robotic Mirror Stage was emphasised in the illustration which found its way into the Guide-catalogue and many other written accounts of the Tortoises: one of the creatures is clearly seen admiring itself in a looking-glass.

The cod-Linnaean name Grey Walter gave his robots, *machina speculatrix*, becomes clearer: these were not only speculative machines, but mirror-gazing machines. The self-absorption of the robots suggests a rival subjectivity which appears able to ignore its human creator. Moreover, the greater the complexity of the programming, the more lifelike the behaviour becomes – if 'lifelike' is taken to mean irrational and unstable. Grey Walter's 1951 paper 'A Machine that Learns' describes a phenomenon he dubs 'experimental neurosis', which he induced is his next-stage robots, *machina docilis*, and which manifested as a state of perplexed paralysis. These were set up with 'learning circuits' which aimed to replicate the classical conditioning described by Ivan Pavlov, for instance by 'training' the robots to associate a ringing bell with a light stimulus. As soon as more than one learning circuit was added, however, the machines began to display dysfunctional behaviour, with one model losing its '"instinctive" attraction to light' so that it 'can no longer approach its source of nourishment':

> This state seems remarkably similar to the neurotic behaviour produced in human beings by exposure to conflicting or inconsistent education. In the model such ineffective and even destructive conditions can be terminated by rest, by switching off or by disconnecting one of the circuits. These treatments seem analogous to the therapeutic devices of the psychiatrist – sleep, shock and psychosurgery.[80]

Grey Walter's anthropomorphic reading of this situation (which later computer-users would understand more prosaically as a crashed operating system) reveals his underlying agenda of using these robots to begin to describe the machinery of human consciousness, rather than purely to advance cybernetic research. The neurosis of *M. docilis* shows the manmade mind responding to self-awareness, not as Narcissus, but as Frankenstein's creature:

> How was I terrified when I viewed myself in a transparent pool! At first I started back, unable to believe that it was indeed I who was reflected in the mirror: and when I became fully convinced that I was in reality the monster that I am, I was filled with the bitterest sensations of despondence and mortification.[81]

The echo of Mary Shelley's 'Modern Prometheus' reveals that Grey Walter's automaton is an essentially gothic apparatus, which enables the inner life of the mind to be made manifest, not via supernatural spectrality, but through the uncanny workings of technology. Indeed, Grey Walter himself draws this distinction: the impulse to impute supernatural life and agency to inanimate objects must be understood only as yet another mirror by which the mind can contemplate itself:

> We are daily reminded how readily living and even divine properties are projected into inanimate things by hopeful but bewildered men and women; and the scientist cannot escape the suspicion that his projections may be psychologically the substitutes and manifestations of his own hope and bewilderment.[82]

'MACHINE WINS'? LACAN, TURING AND THE PROBLEM OF CONSCIOUSNESS

Speaking in his 1954 seminar 'A materialist definition of the phenomenon of consciousness', Lacan refers to Grey Walter's mechanical tortoises as useful metaphors in his attempt to dismantle the Freudian ego. Although he does not refer to their attraction to mirrors, he does imagine what would happen if the robots were programmed to 'jam' unless they could see another machine of the same kind. He uses this to discuss the fascination and desire of the ego for the other:

> You see, by the same token, how a circle can be set up. As long as the unity of the first machine hangs on that of the other, as long as the other gives it the model and even the form of its unity, whatever it is that the first is oriented towards will always depend on what the other is oriented towards.[83]

The advantage of using what he calls 'these courageous little animals' as his model is that 'it doesn't in any way idolise the subject'; instead, it shows that 'the subject is no one. It is decomposed, in pieces.'[84] In other words, by describing consciousness in mechanical terms, he is hoping to demystify the ego and depose it from its reigning position within Freudian psychoanalysis. The attempt to make things that are more like humans inevitably suggests the possibility that humans might be 'mere' things after all, since their claims to any kind of immaterial soul or essence can be challenged by a material construct which seems to present an equivalent type of consciousness without the need to provide it with any supernatural element. For Lacan, the comparison between minds and machines bears fruit; in addition to tortoise robots, the metaphor of the computer enables him to show that the mind's capacity for language can be best understood as a machinic process. Yet this does not solve the problem of the nature of the subject, but merely goes to prove that the subject is fragmented or even non-existent: 'The machine is the structure detached from the activity of the subject. The symbolic world is the world of the machine. Then we have the question as to what, in this world, constitutes the being of the subject.'[85] He has not travelled so far, after all, from Gilbert Ryle's contention that the 'ghost in the machine' concept falsely flatters an essentially biological human consciousness with intimations of the ineffable.

The dialectic of consciousness and materiality took another turn in the research of Alan Turing into artificial intelligence. At the same time that Grey Walter was seeking to map consciousness onto a material medium, Turing was busy attempting to demolish completely the distinction between matter and thought. Computers, as Turing conceives them, both refute and support Ryle's mechanistic description of thought, since they provide an instance of machinic, non-transcendental cognition but also demonstrate that thinking and learning are abstract processes which do not entirely succumb to materialist description. His famous 1950 paper 'Computing Machinery and Intelligence' proposes to answer the question 'can machines think?' by using his now-famous 'imitation game', in which an interrogator directs questions to a human and a computer and must choose, by examining their typewritten answers, which is the machine.[86] This idea appealed to Lacan, who discussed Turing's still-hypothetical computers in relation to the codes of the symbolic realm, and recognised that an important moment had been reached in humanity's ability to conceptualise the process of thought. The validity of the 'Turing test' has been debated ever since, but Turing's original paper can be read, not just as a computing thought-experiment, but as a mid-century gothic text, which responds to the culture's growing sense of a disconnection between mind and body, signal and material, interior process and perceptible output. His stated intention in devising the game was to draw 'a fairly sharp line between the physical and the intellectual capacities of a man.'[87] Yet Turing seems conscious that he is setting himself up to be another 'modern Prometheus' when he attempts to outline scientific methods for creating artificial life by disassembling and analysing fragments of the human – which may be why he specifically excludes as a viable option Victor Frankenstein's chosen methodology of revivifying obsolete human fragments. Understanding intelligence in terms of its mere fleshly clothing, he points out, would involve a radical confusion of form and function:

> No engineer or chemist claims to be able to produce a material which is indistinguishable from the human skin. It is possible that at some time this might be done, but even supposing this invention were available we should feel there was little point in trying to make a 'thinking machine' more human by dressing it up in such artificial flesh.[88]

His quasi-human creature might undergo a process of learning and development analogous to that undertaken by Mary Shelley's monstrous autodidact, however; Turing speculates that the best way to make a machine that can imitate the brain of a human adult is first to 'try to produce one which simulates the child's':[89]

> Presumably the child-brain is something like a note-book as one buys it from the stationer's. Rather little mechanism, and lots of blank sheets. (Mechanism and writing are from our point of view almost synonymous). Our hope is that there is so little mechanism in the child-brain that something like it can be easily programmed. The amount of work in the education we can assume, as a first approximation, to be much the same as for the human child.[90]

Just as Orwell's Winston Smith saw the act of writing in a notebook as somehow essential to autonomous thought, Turing hopes that the artificial child-brain will use its blank sheets to formulate an autobiographical record which will underpin its intelligence. Whereas, for Grey Walter, learning was achieved by means of a circuit which prescribed invariable outcomes from given inputs, Turing's notebook image emphasises the retention of data and the ability to use it in order to deduce further information and instruction. But, like the Thought Police, he is in no doubt that this process will be programmable and controllable; his assumption is that the immature brain resembles an ink-writing oscillograph, mechanically responding to sensory inputs and recording them as coded data.

Turing's optimism about computer memory and its ability to enable original thought falters, however, on the admission that a mechanical child-brain could never learn exactly like a real child:

> It will not, for instance, be provided with legs, so that it could not be asked to go out and fill the coal scuttle. Possibly it might not have eyes. But however well these deficiencies might be overcome by clever engineering, one could not send the creature to school without the other children making excessive fun of it.[91]

Turing clearly sympathises half-earnestly with his bullied Pinocchio-robot, sent off to school to learn how to be a real boy, but he is making a serious point about what he sees as the essential similarity between machines and minds. Like Ryle, he argues against the idea that there is anything unassailably enigmatic going on within human thought processes, citing what he calls 'the solipsistic view' of the neurologist Geoffrey Jefferson's Lister Oration in 1949, in which he proclaimed: 'Not until a machine can write a sonnet or compose a concerto because of thoughts and emotions felt, and not by the chance fall of symbols, could we agree that machine equals brain.'[92] In contrast to this cultural argument for human exceptionalism, Turing presents the image of onion skins to describe the hopeless task of trying to find the ghostly essence of creativity:

> In considering the functions of the mind or the brain we find certain operations which we can explain in purely mechanical terms. This we say does not correspond to the real mind: it is a sort of skin which we must strip off if we are to find the real mind. But then in what remains we find a further skin to be stripped off, and so on. Proceeding in this way do we ever come to the 'real' mind, or do we eventually come to the skin which has nothing in it?[93]

Nevertheless, there is a tension in Turing's writing between his insistence on the increasing perfectibility of a mechanical analogue for human thought and the inkling that there is a quality of 'human-ness' which can be discerned in disobedient machines, at the moment when they reject or supersede their programming. This, again, is an essentially gothic construction: the symbolic apparatus of gothic narratives often depends on the intervention of uncanny, recalcitrant things, especially those over-freighted with significance: Frankenstein's creature is perhaps the archetype of the unruly object, but Winston's dangerously overdetermined and disintegrating glass paperweight is another example. Gothicism refutes the idea of meaning as a simple code; it relies on slippage and elision between mechanical reality and mysterious intimation; it narrates the fragmentation and contingency of the subject and the ultimate illegibility of the thing-world. The out-of-order tortoises which so disappointed Brian Aldiss at the Festival of Britain Exhibition of Science, or the 'neurotic' ones in Grey Walter's learning laboratory, or even the 'jammed' ones of Lacan's thought experiment, all attest to the gothicism inherent in any project which hopes to manufacture a machinic subject, since this artificial consciousness turns out to be as bewildered as its human counterpart. In 1951, when Turing visited the Festival, he encountered the tortoises for himself, as recorded in an anecdote in Andrew Hodges's biography. Turing and a group of friends

> went to the Science Museum in South Kensington where the science and technology exhibits were housed. Grey Walter's cybernetic tortoises were on show, though they seemed to be going round in circles, and Robin [Gandy] said they were suffering from General Paralysis of the Insane. However, they observed one nice and unexpected touch: the feedback-dance that the tortoises performed in front of a mirror.[94]

Gandy's joking reference to a form of dementia which occurs in late-stage syphilis was presumably intended to emphasise the absurdity of a machine exhibiting the frailty of flesh and blood, but the impression left by the 'feedback dance' suggests that Turing, like Lacan and Grey Walter himself, was intrigued by the possibility of cybernetic self-reflection. He and his friends then moved on to the exhibition's most high-tech centrepiece, a computer named Nimrod supplied by the electrical engineering firm Ferranti, which was programmed to play the numbers game Nim. This basic game can be won in most cases by using a simple but somewhat counterintuitive strategy, and an algorithm enabled the computer to beat most members of the public who took it on. As Bronowski's guide to the Science Exhibition put it, 'Although it will not always win, the machine cannot make a mistake!'[95] Turing, however, also knew the winning strategy:

> The Ferranti people were pleased to see Alan and said, 'Oh Dr Turing, would *you* like to play the machine? Which of course he did, and knowing the rule himself, he managed to win. The machine dutifully flashed up 'MACHINE LOSES' in light, but then went into a distinctly Turingesque sulk, refusing to come to a stop and flashing 'MACHINE WINS' instead. Alan was delighted at having elicited such human behaviour from a machine.[96]

Although the computer was mentioned only in a single paragraph in Bronowski's guide, Ferranti published a separate booklet, *Faster than Thought: The Ferranti Nimrod Computer* which explained Nimrod's design and capabilities to a non-specialist audience.[97] The anonymous author stresses that the terms 'mechanical or electronic brains' should be avoided, because they might give 'the impression that automatic computers can think for themselves, which is not true'. However, the machine's autonomy is stressed in the list of 'three essential characters' which define computers, namely,

(1) They can calculate.
(2) They can 'remember'.
(3) They can make decisions.

The random access memory (as it is now known) which allows computers to process data is highlighted as the key to their complexity and power. Although Nimrod itself only needed a simple circuit to equip it with sufficient memory for its single task, more sophisticated machines were already in use which employed cathode-ray tubes for memory storage, with data transformed into patterns on a screen which could then be read back by the computer.[98] In a sense, these memory-enabled machines are the first objects which can claim literally to have a personal history, and not just – as in the case of the uncanny objects of gothic tales – carry the imprint of human histories through time. Nimrod's communicative output is restricted to only two possible alternatives, but its malfunctional insistence on proclaiming 'Machine wins' – although amusing to Turing – carried uncomfortable overtones which were echoed in his 1951 lecture to the 51 Society at Manchester University, 'Intelligent machinery, a heretical theory', which ended with a warning that it seems probable that once the machine thinking method had started, it would not take long to outstrip our feeble powers. There would be no question of the machines dying, and they would be able to converse with each other to sharpen their wits. At some stage therefore we should have to expect the machines to take control.[99]

Once again, the question of whether autonomous objects model human consciousness or represent an alien other remains unresolved. Along with memory, language is at the heart of computers' troubling potential for autogenesis. The opacity of computer code to the human reader, which appealed to Lacan as a metaphor for the occluded workings of the symbolic system itself, was also reflected, perhaps unwittingly, in the name Nimrod – a Biblical figure traditionally credited with building the Tower of Babel.[100]

Even the fact that the leaflet provides a glossary of unfamiliar terms ('computer', 'digital', 'binary') suggests that technology is pulling away from ordinary human discourse. The explanation of binary, meanwhile, recalls the breakdown of Winston Smith's forbidden arithmetical touchstone: while Winston had finally to accept that 2 + 2 = 5, readers unfamiliar with binary numbers were presented with the apparently nonsensical sum 1 + 1 = 10, and forced to recalibrate their perception of common sense in order to make it true.

'GHOSTS AND BOGIES': MACHINE INTELLIGENCE AND THE SUPERNATURAL

The idea that computer technology might change or enhance the mechanics of the human brain was something that clearly interested Turing. In his essay 'Digital Computers Applied to Games', he records an experiment which took place at the Science Museum during the Festival:

> The Society for Psychical Research came and fitted up a room nearby [to the Nim computer] in order to see if operations of the machine could be influenced by concentrated thought on the part of the research workers, most of whom were elderly ladies. When this experiment had failed they tried to discover whether they in turn could be affected by vibrations from the machine and could tell from another room how the game was progressing. Unfortunately this experiment, like the first, was a complete failure, the only conclusion being that machines are much less co-operative than human beings in telepathic experiments.[101]

It might seem that Turing was simply mocking the psychic ladies' experiment, but even in 'Computing Machinery and Intelligence', he was not afraid to tackle the uncanny potential of technologically enhanced thought. In one passage he considers at length, and with an apparently straight face, whether his 'imitation game' test for machine intelligence would be invalidated if the human participant were capable of extrasensory perception:

These disturbing phenomena seem to deny all our usual scientific ideas. How we should like to discredit them! Unfortunately the statistical evidence, at least for telepathy is overwhelming. It is very difficult to rearrange one's ideas so as to fit these new facts in. Once one has accepted them it does not seem a very big step to believe in ghosts and bogies.[102]

A growing popular awareness that the electrical signals of the brain might be transmitted, mediated or made legible by technology resulted in the emergence of stories in which electronic appliances become haunted, although any sense of real horror soon began to abate in the mid-century imaginary as the television set became a familiar domestic object. By the time J.B. Priestley was writing his short story 'Uncle Phil on TV' in 1954, the technology was sufficiently accepted for the uncanniness to be put to comic effect.[103] In this tale of lower-middle-class aspiration and internecine bickering, the Grigson family buy a television with the life-insurance money paid out when their unloved long-term house guest dies of a heart attack. As soon as they get the set home, however, they begin to see Uncle Phil in every programme they watch, at first just in the background, but eventually in close-up as he addresses them by name and accuses them of causing his death. The retributive haunting doesn't merely take advantage of the idea of television as a 'medium' in the spiritualist sense; it implies a direct exchange between the aggravating uncle and the new set as a physical object dominating the room: 'Clearly there was a general feeling,' Priestley writes, 'that fate had been kind in exchanging Uncle Phil, whom nobody wanted, for this new wonder of the world.'[104] The joke is that the Grigsons haven't managed to get rid of Uncle Phil at all, and Priestley is keen to show that the haunting of the new technology arises from an essential similarity between Phil and the television set, as well as hinting at the medium's uncanny potential for surveillance. The Grigsons, we learn, had always disliked Phil's 'determined refusal to leave the fireside even when they were entertaining friends, and hated to have him there watching them.'[105] His physical peculiarity, too, seems to be an omen of the stiffness of the televisual point of view:

> Some accident he'd had made him carry his head on one side, so that he always looked as if he was trying to see round a corner; and even this, to say nothing of the rest of him, got on their nerves.[106]

The accusatory presence of Uncle Phil may be a distant descendent of the all-seeing eye of Orwell's Big Brother, peering into the viewers' living space in order to find evidence of crime. Like Orwell, Priestley reverses the relationship between watcher and watched, but here the television acts more like a traditional haunted object than a mediating third space, its materiality offering a new 'body' for the aggrieved spirit of Uncle Phil. In this, Priestley was responding to a common complaint about the new technology: its intrusiveness into the spatial relationships of the family home. In 1949, *House and*

Garden magazine published an article called 'Make Room for Television', which advocated putting the television near the fire 'where chairs are usually gathered' but warned: 'Most of the day your set will sit lifeless in the room ... As the cabinet is bulky and creates special problems of accommodation, its position shouldn't be obtrusive. Your room must be re-arranged for its new function.'[107]

The less upmarket readers of the *Daily Mail Television Handbook* were treated to extensive advice about the best size of set for small rooms in flats, and the maximum number of viewers possible 'when an exceptional "high-spot" programme is announced':

> For a 9" tube receiver we can say five or six adults when seated and under comfortable conditions, plus several standing.
> For a 12" tube receiver, add two or three more, if space permits.
> For a 15" tube receiver, about the same as a 12" tube, plus a few in the back row who may be permitted to stand on chairs, etc.[108]

In 1947, a BBC audience researcher called R.J.E. Silvey recorded a list of reasons why he would not buy a set if he did not already have one for his job; as well as poor picture quality, which meant that television quickly lost its novelty value when compared to cinema, he mentions 'by no means the least potent factor militating against television in my kind of home', namely 'the sheer palaver involved in having to watch it. It means putting the light out, moving the furniture around and settling down to give the programme undivided attention.'[109]

Mainly, however, he bemoans the lack of serious programmes for 'people like us' who 'just aren't Variety-minded'; his definition of 'my kind of home' includes clear class and intellectual judgements about the kind of home inhabited by people who might enjoy the programmes being broadcast. He was not alone in his dissatisfaction with the BBC's output, however. Readers of the *Sunday Pictorial* were also warned not to expect great things from a medium which had once seemed a threat to every other form of entertainment, but in reality had trouble keeping up with its rivals:

> Are the programmes bad?
> Yes. Transmission most days is only an hour in the afternoon and about two hours in the evening ... Afternoon programmes are mainly old American films. They are terrible ... Major sports promoters are bitterly opposed to television because they know attendances will suffer. Consequently most sportscasts are of amateur events ... Variety programmes are poor because the big combines put a television ban on their stars.[110]

In 1954, Priestley depicted the Grigsons anticipating the luxury of being fully and individually satisfied by what television has to offer: George Fleming, their son-in-law, sells it to them:

What more d'you want? Gives you everything. Sport for me and Dad and Steve. Plays and games and all that for you women. Dancing and fashion shows too. Variety turns we'd all like. Serious stuff for Ernest.[111]

When they install their set, however, the reality is less ideal.

> Una turned it on, not having any trouble at all, and it began showing them a film that looked like an oldish cowboy film, which wasn't exactly their style, still it was wonderful having it in the sitting-room like that. The people were small and not always easy to see and their voices were loud enough for giants, which made it a bit confusing; but they watched it for quarter of an hour.[112]

Despite its poor performance as a source of entertainment, television makes great demands on the family's use of time and space:

> Joyce and Steve ... were in favour of what amounted to a continuous performance by the set. Dad and Ernest were dead against this idea, which they thought wasteful and silly. They wanted to make a sort of theatre of it, with everybody sitting in position a few minutes before the chosen programme was ready to start.[113]

Like the readers of the *Daily Mail Handbook*, they are prepared to make the experience as communal as possible, calculating that they could 'manage a dozen' viewers 'if you brought up the old settee as a sort of dress circle'.[114] In the end, however, they opt to retain the privacy of their space, although they cannot avoid the intrusion of the set itself, which demands a complex programme of tuning and adjustment to keep it in proper working order.

Mid-century viewers pandered carefully to the needs of their sets. First they had to take into account the local topography in choosing and mounting their aerial, and then an engineer would be required to install the set and connect it to the network. Finally, they were responsible for undertaking a daily retune, as the *Daily Mail Handbook* explained:

> The BBC television Tuning Signal is radiated daily for about five minutes before each programme to enable viewers to adjust their Television receiver correctly in readiness for the start of the programme. For satisfactory reception it is important that the correct setting should be found.[115]

And once the set was in place, it tied the householders to their home in a quite emphatic way:

> All receivers will be zoned by manufacturers for use in conjunction with the particular transmitter nearest to the home of the purchaser and, bearing in mind that each transmission zone will have its own particular wavelength, it automatically follows that a receiver specifically tuned at the factory for the London area will not work in the Birmingham area, and vice versa.[116]

In this way conformity and social control were built into the very apparatus of television, and it was not long before anxiety about the loss of individuality began to shift from the medium to its message. In the same year that Priestley's story was published, Theodor Adorno, writing in America, delivered a powerful attack on the standardising influence of mass culture, as epitomised by television, which (like Orwell) he saw as a potential conduit of social brainwashing:

> Rigid institutionalisation transforms modern mass culture into a medium of undreamed of psychological control. The repetitiveness, the selfsameness, and the ubiquity of modern mass culture tend to make for automatised reactions and to weaken the forces of individual resistance.[117]

The medium, he argues, creates its own generic context, which is the opposite of gothic in that it is designed to minimise shock and smooth out the violence of the subject's apprehension of the world. Adorno describes an entirely un-uncanny televisual landscape in which no psychic eructations could spring from any subterranean realm:

> Every spectator of a television mystery knows with absolute certainty how it is going to end. Tension is but superficially maintained and is unlikely to have a serious effect any more. On the contrary, the spectator feels on safe ground all the time. This longing for 'feeling on safe ground' – reflecting an infantile need for protection, rather than the desire for a thrill – is catered to.[118]

Like Orwell, he sees this bland cultural environment as inimical to individuality because it denies the possibility of internalisation: 'inwardness, inner conflicts, and psychological ambivalence' give way to 'unproblematic, cliché-like characterisation.'[119] This insistence on interiority may be at odds with the kind of quasi-mechanical ideas of consciousness which were emerging from scientific, psychoanalytical and philosophical innovations of the mid-century, but for Adorno culture was the essential mirror in which the subject could begin to see, not a perfect image of the whole self, but precisely the kind of non-identical mismatch between subject and object which would facilitate social and political rupture. Gilbert Ryle had been Adorno's supervisor at Oxford University in 1935, while he worked on a dissertation which attempted a critique of the 'resigned, late bourgeois character of phenomenology.'[120] Adorno respected Husserl's thought as 'the final serious effort on the part of the bourgeois spirit to break out of its own world, the immanence of consciousness, the sphere of constitutive subjectivity', but only a dialectical reading such as his, he argued, could break down the false consciousness of phenomenology's bias towards all-encompassing rationality. It seems likely that Ryle's phenomenological argument against introspection would have been read by Adorno as part of this effort, but one of the key differences in their approach is their treatment of culture. Ryle saw fiction and history as proof that the behaviourist paradigm was sufficient to encompass consciousness; 'novelists, dramatists and biographers', he wrote, 'had always been satisfied to exhibit people's motives, thoughts, perturbations and habits by describing their doings, sayings, and imaginings, their grimaces, gestures and tones of voice', and psychology should not 'suffer unnecessary qualms of anxiety' about 'describing the merely mechanical'.[121] For Adorno, the quality of culture and its approach to interiority were vital, and to be satisfied with mere descriptions of plausible human behaviour, such as were common in the bland output of television, was to harm society. For Adorno, the novelistic paradigm of the individual's struggle for autonomy may be essentially a 'middle-class "ontology"' but he sees its modern, mass-cultural iteration as 'increasingly authoritarian and at the same time hollow'.[122] He depicts the clichés of sitcoms and detective shows as a desperate attempt by the prevailing ideology to shore up the consistency and predictability of the population, since 'the more inarticulate and diffuse the audience of modern mass media seems to be, the more mass media tend to achieve their "integration"'. Thus, when 'the perennial middle-class conflict between individuality and society has been reduced to a dim memory, and the message is invariably that of identification with the status quo', then 'the less the message is really believed and the less it is in harmony with the actual existence of the spectators'.[123]

The position in America, where television uptake had not been interrupted by the war and it was already a commercial, multi-channel enterprise, was somewhat different to the beginning of the state-sponsored television age in Britain. In 1948, a *Times* leader had celebrated television as a medium which could be comfortably talked back to by a disobedient and recalcitrant audience. Reminiscing about the joys of silent cinema when 'if we shouted "Six to four the field!" as the sheriff and his posse galloped down a precipice ... we and our friends could be heard above the excitable tinkling of the piano', the writer mourns the noisiness of the talkies and dismisses the possibility of talking back to the radio as unfulfilling. But,

> Television is another matter. There the behaviour of the actors in a play often calls for those comments, ribald or otherwise, which we have to repress in the theatre. If the play is a good one the occasion does not arise; but if, as sometimes happens, it is less than good, implausibility and over-emphasis can be lampooned without anyone being the worse off.[124]

The BBC seems to have responded to accusations that its fare was bland or badly produced by raising the (gothic) stakes, until it was broadcasting such hard-hitting productions that Lord Morrison, among others, protested:

> Sir – How much longer is the British television service going to present Sunday evening plays of horror? For several months now these plays have been more and more morbid and brutal. Madmen, murders, shootings and stabbings, descriptions of eyes being gouged out, dead men arguing with each other ... Can someone please explain what useful purpose is served by these Sunday evening spectacles of brutality?[125]

Responding, the BBC's controller of television Norman Collins, wrote: 'Lord Morrison's letter is timely and, indeed, the corporation has received similar letters from certain of its viewers.' In his defence, he lists a number of upcoming productions, promising less blood-soaked fare:

> The plays already scheduled include *Hobson's Choice*, with Mr Wilfred Pickles; *March Hare*, a comedy; *Promise of To-Morrow*, a new comedy specially written for television; a Shakespeare production for Shakespeare's birthday; *The Master Builder*, *Present Laughter*, *The Insect Play* and a Galsworthy revival.[126]

Clearly, Collins wanted to demonstrate a careful balance between the light entertainment of Wilfred Pickles and Noel Coward and the BBC's bid for serious cultural credentials via Ibsen and Shakespeare. The battle-lines were already being drawn up in the argument over the corporation's monopoly of broadcasting; a month later, the economist R.H. Coase launched a broadside in the form of a monograph, *British Broadcasting: A Study in Monopoly*, arguing that the lack of competition simultaneously gave the BBC too much power and weakened it through an ingrained institutional timidity.[127] In its review of Coase's book, the *Times Literary Supplement* agreed that, with the arrival of television, the nation's culture and economy were in equal danger:

> The glum may think we have invented a toy (like the hydrogen bomb) beyond our means. And perhaps without centralised control it may be impossible to recover the cost of the most costly technique of entertainment ever devised. Culturally, too, television may share something with the hydrogen bomb.[128]

As the 1950s progressed two landmark programmes showed that the BBC's willingness to screen 'evening plays of horror' on a Sunday had not abated. In 1953, *The Quatermass Experiment* featured a dematerialised life-form that floats through space until it encounters a pioneering space rocket from earth. This 'plankton of the ether' – perhaps a metaphor for television broadcasting itself – has no body of its own, being 'pure energy, without an organic structure'. Thus, it is able to penetrate the body of an astronaut, Victor Caroon, who returns to earth apparently physically normal, but gradually transforms into an alien thing, half man and half cactus.[129] The otherworldly life-form has turned the exploratory human subject into a kind of receiver for its remote-control signal, thus proving its technological superiority to Professor Quatermass's team of human scientists, who lost radio connection with the astronauts at the start of episode one. The ground control team tracking the missing rocket indeed resemble radar operators, or even neuroscientists, in their use of complex instruments whose outputs must be interpreted; they hunch intimately around sleek boxes and take readings from screens. But like Powell and Pressburger's Peter Carter, Caroon has detached himself from the earth in order to confront the enormity of space, and like Carter he crashes back into the domestic realm – in this case the cosy home of a harmless old lady – only to find himself drastically remediated by his journey, lost in translation after all.

Television's increasing interest in the gothic possibilities of its own technology came full circle a year later when the BBC broadcast an adaptation of *Nineteen Eighty-Four*. Written by Nigel Kneale, who had also created *Quatermass*, it caused such a sensation that five Conservative MPs tabled a House of Commons motion deploring 'the tendency evident in recent British Broadcasting Corporation television programmes, notably on Sunday evenings, to pander to sexual and sadistic tastes'. A countering amendment conversely deplored 'the tendency of honourable members to attack the courage and enterprise of the British Broadcasting Corporation' and another expressed thanks that 'freedom of the individual still permits viewers to switch off'. The *Times* leader-writer had no truck with anti-television sentiment:

> If anything had been needed to underline the tremendous possibilities of television, the reactions of the last few days have provided it. Orwell's novel has been in circulation for five years. It has been widely read and has made many thinking people uncomfortable ... [But] until last Sunday's broadcast it could be said that the impact of *Nineteen Eighty-four* on the British public had been only marginal. This is no longer the case. Despite their use hundreds of times in newspapers, in broadcasts and in other ways, such phrases as 'totalitarianism', 'brainwashing', 'dangerous thoughts', and the Communist practice of making words stand on their heads have for millions of people suddenly taken on a new meaning.[130]

Television had won the argument. Orwell's gothic warning about its all-consuming media paradigm had not only been consumed by the medium's insatiable appetite for new content, it had been spat out again in remediated form, just as Adorno had described, rewritten to fit into the prevailing Cold War political agenda of the time.

Yet the mid-century's concern with the domestication of uncanny objects was not confined to technological novelties. In the next chapter, the domestic interior is invaded by objects from the past which bear such a clear imprint of past trauma that they can override the present. And whereas computers and television screens helped to initiate a new cultural understanding of the abstractions of the mind, the haunted furniture of works such as Marghanita Laski's *The Victorian Chaise-Longue* began to redescribe the mid-century body.

NOTES

1 'You Need Not Be There', advert in *Daily Mail Television Handbook*, ed. Frank Coven (London: Associated Newspapers, [1949]), p. 10.
2 See René Descartes, *Treatise of Man* (Cambridge, MA: Harvard University Press, 1972), p. 113: 'I should like you to consider that these functions (including passion, memory, and imagination) follow from the mere arrangement of the machine's organs every bit as naturally as the movements of a clock or other automaton follow from the arrangement of its counter-weights and wheels.'

3   See Henri Lefebvre, *The Production of Space*, trans. Donald Nicholson-Smith (Maiden, MA: Blackwell, 1991), p. 118. 'Third space' is the term Lefebvre uses for a space, such as a theatrical stage, which is 'at once fictitious and real'; he writes: 'To the question of whether such a space is a representation of space or a representational space, the answer must be neither – and both.' This is of course distinct from the post-colonial third-space theory of Homi Bhabha and the political-geographical theory of E.W. Soja.
4   W.J.T. Mitchell, *What Do Pictures Want? The Lives and Loves of Images* (Chicago: University of Chicago Press, 2005), p. 33, emphasis in the original.
5   Mitchell, *What Do Pictures Want?*, p. 6.
6   Mitchell, *What Do Pictures Want?*, p. 198.
7   Mitchell, *What Do Pictures Want?*, p. 204.
8   Jeffrey Sconce, *Haunted Media: Electronic Presence from Telegraphy to Television* (Durham and London: Duke University Press, 2000), p. 17.
9   Sconce, *Haunted Media*, p. 19.
10 Sconce, *Haunted Media*, p. 10; p. 14.
11 'Television', lyrics by James Dyrenforth and music by Kenneth Leslie-Smith. See www.screenonline.org.uk/tv/technology/technology5.html [accessed 28 January 2018].
12 Robert Merrill, 'Dr William D. Coolidge and his New Magic Ray', syndicated by Public Ledger, for instance to Salt Lake Telegram, 21 November 1926, p. 12. http://udn.lib.utah.edu/cdm/ref/collection/tgm8/id/44988 [accessed 28 January 2018].
13 'A new tool for the research scientist', *Scientific American*, 135:6 (1 December 1926) www.scientificamerican.com/magazine/sa/1926/12-01/ [accessed 28 January 2018].
14 Sigmund Freud, *The Uncanny*, trans. David McLintock (London: Penguin, 2003).
15 Laura Mulvey, 'Visual Pleasure and Narrative Cinema', *Screen*, 16:3 (Autumn, 1975), 6–18.
16 Freud, *The Uncanny*, p. 139.
17 *The Tales of Hoffmann*, dir. by Michael Powell and Emeric Pressburger (The Archers, 1951); *A Matter of Life and Death*, dir. by Michael Powell and Emeric Pressburger (The Archers, 1946).
18 Peter's quotations are the opening lines of 'The Passionate Man's Pilgrimage' by Walter Raleigh, and the 'time's wingèd chariot' section of 'To His Coy Mistress' by Andrew Marvell. Both poems deal with the idea of impending death.
19 George Orwell, *Nineteen Eighty-Four* (London: Penguin, 2013), p. 9. It is interesting to note that Orwell's son Richard was born in May 1944.
20 'Accurate bombing through cloud', *The Times*, 28 November 1944, p. 4.
21 'Bombing through clouds: a British target-finding invention', *Illustrated London News*, 6 December 1944, p. 689.
22 'Bombing through clouds', p. 689.
23 Friedrich Kittler, *Optical Media: Berlin Lectures 1999*, trans. Anthony Enns (Cambridge: Polity, 2010), p. 216.
24 Kittler, *Optical Media*, p. 216.
25 Kittler, *Optical Media*, p. 217.
26 Kittler, *Optical Media*, p. 218.
27 George Orwell, 'Poetry and the Microphone', in *Essays* (London: Penguin, 1984), pp. 239–47 (p. 244).

28 Orwell, *Nineteen Eighty-Four*, p. 4.
29 Orwell, *Nineteen Eighty-Four*, pp. 31–32.
30 Orwell, *Nineteen Eighty-Four*, p. 5.
31 Orwell, *Nineteen Eighty-Four*, p. 105.
32 Orwell, *Nineteen Eighty-Four*, p. 106–07.
33 Orwell, *Nineteen Eighty-Four*, p. 31.
34 Coven, *Daily Mail Television Handbook*, p. 64.
35 Orwell, *Nineteen Eighty-Four*, pp. 90–91.
36 Orwell, *Nineteen Eighty-Four*, p. 32.
37 Orwell, *Nineteen Eighty-Four*, p. 284.
38 Orwell, *Nineteen Eighty-Four*, p. 169.
39 Mitchell, p. 114.
40 See Jacques Lacan, *The Four Fundamental Concepts of Psychoanalysis* (New York: Norton, 1978), pp. 95–96.
41 Mitchell, *What Do Pictures Want?*, p. 114.
42 Mitchell, *What Do Pictures Want?*, p. 157.
43 Freud, *The Uncanny*, p. 157.
44 Honoré de Balzac, *The Wild Ass's Skin*, trans. Herbert J. Hunt (London: Penguin, 1977).
45 Orwell, *Nineteen Eighty-Four*, p. 173.
46 George Orwell, 'Just Junk – But Who Could Resist It?', in *Complete Works*, ed. Peter Davison (London: Secker & Warburg, 1998), Vol. 18, pp. 17–19.
47 Orwell, 'Just Junk', p. 18.
48 Alan Shadwick, 'Collector's piece', *Manchester Guardian*, 30 December 1948, p. 3.
49 Shadwick, 'Collector's piece', p. 3.
50 'Decline of the junk shop', *The Times*, 28 April 1952, p. 9.
51 Mitchell, *What Do Pictures Want?*, p. 108, emphasis in the original.
52 Orwell, *Nineteen Eighty-Four*, pp. 109–10.
53 Orwell, *Nineteen Eighty-Four*, p. 254.
54 *Citizen Kane*, dir. by Orson Welles (RKO Radio Pictures and Mercury Productions, 1941); Marcel Proust, *The Way by Swann's*, trans. Lydia Davis (London: Penguin, 2003)
55 Armstrong, *Victorian Glassworlds*, p. 14.
56 Armstrong, *Victorian Glassworlds*, p. 11.
57 Armstrong, *Victorian Glassworlds*, pp. 11–12.
58 Armstrong, *Victorian Glassworlds*, p. 12.
59 Gilbert Ryle, *The Concept of Mind* (London: Penguin, 2000).
60 Ryle, *The Concept of Mind*, p. 149.
61 Ryle, *The Concept of Mind*, p. 149.
62 Orwell, *Nineteen Eighty-Four*, p. 32.
63 Ryle, *The Concept of Mind*, p. 152.
64 Ryle, *The Concept of Mind*, p. 153.
65 William Grey Walter, *The Living Brain* (London: Penguin, 1961), p. 63.
66 Grey Walter, *The Living Brain*, p. 61.
67 Lewis Carroll, *Through the Looking-Glass, and What Alice Found There*, in *The Annotated Alice*, ed. Martin Gardner (London: Penguin, 2000), p. 149. Quoted in Grey Walter, *The Living Brain*, p. 45.
68 Grey Walter, *The Living Brain*, p. 45.
69 Grey Walter, *The Living Brain*, p. 46. The 'Minerva myth' may refer to the goddess of wisdom's birth: she springs fully formed from the skull of Jupiter.

70 For a detailed examination of the influence of computing on Lacan's thought, see John Johnston, *The Allure of Machinic Life* (Cambridge, MA: MIT Press, 2008), pp. 65–103.
71 Jacques Lacan, *Seminar of Jacques Lacan, Book II: The Ego in Freud's Theory and in the Technique of Psychoanalysis 1954–1955*, trans. Sylvana Tomaselli (Cambridge: Cambridge University Press, 1988), p. 323.
72 Lacan, *Seminar II*, p. 323.
73 Grey Walter, 'An Imitation of Life', *Scientific American*, 182.5 (May 1950), 42–45 (p. 44).
74 Brian Aldiss, 'A Monument to the Future', in Banham and Hillier, *Tonic*, pp. 176–77 (p. 176).
75 Aldiss, 'A Monument to the Future', p. 176.
76 Basil Taylor, *The Festival of Britain* (London: Lund Humphries, 1951), p. 45.
77 'Bristol's robot tortoises have minds of their own' (BBC newsreel, 1950), www.youtube.com/watch?v=lLULRlmXkKo [accessed 28 January 2018].
78 Jacob Bronowski, 'The Story the Exhibition Tells', in *1951 Exhibition of Science South Kensington: Festival of Britain* (London: HMSO, 1951), p. 32.
79 Grey Walter, *The Living Brain*, p. 115.
80 Grey Walter, 'A Machine that Learns', *Scientific American*, 185.2 (August 1951) 60–63 (p. 63). p. 63.
81 Mary Shelley, *Frankenstein* (London: Everyman, 1963), p. 117.
82 Grey Walter, *The Living Brain*, p. 104.
83 Lacan, *Seminar II*, p. 51.
84 Lacan, *Seminar II*, p. 54.
85 Lacan, *Seminar II*, p. 47.
86 Alan Turing, 'Computing Machinery and Intelligence', *Mind*, 49 (October, 1950), 433–60.
87 Turing, 'Computing Machinery and Intelligence', p. 434.
88 Turing, 'Computing Machinery and Intelligence', p. 434.
89 Turing, 'Computing Machinery and Intelligence', p. 456.
90 Turing, 'Computing Machinery and Intelligence', p. 456.
91 Turing, 'Computing Machinery and Intelligence', p. 456.
92 Turing, 'Computing Machinery and Intelligence', p. 445.
93 Turing, 'Computing Machinery and Intelligence', p. 454.
94 Andrew Hodges, *Alan Turing: The Enigma* (London: Vintage 2014), p. 562.
95 Bronowski, *1951 Exhibition of Science*, p. 7.
96 Hodges, *Alan Turing*, p. 562.
97 *Faster than Thought: The Ferranti Nimrod Digital Computer. A Brief Survey of the Field of Digital Computing with Specific Reference to the Ferranti Nimrod Computer* (Hollinwood: Ferranti, 1951), www.goodeveca.net/nimrod/booklet.html [accessed 28 January 2018].
98 The Harwell Electronic Digital Computer, fully operational in 1951, was one such machine. See E.H. Cooke-Yarborough, 'The Harwell Electronic Digital Computer' in B.V. Bowden, ed., *Faster Than Thought: A Symposium on Digital Computing Machines* (London: Pitman, 1953), pp. 140–43.
99 Turing, 'Intelligent Machinery, a Heretical Theory', *Turing Digital Archive* AMT/B/20 www.turingarchive.org/viewer/?id=474&title=6 [accessed 28 January 2018].

100 In Dante's *Inferno*, XXXI.67, Nimrod is one of the giants who guard the Ninth Circle of Hell, and shouts out the nonsensical (and untranslatable) verse *'Raphèl maí amèche zabí almí'*. Virgil explains that 'every language is to him the same | As his to others—no one knows his tongue.'
101 Turing, 'Digital Computers Applied to Games', in Bowden, *Faster than Thought*, p. 286.
102 Turing, 'Computing Machinery and Intelligence', p. 453.
103 J.B. Priestley, 'Uncle Phil on TV', in *The Other Place and Other Stories of the Same Sort* (London: William Heinemann, 1954), pp. 70–102.
104 Priestley, 'Uncle Phil on TV', p. 75.
105 Priestley, 'Uncle Phil on TV', p. 72.
106 Priestley, 'Uncle Phil on TV', pp. 72–73.
107 Quoted in David Kynaston, *Austerity Britain 1945–51* (London: Bloomsbury, 2007), p. 305.
108 Coven, *Daily Mail Television Handbook*, p. 46.
109 *Sunday Pictorial*, 19 February 1949. Quoted in Kynaston, *Austerity Britain*, p. 213.
110 Quoted in Kynaston, *Austerity Britain*, p. 304.
111 Priestley, 'Uncle Phil on TV', p. 74.
112 Priestley, 'Uncle Phil on TV', p. 75.
113 Priestley, 'Uncle Phil on TV', p. 77.
114 Priestley, 'Uncle Phil on TV', p. 77.
115 Coven, *Daily Mail Television Handbook*, p. 22.
116 Coven, *Daily Mail Television Handbook*, p. 53.
117 Theodor Adorno, 'How to Look at Television', in *The Culture Industry* (London: Routledge, 2001), pp. 158–77 (p. 160).
118 Adorno, 'How to Look at Television', p. 161.
119 Adorno, 'How to Look at Television', p. 162.
120 Letter to Max Horkheimer, quoted in Lorenz Jäger, *Adorno: A Political Biography*, trans. Stewart Spencer (New Haven: Yale University Press, 2004), p. 91.
121 Ryle, *The Concept of Mind*, p. 309.
122 Adorno, 'How to Look at Television', p. 162.
123 Adorno, 'How to Look at Television', pp. 163–64.
124 'Barracking shadows', *The Times*, 29 December 1948, p. 5.
125 'Brutal televised plays', *The Times*, 21 March 1950, p. 7.
126 'Televised plays', *The Times*, 22 March 1950, p. 7.
127 R.H. Coase, *British Broadcasting: A Study in Monopoly* (London: Longmans, 1950).
128 Review of R.H. Coase, *British Broadcasting: A Study in Monopoly*, *Times Literary Supplement*, 14 April 1950, p. 223.
129 Nigel Kneale, *The Quatermass Experiment* (BBC, 1953), script facsimile accompanying DVD, pp. 25–26.
130 'Nineteen Eighty-Four and all that', *The Times*, 16 December 1954, p. 9.

PART II
INTIMACY

4

NEOPHILIA AND NOSTALGIA: THE TROUBLE WITH GENTRIFICATION

Television was not the first uncanny object to disrupt private domestic space. Haunted furniture was an established feature of popular gothic from the beginning of the twentieth century, especially in stories that reflected the rise of suburbia and the new aspirations and mores it seemed to represent. It was no longer necessary for strange phenomena to manifest themselves in the ancestral homes of ancient families, as they had in Walpole, Radcliffe or Poe; nor were they necessarily expressions of a scientific or technological disquiet, as they were for Stevenson and later for Orwell. Instead, psychical disturbances – often female-gendered – might emerge out of the liminality of a burgeoning middle class who colonised developments thrust tactlessly into an older landscape in a way that reflected their occupants' attempt to bulldoze traditional social structures. This chapter will trace this strain of gothic to discover how it reflected and articulated the cultural turn of the mid-century, focusing in particular on two novels which straddle the divide between the pre-war, modernist thing-world – in which subjects began to absorb and reflect the traces left behind by certain objects – and the post-war, liminal moment when objects began to stake out a more intimate claim on human subjectivity, opening the door for the consumerist ideology which was to define subsequent decades. Elizabeth Bowen's *The Heat of the Day* (1948) will be brought into dialogue with Marghanita Laski's novella *The Victorian Chaise-Longue* (1953) to show how both authors were interested in modern negotiations between lost, dazed and traumatised characters and the things with which they chose – or chose not – to surround themselves. First, however, it is worth considering the precursors of this mid-century domestic gothic in order to understand how it developed and expressed its moment.

It is Freud who first points out the uncanny frisson produced by the idea of haunted objects which might inhabit our most intimate spaces alongside us. Towards the end of his essay on *The Uncanny* he mentions a tale published in *The Strand* magazine in 1917, which he read 'during the isolation of the Great War'.[1] He recalls:

a story about a young couple who move into a furnished flat in which there is a curiously shaped table with crocodiles carved into the wood. Towards evening the flat is regularly pervaded by an unbearable and highly characteristic smell, and in the dark the tenants stumble over things and fancy they see something indefinable gliding over the stairs. In short, one is led to surmise that, owing to the presence of this table, the house is haunted by ghostly crocodiles or that the wooden monsters come to life in the dark, or something of that sort. It was a quite naive story, but its effect was extraordinarily uncanny.[2]

The tale Freud refers to – 'Inexplicable' by L.G. Moberly – conforms to the classic conventions of the haunted-furniture sub-genre, characterised by three essential elements: it features a young married couple making a home together; the source of its horror is a domestic object which acts as a conduit for emanations from another time and place; and its ghastly consequences arise from a conflict within the wife, who feels at once attracted to and repelled by an antique's heterotopian promise.[3] Unlike in the junk shop paradigm discussed in the previous chapter, the purchaser in this case is not necessarily warned off by a reluctant shopkeeper – instead, it is the wife's own reservations about the object which are fatally ignored. In 'Inexplicable', the estate agent who shows a rental property to a house-hunting housewife goes out of his way to explain away the foul smell and the air of neglect attached to this 'solidly built, commodious-looking' house in 'the very unromantic suburb of Prillsbury'.[4] This dwelling is an unfurnished house, not a furnished flat as Freud remembers, and the young woman, May, is surprised that the ornate and beautifully crafted crocodile table has been left behind by a previous tenant and 'goes with the house', as the agent explains, 'as a fixture, or as lumber – whichever way one likes to look at it'.[5] May, who is the tale's narrator, immediately replies, 'I should prefer to look on it as a fixture' – indicating her preference for semantic certainty: she does not want the table to fall into the interstitial category of junk or lumber. Despite reacting physically to the table on first sight – she 'shudder[s] and draw[s] away from it', and finds that a 'dimness' has 'temporarily descended upon [her] brain' – she is motivated by social aspiration which overrules her doubts; she gladly takes possession of an object which offers, like the 'too good to be true' house, an opportunity to assume a grander air than she and her husband can quite afford.[6] The table's revenge takes the form of a sharp regression from the civility and gentility of May's aspirations: along with the stench and the terrifying shapes which slither around in the dark, its apparitions regularly trip up the unwary, especially when near the staircase and its symbolic potential for upward (or downward) mobility. Freud, however, does not remark on these aspects of the story, and indeed declines to provide any detailed analysis of it, but he prefaces his account with some remarks 'of a general nature ... about animism and the superannuated working of our mental apparatus'. The uncanny effect, he writes, often arises when the boundary between fantasy and reality is blurred, when we are faced with the reality of something that we have until now considered imaginary, when a symbol takes on the full function and significance of what it symbolises, and so forth.[7]

He remembers the example of the crocodile table because it features a carved image which comes to life – a figuration of an ancient force which jumps the threshold into reality and brings with it the repressed fear that rational modernity may be a fragile illusion. Given that this is a story about home-making, it is telling that Freud alerts us to the association of its uncanny effect with his own feelings of dislocation and homelessness by mentioning that he read it while suffering from the shocks of war. Modernity wishes to assert its mastery of history by means of a style which breaks with the past: it must construct a homely sense of belonging entirely and unambiguously to its own contemporary moment, despite its constant awareness – as Walter Benjamin argued – of the piled wreckage of history which forms its context.[8] The residues of that wreckage, however – in the form of old objects that 'go with the house' – may force the repressed truth about time's mockery of modernity (and forward-looking social aspiration) back up and out into the consciousness of unwary couples who decide to move to a better neighbourhood. Throughout the story May tries desperately to keep such thoughts repressed, doing all she can to dismiss the alarm of her servants and even her guests by desperately ascribing the strange phenomena they experience to an unseen and entirely blameless cat. Hugh's solution is more decisive: he acknowledges the table's ancient power and rids them of it through the primitive ritual of burning it. Even then, he is forced to concede that it may somehow persist. 'It's not a part of the house any more ... It's not a part of anything, except in so far as matter never dies, and the smoke is doing some useful turn elsewhere.'[9]

'SOMETHING AWFUL WILL HAPPEN': 'THE HAUNTED MIRROR' AND THE MURDEROUS BOURGEOISIE

The uncanny nearness of 'useful' things, which shape and mould human experience through intimate proximity, was the theme of several late 1940s and early 1950s attempts to encapsulate the mid-century transition between the shocking newness of wartime atomisation and the hesitancy of a post-war recuperation seeking to balance nostalgia with a neophiliac appetite for the future. The idea that furniture and household goods might be haunted, either literally with a malevolent spirit, or metaphorically with the ghosts of lost certainties, was a powerful mythology.

One striking example is 'The Haunted Mirror', a short segment that forms part of Ealing Studios' 1945 portmanteau film *The Dead of Night* – a film more usually remembered for Alberto Cavalcanti's extended contribution

'The Ventriloquist's Dummy', in which the murderous rivalry between man and object is played out as a psychiatric crisis.[10] Directed by Robert Hamer, 'The Haunted Mirror' is no less interesting in its treatment of anxiety about the agency of inanimate objects. It concerns an affluent young couple and an antique looking-glass which, when brought home to their fashionably modern flat in Chelsea, insists on replaying an indelible recording of its own gruesome past. Presented to her fiancé Peter by a young woman, Joan, this Chippendale antique is a trophy of shared taste, authenticity and luxury. ('It's a beauty!' Peter exclaims. 'Very expensive,' she assures him.) But when Peter looks into the glass he sees, not the bright and streamlined modern furniture of his own room, but a gothic, wood-panelled bedroom complete with elaborately carved four-poster and a roaring fire in the grate. And the scene is not just a passive imprint of the past: 'I feel as if that room were trying to claim me, to draw me in,' he tells Joan. 'If I cross that dividing line, something awful will happen!'

The decorative mirrors of the domestic interior serve a different function from the conceptual mirrors discussed in the previous chapter, which had been used by Lacan and others to elucidate the workings of consciousness. The haunted mirror in Hamer's film is not a metaphor but an active agent – it reflects the intimate and submerged story of Peter's long-dead precursor, and unleashes his own repressed antagonism to Joan. When she returns to the shop for more information about the troublesome mirror, she learns that it had been owned in 1836 by an invalid driven mad by being confined to a single room, who eventually killed his wife and himself. She returns to find Peter equally mad and apparently possessed by the mirror's former owner; when he attempts to strangle her, she can only break the spell by smashing the glass. This moment of symbolic fracture allows the couple to make a definitive break with the past and restores their pact with modernity. Their haunted mirror is a gothically malfunctioning example of the type of superannuated accessory described in Jean Baudrillard's *The System of Objects*, where mirrors are the sign of nineteenth-century interiority; they 'close off space, presuppose a wall, refer back to the centre of the room.'[11] '[T]he mirror is an opulent object which affords the self-indulgent bourgeois individual the opportunity to exercise his privilege,' he writes, 'to reproduce his own image and revel in his possessions.'[12] Peter's mirror does indulge the privilege of its bourgeois possessor, but only by reverting to the interiority of the nineteenth century and the man who looked into it then. Its hold over him demonstrates the pull of an antiquated subjectivity which is – like the mirror's original owner – an emasculated and murderously repressed version of 'manhood'.

Baudrillard's ideal home was furnished with sober, modular furniture which could properly reflect modern personhood – an ideology of the rational which was to some extent anticipated in the British utility furniture experiment which accompanied the rationing of household goods from 1942 to 1952.

Indeed, as Gordon Russell, who chaired the Utility Design Panel from 1943, wrote a decade later in his short guide to popular design, *The Things We See: Furniture*, the utility movement was intended as a way to introduce modern ideas to society beyond the bourgeoisie:

> The interesting feature of the scheme was that there was a definite and conscious effort to grade up both design and general quality standards. ... There is no doubt that the British public has become accustomed to a better type of design than was common before the war. In fact, it is true to say that the later war-time utility designs would only have been available, had they been evolved before 1939, in the more expensive shops.[13]

At the time, however, the scheme had not gained universal public support; in her memoir, Alix Meynell – an influential civil servant at the Board of Trade – recalls that it was the Board's president, Hugh Dalton, who had pushed it through:

> We officials argued at first that it would be going too far along the road to state control to limit the production of furniture entirely to approved Government designs but Dalton was right; his was the only way to avoid the waste of wood, which was largely imported, and of skilled labour, on unnecessary frills. We were very keen on 'clean lines and fitness for purpose'; claw feet, so often to be found in Victorian and Edwardian furniture, was our symbol for all that we thought wasteful, *un*beautiful and to be avoided in utility furniture. We started with six main patterns ranging from the best and priciest made by Gordon Russell and usually sold through Heal's, to the everyday furniture mass-produced by Herman Lebus at his modern factory in Tottenham.[14]

Meynell later embraced the utility philosophy so enthusiastically that she personally instigated the production of 'white, undecorated, domestic crockery and handleless cups. I was unsympathetic to the suggestion that people would burn their fingers; it was a question, I said, of holding by the rim.'[15] Her insights suggest some of the reasons why people who were forced to scorch their fingers, and to buy the less expensive furniture from Tottenham, rejected utility with alacrity as soon as the war was over. This was much to Russell's dismay, who accused the post-war furniture industry of 'indulg[ing] in an orgy of bad taste frequently accompanied, as bad taste so often is, by shoddy workmanship'.[16] In this context, the desirability of old objects, whose value and quality have stood the test of time, is understandable. What happens, however, when old objects tell their own stories, and resist their new owners' attempts to recruit them as avatars of identity?

'ARRESTED ENERGY': IMMOVABLE OBJECTS IN BOWEN'S DOMESTIC GOTHIC

Freud's early example of domestic gothic saw the hopes of aspirant modern youth successfully reasserted through Hugh's intervention, so that, by the end of the story, the rented house finally did express the couple's desired position in life, although for May 'it was many a long day before I could live down those weird experiences'.[17] As the century progressed, however, domestic anxiety developed in more complicated ways. Elizabeth Bowen's interest in domestic interiors and their ability to interpellate the human subject can be traced in the wartime stories collected in *The Demon Lover*. Writing her postscript in October 1944, Bowen looked back on the collection as a form of 'resistance writing' akin to the literature crossing the Channel from occupied France. 'Personal life here, too, put up its own resistance to the annihilation that was threatening it,' she wrote. 'To survive, not only physically, but spiritually, was essential.'[18] But Bowen was not interested in the preservation of a communal or national particularity: cultural artefacts were a reservoir of something emphatically personal. To understand this, she turned for an analogy to the material things that the dispossessed instinctively held close:

> Every writer during this time was aware of the personal cry of the individual. And he was aware of the passionate attachment of men and women to every object or image or place or love or fragment of memory with which his or her destiny seemed to be identified, and by which their destiny seemed to be assured.[19]

Bowen saw that individual self-expression had been curtailed, not just by the constraints on time and freedom imposed by the war, but by the very idea of communal effort and national emergency, which bound strangers to each other while severing the relationships between people and the things by which they were defined.

> You used to know what you were like from the things you liked, and chose. Now there was not what you liked, and you did not choose. Any little remaining choices and pleasures shot into new proportion and new value: people paid big money for little bunches of flowers.[20]

But while rationing and shortages of once-plentiful commodities clearly contributed to this sharp new emphasis on things, it was the nexus of intimate meaning projected into personal objects that interested Bowen as a writer. In the collection, her characters find themselves adrift in London's devastated cityscape, or tumble into a past – on a 'rising tide of hallucination' – that no longer offers the sunlit refuge of nostalgic certainty that it ought to promise.[21] And more often than not, the things they reach out for to anchor them reciprocate by reaching out, disturbingly, in their turn: in 'The Inherited Clock' a woman receives a valuable bequest which unlocks a buried memory of childhood trauma, in which her hand became enmeshed in the mechanism of the timepiece; in 'The Demon Lover' another woman returns to her shut-up London house 'to look for several things she wanted to take away'[22] but finds instead a ghostly message from her dead fiancé, threatening to reclaim her like a piece of lost property. Things are not what they used to be; they invite their human counterparts to look at them differently. Bowen writes of the 'new bare alert senses' which were sharpened by the darkness of the blackout, and of her stories as 'disjected snapshots' which isolate the particular, 'spotlighting faces or cutting out gestures'.[23] The chaos of fragmentation yields sharply refocused perceptions, and this enhanced vision reveals once-humble things to be as resonant as literary and cultural reaffirmations of identity, and just as urgently re-collected from their atomised fragments in the aftermath of disaster:

> People whose homes had been blown up went to infinite lengths to assemble bits of themselves – broken ornaments, odd shoes, torn scraps of the curtains that had hung in a room – from the wreckage. In the same way, they assembled and checked themselves from stories and poems, from their memories, from one another's talk.[24]

These stories were written during the years when she was also composing *The Heat of the Day*; she describes them as 'acting like releases' for the pent-up thoughts which didn't find a place in that novel:

> Each time I sat down to write a story I opened a door; and the pressure against the other side of that door must have been very great, for things – ideas, images, emotions – came through with force and rapidity, sometimes violence.[25]

What they share is a strong sense that London in wartime was a place where time had been frozen, but identities were in flux. In *Urban Gothic of the Second World War*, Sara Wasson describes Bowen's domestic spaces as 'carceral heterotopias' which unsettle the idea of 'home as a stage for confident human action'.[26] Inhuman action, however, always seems possible. The most strikingly gothic of the stories, 'Mysterious Kôr', describes London at night as 'the moon's capital', where 'the soaring new flats and the crouching old shops and houses looked equally brittle', and 'something ... immaterial seemed to threaten', so that 'people stayed indoors with a fervour that could be felt'.[27] Opening the collection, 'In the Square' describes a bright summer evening where the slanting sunlight 'was able to enter brilliantly at a point where three of the houses had been bombed away', and 'the extinct scene had the appearance of belonging to some ages ago'.[28] This is the story which seems most directly to be echoed in *The Heat of the Day*, with its central character of a woman living unencumbered by domestic niceties in a city populated by stripped-back survivalists.[29] In a summary which was published as part of the publicity for *The Heat of the Day*, Bowen described how the wartime distortion of time seeped into the private spaces of her protagonist, Stella Rodney:

> The possibility of there being no present, nothing more than a grinding-together of past and future, enters, at a point in the story, a woman's thought. Against that, there is the actuality of moments, and the power of a moment to protract itself and contain the world. All through *The Heat of the Day*, what might be drama runs into little pockets: this is a domestic novel. Within view of the reader there is

no violent act. Persons hesitate or calculate; and at the same time are inseparable from history.[30]

Stella Rodney is a middle-aged widow who has used the opportunity of the war as an excuse to shake off the trappings of a social identity she was anyway forced to leave behind: first when her husband walked out on her in scandalous circumstances, and then when he abandoned her even more decisively – by dying. Finding herself betrayed by the norms of domesticity, Stella has embraced the sense of ahistoricity which pervades the city; as Bowen writes:

> It was characteristic of that life in the moment and for the moment's sake that one knew people well without knowing much about them: vacuum as to future was offset by vacuum as to past; life-stories were shed as so much superfluous weight.[31]

Stella locates herself instead in a new 'habitat', the 'hermetic world'[32] of her affair with Robert, a stranger whom she met in the parallel universe of the Blitz and who now, two years later, has been unmasked as a Nazi-sympathising traitor by a blackmailer named Harrison. The fact that Harrison offers to keep Robert's treason a secret if Stella agrees to sleep with him contributes to her nightmarish sense of being trapped within an ugly, closed-off world she has herself been determined to construct. At the same time, the narrative power of such unspoken secrets attests to Bowen's sense of drama 'running into little pockets'; the story hinges on the threatened return of repressed truths from these intimate and personal enfoldings.

Indeed, Stella's whole relationship with Robert has been conducted in an atmosphere of gothicism, having begun in the 'heady autumn of the first London air raids' when the dead refused to stay buried,[33] and 'the wall between the living and the living became less solid as the wall between the living and the dead thinned':

> Most of all, the dead, from mortuaries, from under cataracts of rubble, made their anonymous presence – not as today's dead but as yesterday's living – felt through London. Uncounted, they continued to move in shoals through the city day, pervading everything to be seen or heard or felt with their torn-off senses, drawing on this tomorrow they had expected – for death cannot be so sudden as all that. Absent from the routine which had been life, they stamped upon that routine their absence.[34]

Like a ghost, Stella has also become untethered from her pre-war routines, but she is determined to *avoid* stamping herself onto her new environment. The truth about her failed marriage – that she was the wronged party, despite taking the blame – has been put away along with her possessions, which she has placed into storage so that she can move into an anonymous – and, again, time-locked – furnished rental:

> Here in Weymouth Street she had the irritation of being surrounded by somebody else's irreproachable taste: the flat, redecorated in the last year of peace, still

marked the point at which fashion in the matter had stood still – to those who were not to know this room was not her own it expressed her unexceptionably but wrongly.[35]

This description of her flat not only establishes Stella's loss of faith in conventional constructs of selfhood, it also indicates that norms of female domesticity – represented here by fashion in home decoration – have been suspended while war rages in an unseen, external dimension. The Blitz, already distant and sentimentalised in the middle years of the war, had created an illusion of communal purpose among the 'stayers-on', those 'campers in rooms of draughty dismantled houses or corners of fled-from flats'.[36] But by now this communal moment appeared

> apocryphal, more far away than peace. No planetary round was to bring that particular conjunction of life and death; that particular psychic London was to be gone for ever; more bombs would fall, but not on the same city. ... This was the lightless middle of the tunnel.[37]

As in the *Demon Lover* stories, Bowen pays close attention to the other 'stayers-on': the objects which persist in time and seem to interrogate human agency, despite Stella's attempted rejection of them. Apart from the Weymouth Street flat, two sharply contrasted interiors reveal to Stella her own comparative weightlessness: the ancient house in Ireland, Mount Morris, which has been bequeathed to her son Roderick by a distant relative, and Holme Dene, the soulless late-Victorian manor house where Robert's mother and sister continue to live, despite it having been officially for sale for several years. Holme Dene's provisional status appals Stella, perhaps because it reveals the truth about her own relationship with the flat in Weymouth Street: 'How can they live, anyone live ... in a place that has for years been asking to be brought to an end?'; but Robert's reply suggests that his family considers objects and furniture to be mere props in an ongoing pretence of continuity:

> Oh, but there will always be somewhere else. ... Everything can be shifted, lock, stock and barrel. After all, everything was brought here from somewhere else, with the intention of being moved again – like touring scenery from theatre to theatre. Reassemble it anywhere: you get the same illusion.[38]

It is at Holme Dene that Stella – already alerted to Robert's treason by Harrison, yet too stubborn to give in to his blackmail – begins to understand that her monstrous lover is haunted in his own way: 'She, like he, had come loose from her moorings; but while what she had left behind her dissolved behind her, what he had left behind him was not to be denied.'[39] While Stella's family background of impoverished gentility gives her a sense of a fixed origin, even if she has no fixed position in the current world, Robert's self-made, self-defining family offers no such armature of identity – an effect which is both suffocating and annihilating: 'Each time I come back again into it,' he says of his old bedroom, 'I'm hit in the face by the feeling that I don't exist – that I not only am not but never have been.'[40]

In contrast, Mount Morris emanates a sense of implacable permanence which also challenges its human inhabitants to confront their own dependence on, and vulnerability to, time. Its late owner, Cousin Francis, had responded to the weight of history by knitting himself into the material of the house, particularly in the library which he filled with objects that expressed his character (although not that of his wife, who has been banished, in high gothic style, to an asylum). Visiting Mount Morris not long after the funeral, Stella encounters the collection of meaningful junk gathered in the library, including

> colourless billiard balls, padlocks, thermometers, a dog collar, keyless key rings, a lily bulb, an ivory puzzle, a Shakespeare calendar for 1927, the cured but unmounted claw of a greater eagle, a Lincoln Imp knocker, an odd spur, lumps of quartz, a tangle of tipless tiny pencils on frayed silk cords…[41]

These objects immediately offer to resolve themselves into a pattern – the very fact that they are arrayed within a list makes their combination of the natural, the technological and the cultural tantalisingly suggestive. But in fact they are symbolic, not because they show signs of intentional curation by Francis, but because they have been curated by Bowen in order to testify to Francis's engagement with his domestic space, and to demonstrate Stella's surprising response to it. 'The room was without poetry if this could not be felt in the arrested energy of its nature – it was in here that Cousin Francis had had his being,' she notices.[42] When Stella later tells Robert, 'It had not been possible to feel lonely among those feeling things,' she is admitting for the first time that she does feel lonely in her carefully anonymised London.[43] Freud located the uncanny in psychic symbols which sprang to life and demonstrated their own agency; Bowen finds a similar sense of agency in the objects, 'arrested' by death, which awaken with the shock of urgent symbols.

That Mount Morris, like all inanimate things, continues to exist beyond Francis's life-span gives it an uncanny quality which also infects Roderick when he visits the house. Roderick's presence in the novel has been intermittent – he is in the army and appears infrequently when on leave – but his assumption of his legacy is an important driving force in Bowen's narrative. He arrives in the dark and is stalked, not by ghosts of the past, but 'by the sound of his own footsteps over his own land'.[44] Taking possession of the master bedroom and laying his head 'on the old man's pillow', he finds himself unable to sleep; he is haunted by thoughts of inheritance and succession, his possibly imminent death in battle, and the confounding persistence of the non-human: 'It was a matter of continuing – but what, what? As to that, there ought to be access to the mindless knowledge locked up in rocks, in the stayers-on.'⁴⁵

By returning to the idea of 'stayers-on' which had first been applied to the Londoners who endured the Blitz, Bowen brackets Roderick's belief in the wisdom of the ageless rocks with the reckless impermanence experienced by people like Stella in 1940. In the Blitz, the stayers-on had identified themselves with the shattered fabric of the city, and had lost their own sense of integrity in the process; Roderick is just as wrong to expect the frozen timelessness of Mount Morris to model a right way of living. Rather, it is for Roderick to imprint his own way of living onto the place, as Francis had done. *The Heat of the Day* thus encapsulates a key stage of the mid-century turn in domestic gothic: objects do not necessarily have to infest houses with their fearful presence and trip up the assumptions of an aspiring bourgeoisie, as Freud's crocodile table did; in Bowen's world, it is the humans who are uncanny, not the things which furnish their houses. Merely by outliving their owners, things can turn human subjects into spectral presences, barely able to inhabit a space once the inanimate has laid claim to it.

Roderick's rebellion against this annihilation takes the form of lighting match after match in the darkness, asserting his freedom to use and destroy objects at will. The matches comfort him, not just with the light they bring, but because they are objects without any afterlife, fully consumed as soon as they have fulfilled their single function. Even so, as L.G. Moberly's character Hugh pointed out in 'Inexplicable', burnt wood may persist at some mysterious molecular level outside human perception.⁴⁶ The next morning, Roderick wakes full of plans to mechanise and update the estate, but Bowen denies him any triumphant reassertion of his will, giving the last word to the dubious servant Donovan. Roderick's aspirations towards modernity may simply be a way to 'sink a terrible lot of money'.⁴⁷

This late mention of capital serves to highlight how little importance money has had earlier in the narrative. Robert's treason, for instance, has not been motivated by financial gain but by the recognition of his own pathological coldness in the brutality of fascism. Within the novel's twisted narrative logic, Robert's sudden suicide seems to precipitate the end of the war: 'That day whose start in darkness covered Robert's fall or leap from the roof had not yet fully broken when news broke: the Allied landings in North Africa.'⁴⁸ After this, the post-war future begins to chip away at Stella's hermetic stasis, and a brittle new cheerfulness is personified by the figure of Louie, a working-class girl whose search for love and meaning has been interwoven with Stella's, although the latter has barely been aware of Louie's existence. Like Roderick, Louie is young enough to invest in the future, and like him she is sure that spending money will enable her to assert her new identity. Having betrayed her soldier husband in a series of casual encounters with men, she has had a baby and faces potential disgrace. But when her husband is killed in action she is suddenly free to move out of London and assume the identity of a respectable war widow, 'an orderly mother' wheeling 'a still handsome second-hand pram'.[49] As the novel ends, she is 'progress[ing] gapingly along the windows of shopping streets. The baby's intention to survive put itself across her and taught her sense'.[50]

In an essay on language and history in *The Heat of the Day* and Rose Macaulay's *The World my Wilderness*, Phyllis Lassner has argued that both novels are concerned with language, silence and lying, and express the negation of women's experience and utterance in war, and the necessity of self-invention in the face of this erasure.[51] However, there is also another, material, side to Louie's self-definition (and Stella's refusal of self-definition). The loss of identity concomitant with Stella's loss of possessions is the necessary precursor of the consumerism and massification which would rush in to fill this material vacuum after the war. Whereas, in *The World My Wilderness*, Barbary's attempt to conform to this consumerist imperative took the form of shoplifting and precipitated her literal and figurative fall, Louie is smoothly assimilated into the culture of retail desire by the social norms she has absorbed from the popular newspapers she avidly reads. For Marghanita Laski, however, the post-war commodity had as much uncanny potential as the lost objects of the Blitz: her eerie time-slip novella *The Victorian Chaise-Longue* (1953) demonstrates how the self-defining act of making a purchase can also bring to light the clashing temporalities of the human and the inanimate.

'TRUE PURPOSES': THE THINGLY AGENDA OF *THE VICTORIAN CHAISE-LONGUE*

In attempting to emulate forward-looking survivors like Louie, Laski's protagonist, Melanie Langdon, falls into the trap laid for her by a piece of haunted furniture, and finds herself stuck in an uncanny non-space and non-time. Louie had been guided by luck to her handsome second-hand pram, which she assertively 'learned to wheel, brake, tilt, even tow behind her'.[52] Laski's smug and pampered young wife, Melanie, also wants to use her buying power as a way of repurposing old things, but she attempts a much more decisive intervention by disrupting the historical content of a stained Victorian couch, and unwittingly unleashes its past life into her own. Her junk-shop find is a time machine that absorbs her into itself and transports her into the past.

Unlike Bowen, whose gothicism runs into little pockets of the domestic, Laski playfully acknowledges the conventions of popular gothic in this story. The parallels with 'The Haunted Mirror' are clear in the theme of an old object acting as a witness of, and irresistible portal into, the past; both also concern newlyweds and the negotiations between masculinity and femininity. *The Victorian Chaise-Longue* echoes the idea that confinement and illness imbue domestic objects with a concentrated form of congealed emotion and desire; at the start of the novel Melanie is recovering from a bout of tuberculosis, and for the first time is given permission by her doctor to move from her sickbed to the antique chaise-longue in the drawing room, which she had bought just before she fell ill. This chaise turns out to carry a kind of curse; when she falls asleep on it she wakes up to find herself in 1864, where she is trapped inside the body of another sick, trapped young woman, Milly Baines. The overt political burden of the fable is a warning against any retreat from women's hard-won modern independence: the passive and dreamy Melanie is forced to 'remember' the oppression suffered by the Millies of the previous century. Crucially, Laski chooses to draw this comparison in terms of the two domestic interiors and the objects that fill them: both spaces are described with a minuteness which reflects Melanie's sense of enclosure and incarceration in both the 1950s and the 1860s, and tacitly connects the mid-century's disgust at the congested thing-world of the Victorians with an ambivalence towards its own late-modernist tastes.

In fact, the chaise-longue is a dubious object from the start, but not because it is old. On the contrary, Melanie and her husband Guy are very modern in their willingness to discover latent value in old objects which have fallen out of favour with the mainstream. They live in a Regency house in Islington, which was at the time a daring choice: such properties had been rejected by the previous generation, and the Langdons enjoy 'the shocked incredulity of both sets of parents who had insisted that no one could live there, back of the railways, down by the canal, why it was no better than a slum'.[53] But the young couple have spotted that the area is on the cusp between romantic Bohemianism and middle-class respectability, and are

> able to point out that already an artist and architect had bought and reclaimed homes in this hidden forgotten Regency row ... and later two more homes had been reclaimed and converted, one by a young professor and the other by a senior Civil Servant ... leaving only one house still held firmly in working-class hands, the object of complicated plots hatched by the other owners on summer evenings.[54]

In short – although the term had not yet been coined – the Langdons are gentrifiers.

The word gentrification was first used by Ruth Glass in her 1964 introduction to a report by the Centre for Urban Studies entitled *London: Aspects of Change*, and Laski's description of the Langdons' hostile takeover of their canal-side neighbourhood conforms exactly to Glass's disapproving characterisation of this process:

> One by one, many of the working class quarters of London have been invaded by the middle classes – upper and lower. Shabby, modest mews and cottages, two rooms up and two down – have been taken over, when their leases have expired,

and have become elegant, expensive residences ... Once this process of 'gentrification' starts in a district, it goes on rapidly until all or most of the original working class occupiers are displaced, and the whole social character of the district is changed.[55]

The danger, Glass implies, is of a social Darwinism: 'London may quite soon be a city which illustrates the principle of the survival of the fittest – the financially fittest, who can still afford to work and live there.'[56]

By 1979, such gentrification was, in Michael Thompson's *Rubbish Theory*, a perfect illustration of his ideas about the dynamic of changing value, whereby material objects decline from being transient (currently valuable but subject to depreciation), to being rubbish (having reached maximum depreciation) but then, in some cases, can be plucked from the rubbish heap, re-appreciated, and placed in the category of 'durable', where they can stay forever, steadily accruing more value the older they get.[57] Such 'durability' had, in pre-war decades of the twentieth century, been ascribed only to those houses like Mount Morris in *The Heat of the Day* (or indeed Brideshead Castle) which were so far outside fashion that they would remain infinitely, and timelessly, valuable unless a final calamity befell them. By the time Laski was writing about the Langdons, however, a new kind of durability – re-understood as bourgeois desirability – was being ascribed to houses which had once been considered ruins or slums.

Like Laski, Thompson was to identify Islington as a primary case study, focusing on the streets and squares around Packington Street, near the Grand Union Canal, which were once prosperous, but since abandoned by the bourgeoisie who had moved, like May and Hugh in 'Inexplicable', to the leafier suburbs now accessible by rail. He notes that this neighbourhood was once so dilapidated that when 'a winkle-stall-holder and her husband' were offered a four-storey Georgian house there, 'free, by their landlord, they refused to accept it'.[58] The assumption that the working-class residents of a soon-to-be-desirable neighbourhood are simply unable to *perceive* the latent value in their surroundings is a conscience-salving elision of the truth (central to Glass's account) that they simply lack the wherewithal to pay for the renovations necessary to *realise* that value. In both Thompson and Laski, the gentrifiers congratulate themselves on their proper alignment of appearance and value, which they see as disturbingly asymmetric when the properties are in working-class hands. Their 'superior' vision restores a 'proper' order, just as the houses' external decorations are brought into harmony with each other, to form a robustly bourgeois mise-en-scène in which their owners can dramatise their supposedly quirky (but in fact rigidly codified) personal tastes. Thompson describes at length the contrast between the outward appearance of ungentrified properties:

the front doors are often unpainted ... sometimes the tenant has modernised his front door by flushing it with hardboard in which case it displays a rusty chromium-plated letterplate-cum-knocker made of pressed steel and a collection of assorted plastic bell pushes ... the door number is often simply crudely painted on[59]

and the same house post-gentrification:

Immaculately painted, Thames Green with orange front door complete with six fielded panels, brass dolphin knocker and huge brass letterplate to match. The leaded fanlight has been painstakingly repaired and, affixed to the brickwork at the side of the door, is a blue-and-white enamel number plate: a little touch of provincial France proclaiming that the owner drinks Hirondelle Vin Ordinarie with his Quiche Lorraine.[60]

In her novella, Laski draws an intriguing distinction between house and front garden in describing the transformation of this public face, noting

how much the houses had changed since the Langdons had first come there, two years ago. Then they had all looked alike, dirty brick and dirty paint and dirty lace curtains, and only the gardens were different, here a rockery and here a gnome and there some green-and-white miniature palings. Now the gardens were identical, each neatly paved with thick rectangular stones, and, set in each, spindly white-painted iron chairs and table, and it was the houses that had grown apart from their neighbours and changed, what with the grey front door and the turquoise, the shiny black and the consciously amusing light fumed-oak.[61]

Thompson goes on to peek into the carefully staged interior of such a reclaimed house – which he can do through the 'enormously enlarged basement window' – and notes that the bourgeois possessions combine new technology ('a two-bowl twin-drainer stainless steel sink with mixer taps and waste disposal unit') with a collection of gentrified junk-shop objects:

We catch a glimpse of a stuffed pike in a bow-fronted glass case ... Some gilt letters in a bold type salvaged from a Victorian grocers' shop front, and a row of large blue jars with ground glass tops, similarly salvaged from an archaic chemist's and bearing in gold lettering the abbreviated names of assorted poisons.[62]

Such objects constitute a message which can be decoded by the cognoscenti: 'Every feature, every lick of paint, once one has learned the language, [is] a clear statement proclaiming the presence of a frontier middle class.'[63]

Not surprisingly, Laski presents the pioneering Langdons as early exponents of this magpie trend:

Antique-shops, or junk-shops, as they called them, were their common hobby. On Saturday mornings, dressed, so they believed, like people who haggled not from pleasure but because they must, they would leave the car well away out of sight, and wander up and down the Chalk Farm Road, the Portobello Road, St Christopher's Place, looking for the pretty sparkles that would embellish and cement the nest.[64]

On the day Melanie is diagnosed with tuberculosis, she has spent the morning indulging this hobby on her own, looking for an antique cradle for the unborn baby she is carrying. The cradle is a key object for Melanie, just as the pram had been for Louie in *The Heat of the Day*. Motherhood serves a dual symbolic purpose for a bourgeois mid-century wife, re-establishing her domesticity in the wake of wartime disruption of gender roles, and at the same time looking forward to the future by establishing a new generation. Yet the unarguable newness of new life also brings with it the fear of superannuation, the shock of the idea that the moment of modernity may be passing on to those who are younger, and complicating the smooth progress of the generations with anxiety and tension. Whereas Louie's second-hand pram represents her aspiration to replicate as closely as possible the bourgeois version of 'orderly' motherhood to which she has no automatic claim, Melanie's quest for an antique cradle shows her reaching for a timeless aristocratic ideal, even if she has to purchase her own heirlooms instead of inheriting them. No mass-produced cot will do for Melanie: this object is to be a kind of vehicle, transporting her and her family into a fantasy of ease and privilege:

> She remembered the cradle of Napoleon's baby son, the King of Rome, that she had read of as a child, a cradle shaped like a boat with a gilded prow, and she imagined such a cradle standing on the needlework flowers of the rug before the drawing-room fire, rocked by her pretty foot to content the plump drowsy baby who sucked his thumb oblivious of the decorous sherry-drinking above his head.[65]

But this time the 'miracle fail[s]'. The cradle she finds in the Marylebone antique shop is 'Jacobean, dark carved oak and hopelessly unfashionable', and will, according to the shopkeeper 'probably go to America. There's quite a demand for them there, for keeping logs in, you know.' Melanie experiences a thrill at these words which emphasises her belief in the essential, but amorphous, quality of authenticity which has the power to bestow value when perceived by the eye of the gentrifier: '"My cradle will have a baby in it," said Madeline proudly, and she enjoyed a moment of sympathetic superiority, the poor yet well-adjusted English who hadn't lost sight of true purposes.'[66]

The chaise-longue's true purpose, however, is initially obscure. Melanie spots it 'stacked upside down on top of a pile of furniture, its clumsy legs threshing the air like an unclipped sheep that had tumbled onto its back'. She decides it looks 'rather exciting' but adds cautiously, 'Goodness knows what one would do with it'.[67] Laski evokes two images simultaneously in this first encounter with the upside-down chaise-longue. The first is that of the immobilised sheep, symbol of a compromised natural order, protesting clumsily at the unseen force which has imposed this reversal on it – a clear indicator of how Melanie perceives the chaise, as an object in need of rescue; the second, at a deeper level, surely evokes Marx's famous commodity-table, which transforms from 'an ordinary, sensuous thing' into something with an uncanny independent agency, that 'stands on its head, and evolves out of its wooden brain grotesque ideas, far more wonderful than if it were to begin dancing of its own free will'[68] – an image of the problematically animated chaise as it turns out to be. The fact that the chaise has been reversed in space holds a clue to the reversal in time which turns out to be its main narrative and political purpose, but for Melanie its inverted state makes it an icon of the process of gentrification itself, which turns back time, perceives value in rubbish, and remakes historicity as the prime signifier of a 'consciously amusing' modernity.

The chaise tacitly evokes yet another image, too: that of Freud's couch, the symbol of psychoanalysis. Laski's emphasis on Melanie's fantasies and daydreams clearly signposts a Freudian subtext to the narrative. Like the cradle of Melanie's imagination, the chaise-longue is to be a vehicle of desire, the embroidered berlinwork flower decoration on its felt echoing the 'needlework flowers of the rug' by which her dream-baby was to have slumbered obliviously. Yet the fantasy of motherhood falters when confronted by the problematic materiality of the object, with its 'brownish stain on the seat ... as if something had been carelessly spilt there':

> She tried to envisage the frail young mother in the floating clouds of negligee ... but the picture remained in unfelt words, and instead of it there was only her body's need to lie on the Victorian chaise-longue, that, and an overwhelming assurance, or was it a memory, of another body that painfully crushed hers into the berlin-wool.[69]

Here, the contrast between the stained *felt* of the upholstery and the *unfelt* words of the maternal fantasy with which Melanie is trying to comply suggests that codes of taste and behaviour can be confounded by the materials that are supposed to transport them into the real, which instead of bestowing gentility revert back to unexpressed, basic, instincts.

To some extent, Melanie's problems with the cursed chaise-longue can be attributed simply to a gentrification malfunction. She has failed to follow the rules which demand that reclaimed objects must be appreciated at an amused distance, with the eye of irony. Instead, 'it was of love that Melanie had thought when she first saw the Victorian chaise-longue', Laski notes.[70] Even the junk-shop owner, perceiving her category-error – and conforming to the junk shop paradigm described in the previous chapter – tries to steer her away from the object of her desire. 'There isn't much demand for these late ones,' he warns. 'I've got a little Regency day-bed you might like.' Indeed, Melanie realises that

> its Regency ancestor had probably been delicate and enchanting; this descendant was gross, and would certainly have been inadmissible in such a home as Guy's and Melanie's were it not for the singular startling quality of the berlin-wool cross-stitch embroidery that sprawled in bright gigantic roses over the shabby felt, over

the curved half-back and right from the top of the head-rest to the very end of the seat.[71]

Melanie and the dealer find themselves in an inverted negotiation:

'[The stain] hardly shows,' said Melanie, as if she were the salesman now. 'Have you got room for it?' he asked, he too accepting this reversal of roles, and discarding his proper duty of titillating and praising for the customer's part of hesitant withdrawal.[72]

The animated thrashing of the topsy-turvy chaise signals this unnatural reversal, and it also throws into the relief the deadness of Melanie's clotted bourgeois femininity, symbolised by the smothering layers of replica flowers and frozen cherubs which surround Melanie's sickbed. Tellingly, these are described at the very moment when she herself is turned into a kind of valuable domestic accessory by her physician, Dr Gregory, who advises her:

'We've got to go on exactly as we've been doing, no frolics, no excitement, the very utmost care and circumspection. You've got to treat yourself as if –' his eyes roamed round the pretty bedroom, over the creamy silky paper on the walls, the shiny cream curtains printed with huge pink roses, the rosewood bedhead decked with cavorting French brasses, and then to the mirror on the lace-frilled dressing-table, rosy-flushed cherubs clambering in and out of wreaths of coloured posies, and there he found his analogy and ended, '– as if you were a piece of Dresden china.'[73]

At this point Melanie's husband – an up-and-coming barrister – interrupts the consultation with a bizarre outburst in which he unpicks this simile in tones of 'mock – and yet not so mock – pomposity'. This is almost his only utterance in the novella, and it signifies the icy rigidity of his capitalist value structure:

'The use of the phrase Dresden china as a synonym for expensive fragility suggests that there were lamentable gaps in Britain's nineteenth-century supremacy over world markets. And how strange that it should be the Germans, themselves almost synonymous with heaviness, clumsiness, everything that is the antithesis of the object of which we speak, who have provided the very phrase that leaps into your mind when you feel the need to warn Melanie that she must be the object of our incessant, our unremitting care –' it needed a new breath, after all, to complete the sentence; Guy took it as unobtrusively as possible, and ended triumphantly, '– as of her own.'[74]

The messy, female reality of motherhood has been edited out of this reading of Melanie: Gregory boasts that he and Guy have generously 'presented [her] with a fine bouncing baby'[75] – a son she has hardly been allowed to see and who remains as hypothetical as the nursery which she can only picture in plan-view, so that 'she could never perfectly visualise the rooms and be sure how the nursing-chair looked in three dimensions but saw it always as a rectangular patch on a piece of paper with "nursing chair" in Sister's writing inside it'.[76] Now the men deliver the infantilised Melanie into the cradle of the Victorian chaise-longue and stand 'looking down on her in triumph'[77] like proud parents, or perhaps conquering cartographers – or indeed, like the British bomber pilots who pulverised Dresden during the war. In contrast to notions of male-sanctioned female delicacy, the chaise's lumpen ugliness, its resistance to gentrification, is never in doubt. Doctor Gregory calls it 'a monstrous thing' and the fact that he finally decides that 'those hideous roses'[78] may be just the thing for an invalid like Melanie can perhaps be explained by a confusion with the 'pink roses', 'rosewood bedhead' and 'rosy-flushed cherubs' of her bedroom.

But Laski's narrative vehicle, the chaise-longue, is not going to deliver the commodity fantasies of Guy, the infantilising fantasies of Dr Gregory, nor even Melanie's repressed libidinal desires: it is going to strike a blow at all three. Melanie drifts off to sleep 'bathed in sweet soft air', believing herself safely anchored in modernity as she enjoys the sight of bramble flowers in the 'bombed, still desolate waste' across the canal and listens to the 'soft continuous roar of traffic, the whine of the milkman's electric car'[79] and the muffled, reassuringly middle-class sound of a neighbour's daughter practising the oboe. But instead of being the threshold to an aspirational and fashionably reclaimed version of history, the chaise-longue transports Melanie's consciousness – permanently and fatally – into the body of a Victorian woman who is not only sliding rapidly down the social ladder, but is in the shameful position of being pregnant and unmarried and (Melanie somewhat belatedly realises) is at the very point of being viciously murdered by her sister.[80]

Melanie's ability to read the inscription of time in the historicity of junk relies on a highly contingent system of signification which attempts to fuse – dangerously, as it turns out – a modern assumption that the domestic objects she possesses are the infinitely adaptable vessels of her fluid identity, with ownership of a 'possessed' object which asserts its own auratic presence, and demands to tell its own story through its human possessor. Only belatedly does Melanie look beyond the chaise-longue's mere oldness and into its history. Trapped inside Milly's ailing, shamefully fecund body, and about to experience the violent attack which accounts for the stain she tried to ignore in 1953, Melanie finds herself in a nightmare where authentic identity (Melanie's mind) can never be reconciled with external reality (Milly's body); because of this, she loses the ability both to read narrative and to recount history. Milly's sister Adelaide constantly badgers her for information – the name of the baby's father – that she does not possess; yet her own twentieth-century story begins to recede in her mind so that she can no longer speak the words for modern concepts like aeroplanes:

> What did I say, she asked herself when the effort had been made, something about machines that fly, or was it aeronautic machines? Wireless, she screamed in her

mind, television, penicillin, gramophone-records and vacuum-cleaners, but none of these words could be framed by her lips.[81]

Begging Adelaide to tell her about the chaise-longue, she is subjected to a stream of family anecdote which she cannot comprehend because it is so at odds with her preconceptions ('she would never have bought the thing if she had known the kind of background it had, this vulgar tradesman's family, the reticences, the hints, Mother's legs and Chalk Farm and Clapham');[82] yet the schoolroom facts of nineteenth-century history which she ought to know, and ought to be able to use as a psychic anchor in this anachronistic maelstrom, also elude her:

> Instead of talking about these silly women and the weather and the bazaar, they should speak of Queen Victoria and Florence Nightingale and – But what *should* they be talking about? she asked herself. What *did* happen in 1864? Not the Exhibition, of course, and the Crimea must be over. Is the Prince Consort dead? Who is the Prime Minister?[83]

Imprisoned within a synchronic anomaly, history itself appears to have been switched off: 'I know what the Victorian age was like, of course I do, except that being here, it isn't like that at all. It's just like now.'[84] Through the eyes of Milly Baines, Melanie is disabused of the charm and glamour with which she had invested her carefully chosen junk with value. She gazes at a typically overburdened Victorian overmantel full of 'so many small objects that she had only a confused impression of worthless trash.'[85] Looking at

> the conglomeration of crowded, tasteless, worthless objects ... the comment came that these were junk, what you'd see in a junk shop, a real junk-shop, jostled in an open tray on the pavement on Saturday morning, anything for half a crown.[86]

It is not just the chaise-longue's lower-class origins, however, that imbue it with the power to misplace its incumbent in time; it is also its unfashionable date, since in the mid-twentieth century, mid-Victoriana was far from being reclaimed as genuinely fashionable by the mainstream middle class. When Ralph Tubbs published his polemic of post-war modernisation, *Living in Cities*, in 1942, Victorian design and architecture were precisely the bogeys he set out to vanquish: 'The overcrowded homes of the poor ... rapidly became worse,' he wrote of the nineteenth century. 'Speculators discovered a most profitable business in building potential slums for workers. The layout of the town had no relation to a properly ordered social life.'[87] Pictures accompanying this text show back-to-back terraces captioned 'Dreary houses', and a heavily frilled and cluttered interior which is captioned 'Homes were filled with meaningless decoration.'[88]

Gordon Russell's book *The Things We See: Furniture* took a similarly negative line: 'Some of [the Industrial Revolution's] worst features were unplanned, squalid, and filthy towns, poverty of a most degrading kind side by side with flaunted riches, and a kind of festering ugliness which spread over everything unchecked.'[89] He decries the age's pursuit of profit – 'the more money was made the uglier things became' – and its consequential reliance on inferior machine-made copies of once elegant furniture designs. For Russell, the ideal in furniture conforms to a modernist principle of form following function, and a Loosian avoidance of ornament. The mid-century is presented as an opportunity to cast off the past:

> It is worth noting that it is again in those things which had no ancestors, for instance the radio cabinet, that real advances in designing for machine production were made most rapidly. ... These skilled technicians – the engineers – have always been the guardians of precision workmanship and exceptional skill, and have never tolerated slapdash methods. Their whole training encourages them to calculate exactly in advance. Moreover, the engineer always has his eye on the future.[90]

Barbara Jones, meanwhile, in her 1954 illustrated survey *English Furniture at a Glance* makes a distinction between the simplicity of ordinary Victorian furniture and the fussiness of its over-decorated iterations.[91] She separates the era into three phases, beginning with the Industrial Revolution, the 'exciting inspirations' of which were, she finds, largely superseded by the Puginesque gothic revival. 'A tendency to clutter began to make itself felt, for pretty oddments were within reach of many more people,' she admits, before brushing aside the knick-knacks because 'they are in any case not furniture.'[92] The mid-Victorian era precipitated by the Great Exhibition, she argues, has been unfairly coloured by the excesses of that spectacle:

> Clearly a giant penknife with 80 blades bore no closer relation to England in the 'fifties than the Test-match in butter at Wembley Exhibition bore to England in the 'twenties, but the impression is so strong that one's mental picture of mid-Victorian houses shows them crushed under giant sideboards, soaring state beds, drapery, fringes, gothic ornament, red plush curtains, marble statues and cases of stuffed frogs shaving each other.[93]

In reality, she argues, ordinary household furniture of the Victorian age was generally modest, though it tended to be 'lumpish' and 'lacking ... the elegant starkness of the end of the eighteenth century', despite the occasional experiments of designers who 'had a nagging feeling that furniture should now be more exciting.'[94]

Melanie's erotic excitement at discovering her piece of Victorian junk can be better understood if we read it through a Benjaminian lens, for fashion and death were never far from each other in Paris's nineteenth-century arcades, coded as they were with subterranean meaning and haunted by cobwebby layers of stuff sloughed off during modernity's first stirrings.

> Here fashion has opened the business of dialectical exchange between woman and ware – between carnal pleasure and the corpse ... For fashion was never anything other than the parody of the motley cadaver, provocation of death through the woman, the bitter colloquy with decay whispered between shrill bursts of mechanical laughter. That is fashion. And that is why she changes so quickly; she titillates death and is already something different, something new, as he casts about to crush her.[95]

For Benjamin, newness was a kind of divination, with 'each season bring[ing], in its newest creations, various secret signals of things to come'.[96] But this kind of novel hermeneutics comes via the churn and return of history, not by uncritical nostalgia:

> Each time, what sets the tone is without doubt the newest, but only where it emerges in the medium of the oldest, the longest past, the most ingrained. This spectacle, the unique self-construction of the newest in the medium of what has been, is what makes for the true dialectical theatre of fashion.[97]

The gentrification of old objects mimics this process of extracting the new from the old, but it scrambles the signals by creating a new vehicle for value without fashioning a new materiality to contain it. For Benjamin in pre-war Paris, the department store is the primary modern retail space and a direct descendent of the arcades in its dream-like interiority and its optical ability to focus desire. But in mid-century British culture, the department store is strangely absent, replaced by the nostalgic image of the old curiosity shop groaning with untold narratives and embedded in the mythology of what Angus Calder, in *The Myth of the Blitz*, calls Deep England.[98] A symbol of timelessness, the junk shop is also a vortex of retail fluidity, where value slips out of the grasp of economics – shopkeepers give warnings instead of sales pitches, yet shoppers feel an unbearable desire for something they don't want and shouldn't trust. The wartime breakdown of supply and demand brought on by rationing disrupted the eternal return of consumer society which Benjamin read in the ruins of the arcades. In its place came a desire not for novelty but authenticity, while reclaimed junk was arguably more desirable than priceless antiques because it bore witness not just to the past but to the new owner's excitingly modern eye. Indeed, junk's status as junk seems almost to guarantee authenticity, since no one bothers to fake a worthless throw-away. Nor is the retrieval of this authenticity quite the same as a straight retrieval of hidden value; it can magic up value in something – like the Victorian chaise-longue – that wasn't worth much even when new. Like Aladdin's lamp, gentrified junk releases its uncanny power of wealth-creation and wish-fulfilment for the price of a quick clean-up. And by this logic, it follows that *haunted* junk is the most unambiguously and overwhelmingly genuine category of all. It compulsively broadcasts its repressed narrative, and it inscribes its unhomeliness onto its new home: it consumes its reader instead of being passively consumed. Benjaminian 'aura' is weaponised; a deadly game-changer in the battle between people and things.

In the next chapter, things will acquire even more physical intimacy with the human subject, not just inhabiting and defining domestic spaces but, in the form of clothes, coming into close physical contact which describes and defines the human body. The uncanny garments of ritual and conquest which appeared in the mid-century created gothic disruptions in place and time, and the narratives told about them were threaded through with questions about power and resistance.

NOTES

1 Freud, *The Uncanny*, p. 151.
2 Freud, *The Uncanny*, p. 151.
3 For an analysis of how Freud's reference to this story elucidates the uncanniness of reading itself, see Nicholas Royle, *The Uncanny* (Manchester: Manchester University Press, 2003), pp. 133–41.
4 L.G. Moberly, 'Inexplicable', in Jack Adrian, ed., *Strange Tales from the Strand* (Oxford: Oxford University Press, 1992), pp. 183–96 (p. 181).
5 Moberly, 'Inexplicable', p. 185.
6 Moberly, 'Inexplicable', pp. 184–85.
7 Freud, *The Uncanny*, pp. 150–51.
8 See Benjamin, 'Theses on the Philosophy of History', p. 249.
9 Moberly, 'Inexplicable', p. 195.
10 *The Dead of Night*, dir. by Alberto Cavalcanti, Charles Crichton, Basil Dearden, Robert Hamer (Ealing Studios, 1945).
11 Jean Baudrillard, *The System of Objects* (London: Verso, 1996), p. 21.
12 Baudrillard, *The System of Objects*, p. 21.
13 Gordon Russell, *The Things We See: Furniture* (Harmondsworth: Penguin, 1953), p. 50.
14 Alix Meynell, *Public Servant, Private Woman* (London: Victor Gollancz, 1988), p. 212.
15 Meynell, *Public Servant, Private Woman*, p. 216.
16 Russell, *The Things We See*, p. 50.
17 Moberly, 'Inexplicable', p. 195.
18 Elizabeth Bowen, *The Demon Lover*, p. 220.
19 Bowen, *The Demon Lover*, p. 220.
20 Bowen, *The Demon Lover*, p. 219.
21 Bowen, *The Demon Lover*, p. 218.
22 Bowen, *The Demon Lover*, p. 91.
23 Bowen, *The Demon Lover*, p. 223.
24 Bowen, *The Demon Lover*, p. 220
25 Bowen, *The Demon Lover*, p. 216.
26 Sara Wasson, *Urban Gothic of the Second World War: Dark London* (Basingstoke: Palgrave Macmillan, 2010), p. 107.
27 Bowen, *The Demon Lover*, p. 196.

28 Bowen, *The Demon Lover*, p. 9.
29 Bowen, *The Heat of the Day* (London: Vintage, 1998).
30 Bowen, *The Heat of the Day*. Publicity note, Harry Ransom Center archive, box 5 folio 5. Quoted in Allan Hepburn, 'Trials and Errors: The Heat of the Day and postwar culpability', in Kristen Bluemel, ed. *Intermodernism: Literary Culture in Mid-Twentieth-Century Britain*, pp. 131–49 (pp. 133–34).
31 Bowen, *The Heat of the Day*, p. 95.
32 Bowen, *The Heat of the Day*, p. 90.
33 Bowen, *The Heat of the Day*, p. 90.
34 Bowen, *The Heat of the Day*, pp. 91–92.
35 Bowen, *The Heat of the Day*, pp. 23–24.
36 Bowen, *The Heat of the Day*, p. 94.
37 Bowen, *The Heat of the Day*, p. 92.
38 Bowen, *The Heat of the Day*, p. 121.
39 Bowen, *The Heat of the Day*, p. 114.
40 Bowen, *The Heat of the Day*, p. 117.
41 Bowen, *The Heat of the Day*, p. 163.
42 Bowen, *The Heat of the Day*, p. 163.
43 Bowen, *The Heat of the Day*, p. 194.
44 Bowen, *The Heat of the Day*, p. 312.
45 Bowen, *The Heat of the Day*, pp. 311–12.
46 Moberly, 'Inexplicable', p. 195.
47 Bowen, *The Heat of the Day*, p. 313.
48 Bowen, *The Heat of the Day*, p. 291.
49 Bowen, *The Heat of the Day*, p. 329.
50 Bowen, *The Heat of the Day*, p. 329.
51 Phyllis Lassner, 'Reimagining the Arts of War: Language and History in Elizabeth Bowen's *The Heat of the Day* & Rose Macaulay's *The World My Wilderness*', in David Hershberg, ed., *Perspectives on Contemporary Literature: Literature and the Historical Process* (Lexington, KY: University Press of Kentucky, 1987), pp. 30–38.
52 Bowen, *The Heat of the Day*, p. 329.
53 Marghanita Laski, *The Victorian Chaise-Longue* (London: Persephone, 1999), p. 9.
54 Laski, *The Victorian Chaise-Longue*, p. 9.
55 Ruth Glass, ed., *London: Aspects of Change, Centre for Urban Studies Report No 3* (London: MacGibbon & Kee, 1964) p. xviii.
56 Glass, *London*, p. xx.
57 Michael Thompson, *Rubbish Theory: The Creation and Destruction of Value* (Oxford: Oxford University Press, 1979), pp. 44–45.
58 Thompson, *Rubbish Theory*, p. 42.
59 Thompson, *Rubbish Theory*, p. 42.
60 Thompson, *Rubbish Theory*, p. 43.
61 Laski, *The Victorian Chaise-Longue*, pp. 9–10.
62 Thompson, *Rubbish Theory*, p. 43.
63 Thompson, *Rubbish Theory*, p. 43.
64 Laski, *The Victorian Chaise-Longue*, p. 16.
65 Laski, *The Victorian Chaise-Longue*, p. 17.
66 Laski, *The Victorian Chaise-Longue*, p. 18.

67 Laski, *The Victorian Chaise-Longue*, p. 18.
68 Karl Marx, *Capital Volume 1*, trans Ben Fowkes (London: Penguin, 1990), pp. 163–64.
69 Laski, *The Victorian Chaise-Longue*, p. 19.
70 Laski, *The Victorian Chaise-Longue*, p. 15.
71 Laski, *The Victorian Chaise-Longue*, p. 13.
72 Laski, *The Victorian Chaise-Longue*, p. 19.
73 Laski, *The Victorian Chaise-Longue*, p. 3.
74 Laski, *The Victorian Chaise-Longue*, pp. 4–5.
75 Laski, *The Victorian Chaise-Longue*, p. 6.
76 Laski, *The Victorian Chaise-Longue*, p. 10.
77 Laski, *The Victorian Chaise-Longue*, p. 20.
78 Laski, *The Victorian Chaise-Longue*, p. 20.
79 Laski, *The Victorian Chaise-Longue*, pp. 21–22.
80 The text is not quite clear about whether Melanie dies at the end of the book: certainly Milly dies, but for Melanie 'at last there was nothing but darkness, and in the darkness the ecstasy, and after the ecstasy, death and life.' See p. 99.
81 Laski, *The Victorian Chaise-Longue*, p. 58.
82 Laski, *The Victorian Chaise-Longue*, p. 51.
83 Laski, *The Victorian Chaise-Longue*, p. 57.
84 Laski, *The Victorian Chaise-Longue*, p. 57.
85 Laski, *The Victorian Chaise-Longue*, p. 29.
86 Laski, *The Victorian Chaise-Longue*, p. 30.
87 Ralph Tubbs, *Living in Cities* (Harmondsworth: Penguin, 1942), p. 16.
88 Tubbs, *Living in Cities*, p. 17.
89 Russell, *The Things We See*, p. 29.
90 Russell, *The Things We See*, p. 25.
91 Barbara Jones, *English Furniture at a Glance* (London: Architectural Press, 1954).
92 Jones, *English Furniture at a Glance*, p. 63.
93 Jones, *English Furniture at a Glance*, p. 64.
94 Jones, *English Furniture at a Glance*, p. 69.
95 Benjamin, *The Arcades Project*, pp. 62–63.
96 Benjamin, *The Arcades Project*, p. 64.
97 Benjamin, *The Arcades Project*, p. 64.
98 Angus Calder, *The Myth of the Blitz* (London: Random House, 1992), pp. 182–83.

5

STRANGE BEAUTY: COSTUME, PERFORMANCE AND POWER IN 1953

In 1948, a student production called *The Masque of Hope* was presented to the future Queen Elizabeth when she visited University College, Oxford.[1] Written by Nevill Coghill and devised and produced by Glynne Wickham, this specially commissioned piece referenced a dramatic form which flourished in the sixteenth and seventeenth centuries, but it tackled contemporary concerns, celebrating nationalisation and the National Health Service and featuring the abruptly contemporary figure of Black Market, alongside Fear, Gloom and Rumour, as one of the forces vanquished by the power of Hope, Joy, Liberty, Health and Labour. *The Masque of Hope* typified the mid-century's uneasy doubling of incompatible binaries: glorifying tradition while rejecting the past; revering monarchy while exalting in the breakdown of privilege; returning to old forms while improvising new content. Meanwhile, the production of *The Masque of Hope* also materialised its ambiguous claim on modernity through its costumes: although the traditional characters wore highly decorated outfits based on traditional Jacobean designs, Black Market wore a bowler hat and bow tie; and many of the clothes were fashioned from those most contemporary of textiles, black-out material and sacking – the only fabrics which were not rationed at the time.

This tendency towards temporal hybridity was echoed five years later in a much grander production, the premiere of Benjamin Britten's opera *Gloriana*, which similarly played with early-modern forms and conventions, juxtaposing them provocatively with radically contemporary musical and thematic ideas. This chapter will trace the way performance and costume expressed this problematic attempt to reconcile the future and the past, as the very materiality of mid-century apparel began first to enable, and then to demand, new definitions of authenticity, class and national identity. These new definitions inform key cultural artefacts of the period, from Powell and Pressburger's 1948 fairy tale *The Red Shoes* to Iris Murdoch's first novel *Under the Net* (1954); and from the 1951 Ealing comedy *The Man in the White Suit* to *Gloriana* itself, as well as finding expression in the accoutrements of both the Coronation and the ascent of Everest in 1953. Considered together, these very different stories about performance reveal a distinctively mid-century investment – literally, a putting-on of clothes – in the power relationships and gothic temporality inherent in significant garments.

The revivification of the past was a theme frequently brought into play in post-war discourse to offset the futuristic overtones of the prevailing rhetoric of recovery and progress. During the Festival of Britain, for instance, a resurgent interest in architectural modernism – which had been on hold during the war years – was tempered by incorporating updated elements of the traditional within the sleek Scandinavian-inspired pavilions – a compromise that came to be known as 'Festival style'.[2] Similarly, Humphrey Jennings's Festival film, *Family Portrait*, placed a determined emphasis on the survival of eternal British qualities even while urging its audience to embrace social and technological novelty; expressed in a series of voiceover paradoxes such as 'we adore innovations and love tradition', it defined the British character by its ability to combine the 'poetry' of imagination and symbolism with the 'prose' of science and progress.[3] Yet the very fact that this theme required constant reiteration suggests that it was not universally accepted as inevitable or desirable. This was apparent during Elizabeth's 1948 visit to Oxford at which *The Masque of Hope* was staged. This engagement was occasioned by the presentation to her of an honorary Doctor of Civil Law degree, after which she gave a speech praising the university as a place 'where the finest traditions of the past mingle so easily and unaffectedly with the march of events and of ideas':

> Here we can see, better perhaps than anywhere, that peculiar genius of the British people for blending the old and the new, without desecrating the one or blunting the ardour of the other, so that progress may be tempered with wisdom and tradition may be an object of respect rather than a cause of frustration.[4]

Frustration with tradition needed to be assuaged by devising a construct which could hold old and new in the correct balance. The performance of the doctoral ceremony itself suggested performance as just such a construct, and gave Elizabeth a traditional stage from which to outline the standard idealised notion of past and future in harmony. Yet the masque at University College implicitly critiqued this vision of transhistorical concord, not through its (inevitably somewhat anodyne) scripted sentiments, but by foregrounding the metonymic processes of its ironised, obsolete form. The past was presented as a set of trappings and conventions, antique accessories which carry no meaning other than oldness itself, disguising or costuming new ideas rather than nurturing them and bringing them to fruition. The future queen's position as another kind of ritualised object was likewise inscribed into the drama. By choreographing a stylised battle between allegorical figures in order to tell a modern story about social justice, Coghill not only co-opted the Golden Age mythology of Merrie England, he also recruited the future queen as one of the allegorical performers. *The Masque of Hope* did not merely present a spectacle to the princess and her retinue, but transfigured the royal guests into actors in the drama. As *The Times* report noted:

> The Princess was received at the main gate of the college with a fanfare of trumpets and cheers. She took her place in a little pavilion flanked by chairs occupied by senior members of the University in the sunny, many-windowed quadrangle, and the masquers used their immemorial privilege of addressing their royal guest directly.[5]

By seating the princess prominently within the performance space of the 'many-windowed' Radcliffe Quad, and addressing her by name, the masque invoked Elizabeth's own symbolic freight as a walking anachronism. The theatricality of the costumes, props and other trappings of performance which sustain the superannuated idea of monarchy in the modern world were thus revealed, and she was implicated and incorporated into a moment which folded together three temporalities: the fictive time of drama, the progressive sweep of history, and the contemporaneous moment of performance – in this case a unrepeatable occasional drama entirely reliant on the specificity of time and space for its meaning. The mid-century may have been a time of self-conscious aspiration for the future, but it was also a moment of anxiety about the fragility of past certainties – norms which might vanish if a sense of tradition and national identity was lost. The adoption of an early-modern dramatic form here reiterated the link between the two eras, yet the use of ritualised performance to express this insinuated a subtle critique of the processes of display, fictivity and artifice at work, not only in the theatrical celebration, but also in the reframing of the royal figurehead as a totemic object called upon to embody both antique changelessness and thrusting modernity. It was a pattern of superficial reverence erupting with gothic gusts of repressed critique which would be repeated in several of the cultural events examined in this chapter.

'IT'S THE RED SHOES THAT ARE RUNNING AWAY': THE UNCANNY POWER OF COSTUME

The same year that the future queen experienced her double performance in Oxford, she was also in the audience for a more intimate show: a private screening of Powell and Pressburger's *The Red Shoes*, attended by her parents and her sister Margaret and organised by Alexander Korda. In his memoir *A Life in Movies*, Powell relishes the effect the film had on its royal audience: '[Korda] told me they were all devastated by the ending of the picture, as they were intended to be, and thanked him with tears streaming down their faces for showing them "such a lovely – boohoo! – picture".'[6] The film takes its title from the Hans Christian Andersen fairy tale about a vain and selfish girl whose red shoes are bewitched to punish her for her godless ways: they dance day and night and cannot be removed. Even when she asks a woodcutter to chop off her feet, the amputated shoes continue to dance, and prevent her even from going to church to repent. Finally a merciful angel arrives, carrying such a powerful charge of overwhelming grace that the girl's heart bursts with joy, and she dies. In their very different version, Powell and Pressburger replace the tale's Christian morality with a strictly aesthetic imperative, framing it around a conflict between art and reality which the film itself performs. Here, the bewitched shoes are not a punishment for vanity but become a symbol of the brutal sacrifices required by art; Moira Shearer plays a ballerina, Vicky, torn between the demands of her charismatic and demanding mentor Lermontov (Anton Walbrook) and the domestic role offered by her husband Julian (Marius Goring). At the climax of the film, with both men demanding her absolute commitment to them, she runs from the theatre, wearing the red shoes, and leaps from a parapet onto a railway track to her death. On a psychological level, the explanation for this act is that she has committed suicide rather than choose between her two identities, but the film (and the source tale) strongly imply an uncanny material intervention. Powell states in his memoir: 'It isn't Vicky who's running away from the theatre, it's the Red Shoes that are running away with Vicky.'[7]

Indeed, the shoes' magical powers have already been established in the lavishly staged and expansively shot *Red Shoes* ballet which forms the film's centrepiece. Here, the shoes' demonic agenda is made explicit, although Andersen's Christian motivation is absent and the unnamed Girl, as danced by Vicky, is tormented by the shoes' demands simply because she has made the mistake of admiring them in a shop window. Their power is not limited to mere unstoppability either – from the point of view of the film, they appear able to subvert time and place: the ballet is ostensibly performed on an ordinary theatre stage, but the dance unfolds within a dreamlike, filmic space which extends and contracts according to the demands of the choreography rather than adhering to any realist constraints. The film thus foregrounds the artifice of staged performance, with the shoes acting as a focus for a prosthetic enhancement of reality and the ambiguous status of the actor/dancer's body. When Shearer puts them on her feet, she is called upon to represent a collection of nested identities: she is the ballerina Vicky as well as her various stage personas; she is the character of the Girl in the *Red Shoes* ballet, as played by Vicky as played by Shearer; and as far as the audience is concerned, she is also presenting the character of 'Moira Shearer', a newly minted film star in her first acting role, and thus another deliberately constructed identity.

Clothes played a crucial part in this latter transition. Powell's memoir describes at length how Shearer reacted to her traumatic induction into the sartorial demands of her new profession: she arrived on her first day already 'at the end of her tether. With our fittings and the ballet fittings and make-up tests, she had not had a second to herself for about three weeks.'[8] Her first day of filming began with Vicky's death-leap from the balcony:

> She is only in the air for about eight frames, but it is one of the most beautiful cuts in the film. By now the camera crew were her devotees. The whole sequence of her running out and dying on the track was completed by lunchtime. Moira spent the afternoon having fittings with Mme Jacques Fath and her dressmakers for the clothes in the film. Towards six o'clock she had hysterics, went to bed and slept for twelve hours. Her career as a film star had begun.[9]

Powell's account suggests that Shearer's lengthy encounters with her new wardrobe were as exhausting and traumatic as the physically and emotionally demanding death-leap set-up; by conflating the two, he implies that her 'hysterical' reaction is a much to do with the shocking redefinitive power of her new apparel as it is to do with stress or fatigue. It is the red shoes – the one constant feature which remains changeless throughout Vicky/Shearer's many transformations – that mark the body as the site of these multiple meanings. Yet, as gothic objects of the mid-century moment, these shoes also critique their own symbolism, calling into question the ritualistic power invested in costume.

Critics including Andrew Moor have commented that the role of Lermontov, as the demanding star-maker, echoes that of Powell himself, who is thus interpolating himself into the film's complex system of identity-doublings.[10] Lermontov often appears wearing sunglasses, and while this can be interpreted as a visual signifier of his shadowy nature, the glasses also signal a Powell-like vision which mediates the world through an aesthetic lens, and links Lermontov with the demonic optician in Powell and Pressburger's other ballet film, *Tales of Hoffmann*.[11] Lermontov's quasi-supernatural ability to discern and develop raw talent in his dancers is also expressed in the screenplay through a sartorial metaphor: 'Not even the best magician in the world,' he says, 'can produce a rabbit from the hat if there isn't already a rabbit in the hat.' This debunking of the conjurer's trickery subtly problematises the notion of the magic shoes as the implacable agents of the film's narrative: the hat appears to possess the magical power, but the audience knows it can only express the work of the magician who has carefully secreted the rabbit in its place. Likewise, the shoes appear to kill Vicky, but it is her own dual impulses, as artist and wife, that have done the preparatory work. Hat and rabbit, shoes and dancer form a dialectical image of the work of art as both the most intimate expression of the agency of the artist, and the autonomy of the finished work which threatens her annihilation.

To the royal audience who wept their way through Korda's screening, Vicky's relationship with the costume and trappings of her public role might have had a particular resonance. In a key early scene, Vicky is invited to Lermontov's villa for what she thinks will be a party, and arrives dressed as a princess, in full-length evening gown complete with cloak and coronet. Instead of enjoying a social evening, however, she gets a brisk and business-like meeting in which she discovers that she is being recruited as the company's new prima ballerina and will have the lead in the *Red Shoes* ballet. Although her royal costume is inappropriate at the level of narrative realism, it is not, after all, a mistake: Vicky has been inducted into an artificial world, like royalty, in which her public identity – marked by theatrical spectacle and ritualised costume – attempts to obliterate her individual will and simultaneously implicates her in her own obliteration. Vicky – whose upper-class background is always made clear – might seem to have been stripped of the trappings of aristocratic finery when she enters Lermontov's ballet company and dons the practical workwear of the rehearsal room, but in reality she is merely exchanging one regime of symbolic apparel for another. Yet although she cannot escape this oppressive overdetermination, the red shoes turn out to have unexpectedly subversive potential: they bring about a rift in the spectacle, first by shattering the hermetic space of the stage on which the ballet is supposedly performed, and then by dragging its principle performer out of the theatre completely and flinging her to her death.

Jonathan Faiers' study of unruly cinematic clothing, *Dressing Dangerously*, identifies several categories of filmic garments which exceed the 'fundamentally recognised function of clothing to protect from the elements and preserve modesty' – clothes that 'manifest an excess of meaning' such as the *film noir* trench coat or the stained and torn costumes of melodrama.[12] Such 'objects of sartorial agency' establish a 'negative cinematic wardrobe', Faiers argues, which accesses directly the viewer's personal experiences with clothing, rupturing the narrative and 'interrogat[ing] the authority of mainstream film's ability to immerse the viewer within the film's action.'[13] He invokes Lacan's formulation of the term *suture* – as adopted by the film theorist Jean-Pierre Oudart – to describe the process by which a spectator is 'stitched' into the action of a film, and argues that the unstitched nature of dysfunctional garments that are lost or torn away creates 'an oscillation between our lived experience of clothing and the fantasy of cinematic clothing' that troubles this immersive suturing.[14]

In *The Red Shoes*, however, it is not the shoes themselves that come undone, but the woman wearing them; the mythical red shoes are impossible to take off, even when cut from the legs with an axe. Their intimacy derives from the wearer's consenting decision to be enchanted and defined by them. The cinematic suturing achieved, according to Oudart's theory, by the montage effect of film's shot/reverse-shot formulation, is thus presented by the film as a warning against such tight fastening; the spectator is shown an image of her or his own entrapment as Vicky is all too firmly stitched into a spectacle which has been initiated by Lermontov/Powell, but is followed through to its inhuman conclusion by the shoes' own thingly agenda.

'CLOTHES DISAPPEAR'? LIBIDINAL TRANSACTIONS IN *CORRIDOR OF MIRRORS*

Terence Young's *Corridor of Mirrors* (1948) tells another uncanny story in which the sexual and social capital attached to glamourous clothing brings about a gothic transformation. It tells the story of a man, Paul Mangin (Eric Portman), who lives in a grand palazzo-style house somewhere near Regents Park, and believes he is the reincarnation of a Borgia princeling.[15] When he meets Mifanwy (Edana Romney) in a nightclub, he is struck by her resemblance to a fifteenth-century portrait of the woman he believes betrayed and abandoned him in his previous life in Renaissance Italy. She in turn is seduced by his otherworldly charm and by the elaborate dressing-up games that they play in his corridor of mirrored closets, each containing a mannequin uncannily resembling her and wearing a selection of sumptuous gowns, robes, tiaras and jewellery – all of which Paul has commissioned or collected over many years, apparently waiting to find the right woman to wear them. As their intimacy grows, he begins to dictate every aspect of Mifanwy's appearance and behaviour, and their sexless affair becomes more and more involving for her. The spell is broken, however, when she discovers that another woman, Veronica, has been hidden in the house all the time, watching them. Veronica claims that, far from being unique, Mifanwy is merely one in a series of interchangeable playthings, and that Paul will soon tire of her. Mifanwy ends the affair and gets engaged to another man, choosing to break the news to Paul at an elaborate Renaissance-themed costume ball he is holding in her honour. The next day a woman, who had been drunk at the party, is found dead in Paul's house; he admits to murder and is duly hanged, and only later does Mifanwy discover that Veronica was the true killer and Paul was, after all, just a psychologically repressed eccentric with a penchant for old clothes.

The film has some interesting similarities to *The Red Shoes* in its fairy tale overtones (this time it is Bluebeard that is evoked) and its makeover fantasy involving a man who wants complete control over his creation, and a woman who gradually cedes her autonomy as she comes under the spell of a fictional world and the very specific costume that goes with it. But whereas Vicky's personhood was to be abstracted and subsumed into Lermontov's artistic vision, Mifanwy's transformation is far more solidly material and explicitly gothic: at the very beginning of her affair with Paul she is alarmed by an image of herself as a faceless and sexless mannequin, but later she comes to accept this role, even describing herself as 'a wax doll – all head and shoulders'. The clothes, she implies, not only hide but have entirely replaced her body, so that sex becomes an impossibility; even her head and neck have been reduced to mere placeholders for a succession of accessories. This reification seems to be the primary intention of the libidinally stunted Paul, and it extends to himself, too, since he is also turned to wax; after his execution, his effigy is displayed in the Chamber of Horrors at Madame Tussauds. Indeed, because the film is told in flashback while Mifanwy gazes at this simulacrum, the waxwork precedes the appearance of the living actor, who is introduced via a dissolve which blends wax and flesh into a single image.

Since Paul also dresses in antiquated garb, he is equally implicated in the negation of autonomous subjecthood into which he inducts Mifanwy, but it is his practice as a collector which brings him most dangerously into proximity with the object world. A collector has what Walter Benjamin called 'the most intimate relationship that one can have to objects. Not that they come alive in him, it is he who lives in them.'[16] The collector creates an artificial world in which he believes he can live freely, without reference to the rest of society; but this apparent liberty is a trap: he is consumed by his own collection. The film makes the hermetic isolationism of the collector explicit: the couple always stay inside the house when they are dressed up, because to go outside would break the spell; Paul's fatal crisis occurs when he makes the mistake of opening up their private world for a public party. Benjamin's collector experiences 'the most profound enchantment' of 'locking ... individual items within a magic circle in which they are fixed as the final thrill, the thrill of acquisition, passes over them.'[17] But by finding Mifanwy, Paul is on the point of completing his collection and losing this acquisitive drive; he is thus destined to move definitively, via death, to the status of objecthood himself.

Benjamin emphasises that objects in a collection accrue value which is outside the system of mass-produced commodities: 'The purchasing done by a book collector has very little in common with that done by a student getting a text book,' he writes, and goes on to detail the thrill of auction bidding and the ways in which his own drive to collect has influenced his travels – 'How many cities have revealed themselves to me in the marches I undertook in the pursuit of books!'[18] But historical authenticity is not a necessary attribute for the clothes in *Corridor of Mirrors*, where the pseudo-sexual thrill of the chase is replaced by a painstakingly elaborate pastiche. In the original novel by Chris Massie, the collector, here called Douglas, has filled his wardrobes both with antiques and with replicas made to his own specifications because he has been unable to find sufficient original pieces:

> Have you ever thought, Mifanwy, how extraordinary it is that clothes disappear so quickly, as quickly as the fashions they illustrate? People preserve books and furniture from generation to generation, but clothes disappear. Have you ever wondered about that?[19]

In Young's film version, Paul is seen visiting a dressmaker to order clothes for Mifanwy, and there is less emphasis on his interest in genuine antiquities: he is presented as fabricating an elaborate fantasy around one true antique, the painting of the Renaissance woman whom Mifanwy uncannily resembles. The problem of which is the original – the portrait which Mifanwy is manipulated into impersonating, or Mifanwy herself as the painting's sitter, reborn – coalesces around clothing's negative dialectic and its libidinal transitionality: clothes must not be allowed to disappear in an act of intimate undressing. Mifanwy's costumes are commodities which both express and negate the fluidity, cyclical temporality and commodification of fashion, and at the same time they both stand in for and repress her desire for physical contact with Paul.

'AN UNEASY QUEEN': LOST COSTUMES AND MISPLACED DESIRE IN IRIS MURDOCH'S *UNDER THE NET*

As the 1940s turned into the 1950s, a young philosopher called Iris Murdoch started work on a novel which took up the themes of sex, power and performance and recast them as a wry commentary on the clash between metaphysics and embodiment.[20] *Under the Net* (1954) takes its title from Wittgenstein's description of linguistic discourse as a 'net' which is superimposed on reality and allows perception and description to take place, but which necessarily obscures – or at any rate fails to express – the true nature of things.[21] In Murdoch's hands, this metaphor becomes concrete as her narrator, a young drifter and would-be novelist called Jake Donaghue, attempts to understand the true nature of Anna, the woman he loves. Instead of encompassing her particularity, the more he tries to understand her, the more he finds himself entangled and enmeshed in the literal and perceptual fabric with which he seeks to bind and define the abstract object of his desire.

This perceptual failure plays out in a crucial scene, in which Jake tracks Anna down to a small avant-garde theatre in Hammersmith, which she has set up with the help of Jake's erstwhile friend, Hugo. The wealthy Hugo – another lost object, like Anna, whom Jake pursues doggedly and unsuccessfully through the pages of the novel – embodies the conceptual core of Murdoch's philosophical critique; his enigmatic pronouncements about the impossibility of language, which Jake calls his 'philosophy of silence', offer one way of reading Wittgenstein, but are revealed as perspective of other-worldly material privilege, and in any case turn out to be impossible to live by in any practical sense, even for those, like Hugo, who have access to apparently infinite funds. Nevertheless, inspired by Hugo's distrust of words, Anna has made the mistake of giving up a good career as a singer in order to set up a theatre that produces work entirely in mime: a policy by which she intends to create a purified aesthetic environment free of the muddying confusion of base language.

Stumbling into the auditorium one afternoon, Jake is baffled but hypnotised by the austere drama on stage, in which masked actors, dressed in uniform white, slowly 'execute their movements in the extraordinary silence'.[22]

As if to make up for this absence of words, however, the backstage area of the theatre is overflowing with redundant clothes and other objects which clamour to speak, like a material ramification of the Freudian uncanny, in which the repressed wells up from its hiding places by means of a supernatural animacy. Jake finally locates Anna in the jumbled prop store, which looks 'like a vast toy shop that had been hit by a bomb':

> Here was every kind of thing ... In my first glance I noticed a French horn, a rocking-horse, a set of red-striped trumpets, some Chinese silk robes, a couple of rifles, Paisley shawls, teddy bears, glass balls, tangles of necklaces and other jewellery, a convex mirror, a stuffed snake, countless toy animals, and a number of tin trunks out of which multi-coloured costumes trailed.[23]

This zone of riotous excess and turbulence is the opposite of the chaste sterility he has witnessed on the silent stage, and Jake considers it an 'enchanting chaos' from which Anna seems to emerge 'like a very wise mermaid rising out of the motley coloured sea'.[24] Yet there is a tension here: on the one hand, Jake seems to be on the point of acknowledging that perception, description and meaning in the world can only arise from a jumble of material redundancy and semiotic noise; on the other hand, he retains his Hugo-inspired desire to reject such provisional signification since it can never approach the status of absolute truth. Within this ambiguous semantic regime, Jake's interpretation of Anna remains relentlessly subjective – we later learn that he has completely misunderstood her relationship with Hugo – and indeed, in practice her position among a superfluity of objects simply gives Jake licence to objectify her in turn, so that she can be fitted – as Mifanwy was in *Corridor of Mirrors* – into the role he wants and needs her to play.

It is for this reason that he is disturbed by Anna's own ambivalence towards the randomly assembled bits and pieces which she picks up and puts down distractedly while they talk, all the while 'averting her eyes from me'.[25] In an act of violent appropriation which is only half jocular, he throws her down 'onto a pile of velvet costumes' and they are instantly buried in an avalanche of 'scarves, laces, tin trumpets, woolly dogs, fancy hats and other objects'.[26] After they have made love, Anna lies 'amid the coloured debris like a fairy-tale princess tumbled from her throne':

> She lay still for a moment, receiving my gaze, her foot arching with consciousness of it.
> 'Where's your crown?' I asked.
> Anna searched under the pile and produced a gilded coronet. We laughed. I helped her up and we dusted bits of tinsel, gold dust and loose spangles off her dress.[27]

Jake believes that he has rescued Anna from a realm of pseudo-royal intangibility, by clothing her in colourful and material artifice. He has decided that the theatre itself is a costume which does not fit Anna's true essence; it is, he thinks,

> a house for Anna, a house which Hugo had built and in which Anna would be queen. An uneasy queen; I recalled her restlessness, her nervousness, when I had been at the theatre. She was clearly not at peace with the role which Hugo had created for her.[28]

Jake, in his determination to deny Anna any artistic autonomy, has misread her unease, which really stems from her ambivalence towards him and his desire to define her. We later learn that the mime theatre has indeed been her own idea, and that, far from being under Hugo's influence, Anna – apparently embittered by her failed love affairs – is the author of a sincere attempt to attenuate and even abolish her own bodily materiality. The scene she shares with Jake in the props room has been a performance designed self-consciously to 'receive his gaze' while concealing the truth about her own feelings. The glittering junk and spangled costumes have performed an act of uncanny enchantment which remains ambiguous in intent: is Jake right to fall in with this raucous code of chaotic meaning and accept its contingency and fragility? Or is Anna right to try to strip away the chatter of ideas, in order to pursue some ever-retreating spectre of metaphysical reality and value? Jake, Murdoch implies, will never develop his own truth as a writer until he sees the enchanting net for what it is, yet the novel also depicts Anna as a doomed absolutist unable to partake of the mid-century's vibrant ambiguity.

To some extent, despite her bohemian aspirations, Anna's failed mime aesthetic shares the kind of snobbish disdain for everyday things that Barbara Jones wanted to contest in *Black Eyes and Lemonade*. The silent theatre attempts to frame the world according to the discriminations of a 'sophisticated' eye which supposedly sees past the clutter and squalor that obscures the realm of platonic idealism. In contrast, like Jones, Jake is alert to the gothic energy that these abject and unruly objects harness in order to resist demotion from the zone of visibility. When he spends the night in the crowded prop room, he is disturbed by the 'uneasy feeling of being observed' and although he 'could find no living thing' to account for this uncanny sensation, he eventually realises that it comes from 'a set of masks, similar to those I had seen on the stage, whose slanting eyes were turned mournfully in my direction':

> Then I began to discern that the room was full of eyes, the big vacant eyes of the rocking horse, the beady eyes of teddy bears, the red eyes of the stuffed snake, the eyes of dolls and puppets and gollywogs. I began to feel extremely uneasy ... Something in the far corner subsided softly. I sat down cross-legged in the middle of the floor and tried to think about something realistic.[29]

Meanwhile, having set Anna and Jake up against each other in relation to the clamorous profusion of the mid-century thingscape, Murdoch introduces the elusive Hugo, who has chosen to concern himself with another way of seeing and has invested his considerable wealth into a film company. Determined to re-establish contact with his lost friend, Jake travels to the studio to find him, and stumbles into a world which, far from partaking in the overdetermined chaos of the uncanny, upstart object, instead consists of layers of flattened fakery. Hugo's film set teeters on the brink of semantic collapse, not because of any elaborate plenitude, but because its flimsy two-dimensionality cannot sustain any reliable articulation with reality. A mocked-up version of an ancient Roman forum turns out to be the setting for a real political rally, with disgruntled, toga-clad extras mingling with communist agitators amid the false walls and vistas of a make-believe city:

> In the background, rising up in an explosion of colour and form, was a piece of ancient Rome. On brick walls and arches and marble pillars and columns there fell the brilliantly white radiance of the arc lamps, making the building stand out in a relief more violent than that of nature and darkening by contrast the surrounding air into a haze of twilight. Nearer to me was a forest of wooden scaffolding festooned with cables in which were perched the huge lamps themselves; and in between, mounted on steel stilts and poised on cranes, were the innumerable cameras, all eyes.[30]

The film set's scopic regime of hypervisibility obliterates reality rather than illuminating it. And, just as it did in the Renaissance ball staged by Paul in *Corridor of Mirrors*, the hubristic materialisation of a fetishised historical fantasy invites the destruction of both its own fabric and the dreaming subject's complexly entangled assemblage of technology and desire.

The politics of the scene provides an incidental gloss on the action. In the Dome of Discovery anecdote recorded by Mischa Black and discussed in this book's Introduction, a flock of liberated paper plates, picked out in the darkness, had materialised the recalcitrance and the will to freedom of an aggrieved workforce; in contrast, in the harsh light of a film set, where the intersection of capital and culture necessitates conformity to a strict grid of sanctioned meaning, no such attempts at flight can be permitted. Instead, Murdoch presents the campaigner Lefty Todd – 'the eccentric leader of the New Independent Socialists' – making an impassioned speech about workers' rights, only to be drowned out when the meeting is invaded, first by right-wing nationalists who fight a pitched battle with the socialists, and finally by the authoritarian intervention of the police.[31] Trapped in a corner, Hugo and Jake can only escape to safety though an act of ersatz terrorism, using a small 'domestic detonator' (which Hugo happens to have in his pocket) to blow up a section of fake wall in the fake Roman forum:

> The shock of the explosion must have dislocated something in the fabric of the city. For now suddenly the whole structure was beginning to sway and totter in the most alarming fashion. I looked up and saw as in a dream the brick and marble skyline vacillating drunkenly while there was a slow crescendo of cracking and splintering and rending.
> 'Damn, that's torn it!' said Hugo. 'It's all right,' he added. 'It's only made of plastic and Essex board.'[32]

In a passage which directly echoes William Sampson's accounts of his Blitz experiences, Jake is convinced that he will be crushed:

> Directly above us the wall began to lean inwards. To see what looks like fifty feet of solid brickwork descending on you is an unnerving sight, even if you have been told that it is only made of plastic and Essex board. With a sickening roar it began to fall.[33]

The wall may be a sham, but Jake's reaction to it is genuine. His recent experiences during the war are never detailed, but he has told us that it is 'important for the purposes of this tale' that 'I have shattered nerves. Never mind how I got them. That's another story, and I'm not telling you the whole story of my life.'[34] His description of the carnage that ensues after the explosion nevertheless becomes a comedic act of discursive recuperation, with shattered bodies brought back into wholeness by the revelation that the destruction has, after all, been an illusion:

> The foreground looked ... like the moment after the battle. The ground was strewn with legless torsos and halves of men and others cut off at the shoulders, all of whom, however, were lustily engaged in restoring themselves to wholeness by dragging the hidden parts of their anatomy out from under the flat wedges of scenery, which lay now like a big pack of cards, some pieces still showing bricks and marble, while others revealed upon their prostrate backs the names of commercial firms and the instructions of the scene shifter.[35]

Jake finally escapes from this nightmarish confusion of death and comedy with the help of another performance, this time by a novelty-act dog, the Marvellous Mister Mars, whom he has acquired earlier in the narrative through a series of bizarre misadventures. Finding the gates of the studio barred by police who want to detain the rioters, Jake orders the trained dog to play dead and rushes through with a cry of 'The dog's hurt! I must find a vet!'[36] Like much of the comedy in the novel, this moment underlines a philosophical point: even death and life are revealed as a sham, the transition between the two simply a matter of will, utterance and perception. As an animal, Mars cannot partake of the lies of language, yet he can still lie, in his actions: a refutation of Hugo's failed philosophy of silence, and of the hypothesis that a rejection of language could enable the net of falsity to be lifted from reality.

It is worth pausing to consider this dog more closely. Throughout the novel, a recourse to animality has been presented by Murdoch as a defence against the incursions of a sterile and lonely metaphysicality. Earlier, when Jake had been alarmed by the eyes watching him in the darkened props store of Anna's theatre, his defensive need to 'think about something realistic' and not to 'find myself alone in the dark in such a room' had led him to don an animal costume: selecting 'a bearskin complete with snout and claws', he 'thrust[s] [his] hands and feet into the bear's paws and let[s] the great snarling snout fall over [his] forehead. It made a snug sleeping suit'.[37] This animal suit is the opposite of the artificial royal regalia which has defined his false vision of Anna as the helplessly entangled object of his desire. It crystallises the necessity – which Jake cannot as yet perceive – for him to become a hybrid figure, whose receptiveness to ambiguity and contingency can protect him from the uncanny surplus of meaning that plagues him on his journey through the material assertiveness of post-war London. Murdoch gradually strips him of the monolithic certainty with which he has pursued both Anna and Hugo, until he ends the novel with an understanding that all his philosophical struggles have been essentially synthetic. Once divested of his pretensions, he can transform himself from a hack translator of others' ideas into a novelist with his own idiosyncratic narrative to tell.

Anna, on the other hand, has lost her physicality completely by the close of the novel. Last seen in Paris, drifting through the darkness of the Tuileries Gardens after the fireworks of Bastille Day, she removes her shoes in a symbolic act of undressing, and disappears from view. In the final scene, Jake encounters her as a disembodied voice on the radio, where she is singing 'an old French love song' whose words 'came slowly, gilded by her utterance'.[38] Both she and Jake have rejected silence, but while Jake firmly grasps the material world, Anna, the uneasy queen, has become entirely conceptual, a celestial being transmitted across the ether.

'CHEAP MATERIAL CANNOT PLEASE': SARTORIAL STATUS AND HUMAN FINERY

For the art critic Quentin Bell, there was no doubt that clothing in the mid-century was saturated with meaning and desire, but he was more interested in the armature of taste and class which underpinned these affective and semantic structures. His idiosyncratic account of the sociology of fashion, *On Human Finery* (1947), was not concerned with theatrical costume as such, but he analysed the mechanisms of sartorial display as a quasi-theatrical spectacle which had real effects on the human subject:

> Fashion for those who live within its empire is a force of tremendous and incalculable power. Fierce and at times ruthless in its operations, it governs our behaviour, informs our sexual appetites, colours our erotic imagination, makes possible but also distorts our conception of history and determines our aesthetic valuations.[39]

This complex of temporal, political and libidinal power is presented by Bell as something imposed onto wearers by their clothes and has serious consequences for their agency and status. While the post-war bohemianism of Iris Murdoch's Jake and Anna was beginning to stir in unfashionable districts like Hammersmith and Shepherd's Bush, disorderly dress still denoted, for Bell, a loss of social status and implied moral degradation. 'So strong is the impulse of sartorial morality,' he writes,

> that it is difficult, in praising clothes, not to use adjectives such as 'right', 'good', 'correct', 'unimpeachable' or 'faultless', which belong properly to the discussion of conduct while, in discussing moral shortcomings, we tend very naturally to fall into the language of dress and speak of a person's behaviour as being 'shabby', 'shoddy', 'threadbare', 'down at heel', 'botched', or 'slipshod'.[40]

Later, he draws a firm connection between sartorial morality and hierarchies of class and wealth – 'pecuniary standards of value', as he calls them.[41] Discussing the 'vulgarity' displayed in 'the ornate costume of the nouveau riche', he asserts:

> [A] certain minimal display of wealth is usually considered essential; no excellence of cut, hue, or design will serve to redeem the sin of poverty. A cheap material cannot please, only 'good' materials are permissible, and these must be expensively worked.[42]

Bell's assumptions were already being undermined, not only by the incipient bohemianism and multiculturalism of mid-century subcultures, but by the invention of new materials and manufacturing techniques which would threaten such strictly enforced networks of value and meaning. Indeed, Bell himself saw these structures as irrational and in need of critical scrutiny: 'The study of clothes,' he points out in his introduction,

> is a study of monstrosities and absurdities. It is ... a borderline science important to the historian in that it exhibits in a pure form the pursuit of status, and particularly interesting to the art historian in that here, if anywhere, we can trace a direct relationship between aesthetic and social feelings.[43]

Bell's historical and sociological method includes tracing the history of what he terms 'sumptuosity' as a form of conspicuous consumption intended to signal status from the early modern period onwards. He is unconvinced by social or political influences on changing tastes; his explanation for the 'mechanism of fashion' is hydraulic: innovations adopted by the aristocracy eventually overflow and trickle down to the working classes, become 'vulgar', and fall out of fashion only to cycle back to the top in the form of another novelty. It is the clothing that exists outside this system, such as military uniform and ceremonial regalia, which imparts lasting status; and it achieves this by referring back to a pre-modern time when apparel was rigidly codified and the trickle-down of fashion was outlawed:

Until the emergence of modern capitalism every civilised country has enacted sumptuary laws for the preservation of class distinctions, morality, thrift and industry ... Nothing was spared in the effort to curb fashion, but the history of sumptuary laws is a history of dead letters. All that remains today ... is a kind of legal ghost: the regulations which still govern the dress of peers and peeresses when the Sovereign is being crowned.[44]

Taking place at the post-war turning-point of the century, then, the Coronation of Elizabeth II crystallised the tension between timeless apparel and the flux of history. The ritual putting-on of clothes which conferred her status as monarch highlighted the dynamic process of meaning which took place when commoners – like Galahad in Sam Selvon's *The Lonely Londoners* – dressed dangerously.

'DAZED BY RITUAL': MATERIALISING EXCESS AT THE CORONATION

Maurizia Boscagli's recent post-Benjaminian analysis of the twentieth century's material turn, *Stuff Theory*, argues that clothes perform a dual function, both as a 'site of female spectacle' and as a 'mode of dissent against how subjects and objects are supposed to relate'.[45] Clothes, she writes, 'partake of the duplicity of the talisman: as aesthetic objects they are charged with intimacy and thus occupy a potentially synaesthetic position in regard to the subject. Fetishistically invested, they *also* speak directly to, and of, desire and fantasy'.[46] According to Boscagli, consumer culture determines that 'the "use" of clothes is always unnatural, for it is contra use value, and is, instead, semiotic and libidinal'.[47] In certain instances, she argues, this dissonance creates 'rifts in the modern protocols of visuality, moments of break with the bourgeois systematisation of subjectivity and materiality indexed by the spectacle itself'.[48] Such rifts occur when the wearers of clothes – and these are all women in Boscagli's deliberately gendered analysis – become conscious of this unnaturalness and perform it by misusing or subverting conventional dress. However, although she argues that 'the Spectacle increasingly intensifies during the twentieth century', and chooses literary examples from 1922 (the Nausicaa episode in Joyce's *Ulysses*) and 1983 (*Die Klavierspielerin* [*The Piano Teacher*] by Elfriede Jelinek), she passes over the mid-century hiatus in the commodity system and the rupture that this itself caused in the smooth workings of fashion's regime of gendered decoration and desire.[49] As the most spectacular female object of an all-pervasive cultural gaze, the queen at the moment of her Coronation raised questions about the agency and autonomy of the mid-century woman, in that her power and presence were explicitly symbolic, constructed from the royal trappings superimposed onto her body and carefully designed to promote themselves as objects in a fantasy of affluence, while preventing her from becoming a focal point of sexual desire.

The Coronation gown, designed by Norman Hartnell and thickly embroidered with symbolic references to the Commonwealth countries, was presented as a solid, impenetrable casing: 'When I first saw the dress on the stand at Hartnell's workroom,' one newspaper reporter confessed, 'I got the impression that it was made entirely of glass. Such is the effect of the thousands of seed pearls, each set in its equally small saucer of silver, which entirely cover the white satin bodice and skirt.'[50] Far from subverting fashion, the royal personage retreated from it as much as possible and allowed her symbols to speak for her. The queen's metaphysical status depended on her invisibility as a woman.

During a Coronation the crown – the traditional textbook exemplum of the trope of metonymy – implicates monarchy into the very mechanism of symbolic imagery; just as it condenses and concentrates the power of royalty within its own materiality, so it emphasises the superstitious origins of the monarch's supernatural potency by foregrounding a totemic object. The material symbol of the crown also conforms to Freud's definition of the uncanny by summoning a superannuated (or even atavistic) cultural belief-system, and its autonomy and agency appear in the way it creates meaning and bestows it onto a human object. Bill Brown, in his essay on trivia, 'The Tyranny of Things', examines such royal regalia as a way of explicating 'the dialectic by which human subjects and inanimate objects may be said to constitute one another.'[51] Meaning within this system is always contingent, according to Brown – produced by the communal agreement of those who participate in the symbolism: 'Different subjects materialise the physical object world differently. And thus the appropriate analogy may be that the human subject must produce the material object no less than subjects must produce their king.'[52] Brown goes on to read Mark Twain's *The Prince and the Pauper* as an examination of fetishisation. In this fairy tale about sovereignty and symbolism, Prince Edward (son of Henry VIII) changes places with a poor boy called Tom, and when he returns to the royal palace for his Coronation, he can only prove his identity by producing the Royal Seal which he had hidden inside a suit of armour before he began his adventure. This is the 'trivial thing' which 'materialise[s] the immaterial excess that differentiates a royal body from its brute physicality, the aura that is at once absent yet present: the royalty, phantasmatically transmitted by blood, that is in fact metaphysical.'[53] Just as commodities congeal excess value in Marx's description of capitalism, so ritual objects congeal excess meaning within themselves, which is only released when subject and object fall into their correctly dialectical positions relative to one another.

In keeping with this understanding of symbolic value, the Coronations of the twentieth century were larded with layers of new traditions. A monarch called upon to function as a symbol is best presented within a context replete with other symbols. As David Cannadine pointed out in his contribution to the essay collection *The Invention of Tradition*, the public performance of royal pageantry was not the ancient practice it purported to be, but was introduced with the Coronation of Edward VII as a bulwark against social unrest and new democratic rights:

> In England, as elsewhere in Europe, the unprecedented developments in industry and in social relationships, and the massive expansion of the yellow press, made it both necessary and possible to present the monarch, in all the splendour of his ritual, in this essentially new way, as a symbol of consensus and continuity to which all might defer.[54]

Apart from the symbolic regalia worn and carried by the Queen herself, the trappings of all participants at the Coronation in 1953 were also intended to materialise a differentiating excess; descriptions of the build-up to the ceremony dwelt at length on the excessively luxurious accoutrements of power:

> In this roomy and lofty vestibule ... the robes and uniforms of many centuries began to assemble at 6am. The eye noted the Tudor anachronism of the Yeomen Warders and the axes carried by the Gentlemen-at-Arms which, on some Darwinian principle, have atrophied by disuse from weapons into glittering and tasselled ornaments; and then turned to the familiar red and blue and bearskins of the Queen's Company of the Grenadier Guards, who lined the walls.[55]

This anonymous *Times* correspondent wryly but tellingly emphasises the superfluity of the layers of ornament, which occlude the human beings inside them and turn them into so much wallpaper, even as they materialise their status; such atrophied anachronisms embody the same metaphysical surplus which imbues Elizabeth's crown (and Twain's royal seal). A later passage in the same newspaper report explicitly juxtaposes the use-value of a team of servants with the regalia of the leisured aristocracy:

> Two interludes which occurred just as tension was rising in anticipation of the arrival of the Queen and the Duke of Edinburgh were typical of the contrast between the formality and the informality of most of the scenes and moods in the annexe. First a party of women in white overalls moved briskly over the deep blue carpet with soft brushes, making great men do their will and move aside. Secondly, there was a stir of concern as it became apparent that a nobleman, with an indispensable part to play, had mislaid, or had mislaid for him, his coronet.[56]

Presented as comedy, these interludes in fact betray the fragility of the hierarchical distinctions supposedly marked by the white overalls and the coronet. The briskness of the women exposes the incompetence of the nobleman, who is not only incapable of looking after his own coronet, but depends on blundering – or recalcitrant? – servants who mislay it for him. Just as in *The Prince and the Pauper*, a missing token threatens the whole structure of the ceremony. Without the material symbol of the nobleman's phantasmagorical potency, a revolutionary tide threatens to turn; the cleaners '[make] great men do their will', begging the question of who really has 'an indispensable part to play'. Like an actor in costume, the players in the ritual risk exposing the fetishisation on which their double-identity depends, if they become separated from the clothes by which their role is instantiated.

The Coronation's presentation of a monarch as a mediated object, a symbol semantically fixed in a network of social and class tradition, is designed to emphasise and exalt her status and prestige. But in mid-century culture there was a strong countervailing assumption which resisted such inflexible systems of meaningful display. Just as, in Cannadine's words 'the archaic traditions of the Middle Ages were enlarged in their scope so as to include the modern splendour of a mighty [Victorian] empire',[57] so, in 1953, the splendour of monarchy had been quietly reconfigured to conform to new empires which were seeking to serve and exploit the mass-market desires of an incipient generation of consumers.

The fantasy that sartorial power structures were unchanging was challenged by the new textiles and materials which were starting to reflect and enable post-war popular culture. The crowds who camped out in rain-lashed central London to catch a glimpse of the Coronation procession were likely to be sheltering under the new synthetic raincoats which heralded a mass-market aspiration towards affordable utility. Lady Violet Bonham Carter noted in her diary the good humour of the crowds 'wrapped in soaked newspapers & plastic mackintoshes but burning with loyalty & full of good humour'.[58] But a newspaper correspondent reporting on the street-campers made a point of noting another coat's absence: 'The crowds, in which women predominated, were clearly uncertain whether to wear overcoats against the cold or mackintoshes against the wet. Some wore both: but the duffel coat, now de rigueur for so many occasions, was strangely absent.'[59] Duffel coats – introduced by the Royal Navy in First World War and reissued in their thousands to Second World War servicemen – had flooded onto the army-surplus market in the post-war years, marketed by a glove and overall manufacturing company called Gloverall. By the mid-1950s this article of military uniform had become the uniform of a certain kind of non-conformist, having been adopted both by the dissident agitators of the left and by a certain type of no-nonsense urban creative. Hugh Casson's 1957 portrait of his friend and fellow Royal Academician Sir Robin Darwin depicts the artist wearing his own army-issue duffel coat with pride; Sylvia Townsend Warner's diary from the 1950s recalls a visit by the epicene scholar and translator Enid Starkie, who appeared wearing 'bright blue trousers, very baggy, a baggy scarlet duffel coat, a red beret, too large, and some bunches of red-gold hair'.[60] And the actress Sandra Caron, when offered a new mink coat by her sister, the singer Alma Cogan, chose instead the gift of a duffel coat because she wanted to look like 'a sort of beatnik'.[61]

Duffel coats, as salvaged objects, reactivate their historical surplus and transform one meaning (military utility) into another (the refusal of capitalist fashion). Plastic macs, in contrast, rely on and perpetuate the surplus value generated by capitalism. While the duffel coat is a heavy object, disguising the body and offering the illusion of uniformity, the plastic mac is flimsy and transparent, its cheapness suggesting that it should be taken lightly, thrown away and replaced by ever cheaper mass-produced versions of itself. The fashion correspondent of *The Times*, in 1955, summarised the appeal of the earliest plastic macs:

> Plastic raincoats which can be rolled up small and stuffed in pocket, handbag, or suitcase owed little to fashion when they were first introduced and everything to function. They were utterly unbecoming, but they served as convenient cocoons, dispensed with the need for a raincoat proper, and were cheap enough to be thrown away and replaced by a new one when the plastic began to tear away from the buttonholes and rain seeped through the stitching.[62]

But while disposable synthetics were beginning to blur class distinctions among the middle classes, the position of commoners in relation to royalty remained carefully circumscribed in order to preserve the element of fetishisation which characterised the Coronation spectacle. For the royalist mainstream – whether fur-coated or plastic-macked – the Coronation not only situated the new queen within a sanctioned historical narrative of continuity blended with progress, it was a performance which carefully staged their response in order to assert the consensual nature of class hierarchy. Spectatorship at the event was precisely modulated according to status, with the aristocratic audience in Westminster Abbey co-opted as lavishly costumed extras in the drama, while the well-off bought tickets for grandstand seats along the procession route, leaving the masses to jostle for any vantage point they could lay claim to. A ticket-holder in the £30 seats – *Daily Express* columnist Eve Perrick – noted the strict dress code of the middle-class spectators, which was both aspirational and bathetically practical:

> We seemed to have, although it was all quite unofficial, a kind of regulation dress. No ermine, mind you, but nearly all the women wore mink. And in place of coronets the men had come prepared with little plastic cosies which they fitted over their light-weight trilby hats.[63]

Many non-ticket-holders found vantage points in the shopping districts of the West End. The royal route included Regent's Street and Oxford Street, thus appropriating the resonance of spaces already imbued with acquisitive desire; the gold-and-glass carriage presented the new queen like an expensively dressed mannequin in an ever-receding vitrine display or an inaccessible shop window. It is notable that Queen Sālote of Tonga briefly became a darling of the British press because she chose to brave the rain in an open-topped carriage, making her more accessible to the crowds than any of the home-grown dignitaries. It was popularity tinged with loss of status, however; Margaret Thatcher – who also had tickets for the stands and was protected from the elements – noted sniffily in her diary, 'The queen of Tonga never wore *that* dress again. Mine lived to see another day.'[64]

Meanwhile, for those not in London, the Coronation was a television event rather than a live spectacle. The *Daily Express* championed the new technology which not only caught a 'secret smile' from the Queen at the moment she was crowned, but also 'spread [it] across Britain into Europe and even behind the Iron Curtain into Berlin'.[65] Angus Wilson, writing in the *New Statesman*, described his experience as part of a communal television audience 'dazed by ritual' at a hotel in Essex. He was impressed by the way this experience broke down both his own 'innate Republicanism' and the 'Rotarian, have-the-next-one-on-me-old-boy jollity' of 'the saloon bar gang':

> It was fascinating to see them fight the strange beauty, the formal Byzantinism of the ceremony that appeared on screen. They were prepared, of course, for an occasional catch in the throat, a moment of lowered head, but the elaborate grace before them demanded less perfunctory reverence ... It was nice to see the 'gang' so put out when they least expected it.[66]

The phantasmagoria which so dazed the viewing public demonstrated the power of objects to produce metaphysical transformations, and because this phantasmagoria was itself mediated by the television screen it became even more uncannily powerful. Arguably, this moment summoned in the public a desire for objects which could perform a similar transformation on themselves – a desire never fulfilled by the eternal postponement of satisfaction offered by mass consumerism. If the Coronation promoted a consumerist motive force within society, it also provided its own critique in the way it turned the new queen into a spectacular ghost, an image on a screen, immaterial herself within the materialist spectacle of the occasion.

Wilson goes on to describe the way local communities answered this performative paradigm by staging their own productions and inserting themselves into networks of meaning more politically nuanced than the distant event in London: a historical pageant which mixed Tudor themes with Norman architecture and a Victorian sensibility; a village sports day; a Morris dance patronised by

> a large crowd contain[ing] a sprinkling of first-rate Osbert Lancaster intellectuals, including an old lady with grey earphones, purple ribbons round her hair and throat, a purple cloak, and a flatly benign expression that smiled at once upon a Co-operative Guild future and a Maypole past.

His piece ends with a description of a dinner at which the guests recount their experiences as performers at another pageant, in Toppesfield.

> I was told the hostess had been a great success as Roxana; another guest told me he had been playing Wamba the Jester, while a lady who arrived late explained how

exhausted she was 'what with the rehearsal of Benjie's opera and playing Katharine Howard'.

The mention of Daniel Dafoe's *Roxana* and Raleigh's *Ivanhoe* suggest that this pageant had high cultural ambitions, but the throwaway reference to Benjamin Britten's *Gloriana* – and the fact that Wilson does not elaborate further on it – is indicative of the ambivalent response that particular dramatic spectacle provoked in Coronation year.

'AS CROOKED AS HER CARCASE': THE FAILURE OF ROYAL GLAMOUR IN *GLORIANA*

Britten's contribution to the royal moment was not intended to elicit either a perfunctory catch in the throat nor an upsurge of spontaneous royalism in otherwise Republican spectators; it was, in the words of librettist William Plomer, 'an original opera with a serious theme'.[67] The project had first been suggested by Lord Harewood, the queen's cousin, in 1952, and he was instrumental in choosing the theme of the reign of Elizabeth I, suggesting Lytton Strachey's *Elizabeth & Essex: A Tragic History* as source material.[68] But it was Britten who decided to frame this portrait of an elderly monarch, whose royal dignity is threatened by foolish infatuation, in terms of the material trappings of the queen's constructed identity and status, and her vulnerability to human failings without them. The opera presents the first Elizabeth as holding two incompatible identities in an uneasy balance: first she is the impermeable Renaissance monarch whose totemic glamour and rich apparel are worn as a carapace while plots, politics and intrigue swirl around her; then she is a vulnerable private woman in love with a man, Essex, who only professes to return her affection in the hope that he will gain preferment and influence. Six days after Elizabeth II had performed her role in the drama of the Coronation, the new queen was now once again in the audience instead of on the stage. Just as she had been literally hailed by the players in *The Masque of Hope* while still a princess, now she was being hailed symbolically by an opera which all too openly sought to suture her into the spectacle of the symbolically and physically divested monarch on the stage. The numerous brickbats hurled at the opera after the premiere arose partly from the sense that the living queen in the audience had been stripped bare by the treatment of her namesake – as indeed, metaphorically, she had been. Lord Drogheda, who was to become chairman of the Royal Opera House five years later, described the gala in his autobiography:

> Long remembered it was, but as a fiasco ... *Gloriana* was quite long, the evening was warm, the intervals seemed endless, stick-up collars grew limp, and well before the end a restlessness set in. 'Boriana' was on everyone's lips. Most distressing was that in one scene the elderly Queen Elizabeth I removed her wig from her head

and was revealed as almost bald: and this was taken, for no good reason at all, as being in bad taste.[69]

The scene in question – Act 3 Scene 1 – depicts the return of the Earl of Essex from his campaign in Ireland, where he has failed to defeat the rebellious Tyrone. Despite the protests of the queen's ladies in waiting, he insists on pushing through into her private chamber for an audience. As the stage directions put it:

> He steps forward and sweeps the curtain back, disclosing the Queen seated at her dressing-table, wearing an old, plain dressing-gown ... Her red-gold wig is on a stand before her, among the paraphernalia of her toilet. She has a looking glass in her hand ... Wisps of grey hair hanging round the Queen's face make her look old, pathetic and vulnerable.[70]

The visual effect of the shabby, de-wigged queen was striking. Like Essex, Britten had broken the first rule of a constitutional monarchy; in Walter Bagehot's phrase, he had 'let in daylight upon magic'.[71] And Britten, like Essex, was punished for it.

William Plomer responded to the bad reviews by attacking the opera's critics as jealous mediocrities, whom he characterised as 'philistine and puritan art-saboteurs, iconoclasts and ignoramuses, and those who fear and hate anything which does not flatter their prejudices and pander to their appetites'.[72] He went on to dismiss the original gala audience as a group of shallow socialites, excessively interested in clothes and finery:

> An unmusical audience, consisting largely of important persons ... who were there for official or social reasons or out of loyalty and courtesy to the Queen ... Were these chatterers interested in anything beyond a plenteous twinkling of tiaras and recognizable wearers of stars and ribbons in the auditorium?[73]

Plomer's description suggests that the relationship between stage and auditorium was reversed at the opera's premiere: the audience themselves, with the queen as their diva, sought both to provide and to consume a shallow and primarily sartorial spectacle, while, for Plomer, the players on the stage represented a more authentic version of reality. Indeed, he and Britten had been determined 'to shun anything that might smack of Wardour Street, Merrie England, Good Queen Bess, or the half-baked half-timbering of debased twentieth-century "Tudor" stylings', and had thus left an opening for a rival, crowd-pleasing phantasmagoria to be staged in the stalls and boxes.[74] But the idea that the lèse-majesté of the dressing-room scene was merely a by-product of aesthetic high-mindedness, with composer and librettist too wrapped up in the purity of their art to consider protocol, is unconvincing given the brazenness of the irreverence.

In fact, clothing is central to the opera's commentary on the ceremonial fictions of the Coronation it celebrated, and the second half of *Gloriana* plays out the rapid decline in Elizabeth's power explicitly through images of performance and costume. While Act 1 shows the queen in full control of her royal glamour, and determined to quell her love for Essex in order to 'die in honour, / Leave a refulgent crown!', Act 2 begins the unravelling of her carefully constructed persona.[75] The act opens with a masque in her honour – a crowd-pleasing interlude which nevertheless impedes the main narratives of love, ambition and duty and forces the queen into a ritual role at a time when action is called for. At least one contemporary critic, John W. Klein, considered this supposedly meaningless digression a bigger mistake than any potential insult to queenly dignity later in the opera: '[Britten] devotes practically one whole scene (which is almost entirely irrelevant) to pageantry. This was obviously necessitated by the exigencies of the festive occasion, but inevitably – from a purely dramatic point of view – it tends to weaken his work.'[76] Arguably, however, this play-within-a-play reflects the events of 1953 somewhat pointedly. Like *The Masque of Hope* in 1948, it places the new queen into the heart of the drama by showing her proxy as a captive audience co-opted into a role within the spectacle, forced to sit and listen appreciatively to what Essex, in an aside, calls 'Tedious orations / Dotards on their knees – / I for one could yawn myself to death.'[77] While the stage Elizabeth is hemmed in by duty, trapped inside an empty piece of theatre, her courtiers, including Essex, plot in asides to take control of the kingdom. It is from this position of weakness that Elizabeth takes the drastic step – in Scene 3 of Act 2 – of humiliating her romantic rival, Lady Essex, for choosing the wrong dress for a dance. In this scene, Lady Essex has entered wearing a particularly fine gown in an attempt to persuade the gathered nobles of Essex's high status. But Elizabeth is furious at being outshone, and rather than fall back on the laws of sumptuary which (as Bell pointed out) specifically outlawed this kind of threat to her status, like a petulant child she plays a prank on her rival. When the ladies retire to 'change their linen' after a vigorous dance, Elizabeth steals the gown in question; the stage directions describe how 'the Queen suddenly returns, unheralded and unattended, and wearing Lady Essex's missing dress. It is much too short for her, and she looks grotesque.'[78] She taunts Lady Essex:

> Too short, is it not?
> And becometh me ill?
> ...
> If, being too short,
> It becometh not me
> I have it in mind
> It can ne'er become thee
> As being too gaudy!
> So choose another![79]

These bullying tactics do not strengthen the queen's position; the conspirators agree that this is 'what comes of being ruled / By a king in a farthingale' and Essex's indignation leaves us in no doubt that his previous protestations of love for the queen have been merely tactical when he exclaims 'Conditions! Conditions! / Her conditions are as crooked as her carcase!'[80]

The incident with the dress was very important to Britten. He borrowed it, almost exactly, from an unrelated scene in Strachey's book, in which the owner of the dress was Lady Mary Howard;[81] by transferring it to Lady Essex, and making it a crucial narrative turning point, he loaded it with political significance. Correspondence in the Britten archive shows that Plomer had wanted to have Lady Essex parade in the dress during an earlier scene in a private garden, but Britten insisted the incident be moved into the dance at court.[82] It seems likely that Britten wanted the dress incident to be concentrated in a scene of public power and status because he was making a point about how power is produced by costume. And the scene works in another way; along with the dressing-room scene which follows after the interval, it separates the actors on stage from their costumes, and places the material object centre-stage. Elizabeth's removable clothes are redefined as pieces of costume in royalty's ongoing theatrical performance, thus revealing that the character is in turn an actor herself, playing a further character in another level of fictivity. Just as in *The Red Shoes*, this creates nested layers of identity, but whereas in Powell and Pressburger's film it is the impossibility of removing the shoes that contributes to their uncanny agency, in *Gloriana* the queen's ritual trappings repeatedly slip away from her and threaten to reveal the private self which might come unstitched from her royal status.

Heather Wiebe has argued that the dewigging of the queen in the third act 'unveiled an uglier reality behind the Coronation's carefully produced fantasy of the Elizabethan era':

> The opera's peculiar darkness speaks to an ambivalence within the Coronation celebrations about the structures of British – or, to be more precise, English – identity. ... It probed a problem at the heart of this construction of identity, faltering at the line between domestic and expansive versions of Englishness.[83]

For Wiebe, the Coronation's 'self-consciously imperial character' was challenged by Britten's depiction of the first Elizabethan era, which right-wing commentators celebrated as the seminal incarnation of British achievement in culture and outward-bound imperial power.[84] Indeed, the arts in general, in her view, 'fit uneasily into the Coronation display as a whole.'[85] However, she tends to overestimate the extent to which the Coronation itself 'presented the age of Elizabeth I as the original imperial moment';[86] as Cannadine has shown, the ceremonies and rituals were designed to bolster a Victorian construct of monarchy, not an Elizabethan one, and most references to the first Elizabeth were not politically aspirational but were blurred into a decorative fiction of 'Merrie England', along with maypoles and Morris dancing. What Wiebe does pinpoint, however, is the way in which Britten's music complicates the opera's claims to historical authenticity. She focuses on the musical significance of 'Happy were he', a melancholy lute song which Essex plays to Elizabeth, and which is among the most beautiful moments in the opera:

> Happy were he could finish forth his fate
> In some unhaunted desert, where, obscure
> From all society, from love and hate
> Of worldly folk, then might he sleep secure.[87]

The lyrics are based closely on a poem that the real Essex composed, so that the song seems to offer an authentic Elizabethanism rooted in what Wiebe calls 'an English pastoral already cloaked in melancholy – austere, solitary, unattained and unattainable'.[88]

The postulated 'realness' of this moment creates a crisis of credibility within the fiction of the opera; a crisis which reaches its climax in the final scene, where the dying queen, picked out in a spotlight on a darkened stage, stops singing and begins to utter spoken quotations from the recorded speeches and letters of the historical Elizabeth I, producing an intimation of fictional collapse which resonates also in the 'lost objects' of the opera, namely, the wig and dress which become detached from their wearers. Essex's fantasy of a simple hermit's life, 'content with hips and haws and brambleberry', is based on a release from culture and a return to nature – a dream of objectlessness and an escape from surplus value and meaning. Perhaps the pervasive sense that this opera was somehow disrespectful to the second Elizabeth arose, not just from its suggestion that her namesake was old, bald and weak, but from a more ambitious revelation of monarchy itself as a fiction which, like all fictions, must eventually collapse when confronted with the turning wheel of history. Like the masquers in Oxford five years earlier, Britten was using the privilege of artistic licence to evoke the queen as a symbol of fictivity, and his message was not so much about nationalism and empire, but something more personal about the fragility of metaphysical excess and the obliteration of the self demanded by the metonymic trappings of status.

'IT LOOKS AS IF IT'S WEARING YOU!': SCIENCE, SYNTHETICS AND SOCIETY IN *THE MAN IN THE WHITE SUIT*

The spectacle of the Coronation itself was, as design historians Christopher Breward and Ghislaine Wood have described it, 'a sophisticated design event, operating across the fields of photography, fashion and performance to project a new version of the Crown's role in the life of the state'.[89] In particular, they examine the queen's Coronation portrait by Cecil Beaton, which shows the queen in ermine, crown, densely embroidered gown and full regalia, seated in front of a clearly fake projected backdrop depicting Westminster Abbey.

This, they argue, is a complex fiction and declares itself as such through its use of synthetic materials; the threshold between the flesh-and-blood monarch and the virtual background is marked by a curtain, a 'bolt of blue and gold "Queensway" rayon silk, designed for Warner and Sons by Royal College of Art professor Robert Goodden to decorate the Abbey interior'.[90] This 'embodies the contradictions: a synthetic rendering of age-old symbols drawn back in a technicoloured sweep, like set-dressing on a Hollywood film set'.[91] Arguably, indeed, this image not only 'suggests the contingent and artificial nature of a grand state event in a democratic age', but seems to emphasise the intransigent materiality of the royal regalia, and threatens the autonomous personhood of the sovereign wearing and holding the symbols of power.[92] The rayon curtain, which is intended to link the seated queen with the religious, historical and ceremonial context represented by the fake, blurry and unconvincingly lit abbey, instead threatens to close behind her, and leave her stranded in possession of some elaborate but meaningless baubles.

The tension between the fabric of tradition and the technological modernity represented by the rayon silk curtain had been played out in a more overtly political way in Alexander Mackendrick's 1951 Ealing comedy *The Man in the White Suit*.[93] The film follows the fortunes of an idealistic chemist, Sidney Stratton (Alec Guinness) who upsets the status quo in a northern mill town when he invents a thread that cannot break and never gets dirty. When he dons the first suit to be made of this pure white fabric, he is greeted by his employer's daughter, Daphne (Joan Greenwood), as the harbinger of a social justice enabled by clothes which are eternally pristine:

> It makes you look like a knight in shining armour. It's what you are. Don't you understand what this means? Millions of people all over the world are living lives of drudgery fighting an endless losing battle against shabbiness and dirt. You've won that battle for them. You've set them free. The whole world's going to bless you!

But instead of being the people's champion, Sidney remains the underdog, harried both by the textile consortium running the weaving industry, who see a threat to their profits, and the mill's workforce, who see a threat to their jobs. That the fur-coated industrialist and the dungaree-wearing shop steward should join forces against the Oxbridge scientist in his college scarf and cricket jumper is typical of the fundamental social conservatism which underlies many of Ealing's ostensibly anti-authoritarian tales of insubordination, such as *Passport to Pimlico* (1949) and *Whisky Galore!* (1949). The film strives to restore its characters to the traditional balance which has been disrupted by the novel material of the white suit. That the material has its own agenda, quite separate from Sidney's, is suggested by the fact that he disappears completely inside the suit when he wears it in low light, his face and hands blending into the shadows while the fabric's artificial whiteness sings out – an effect remarked on by Daphne, who declares 'It looks as if it's wearing you!' Just as the queen's personhood is occluded by the opalescent, shell-like trappings of the Coronation vestments, Sidney becomes, in effect, a version of H.G. Wells's *Invisible Man*, who can be manifested only by means of his clothing.[94] When, in the film's climax, Sidney makes a desperate run from the combined forces of capital and labour who are determined to suppress his invention, his mad dash through the dark streets of the mill town is made ridiculous by the fact that he is wearing a luminous suit which makes it impossible to hide. He is cornered, but as hands grab him, the white fabric falls apart like blotting paper. Technology turns out to be unreliable, the textile industry is saved, and Sidney – like the Emperor in his delusional New Clothes – is left standing in his underpants, revealed as a clown.

Although Daphne has compared him to a knight in shining armour, Sidney's suit is not so much the emblem of a warrior, as the battleground itself. Yet only at the end of the film, when the glaring suit is threatening to give him away, does he realise he is in the wrong clothes. He bumps into his landlady, Mrs Watson, who is carrying the laundry she takes in to make ends meet, and begs her for a garment to cover himself. Instead of helping him, the once kindly Mrs Watson refuses him, unleashing a rebuke that makes Sidney understand the folly of his aspiration, and strikes the keynote of the film's conservative condemnation of high-minded scientific utopianism: 'Why can't you scientists leave things alone? What about my bit of washing when there's no washing to do?' At this climax of its illusory supremacy – in the next scene Sidney's suit will fall apart amid gales of laughter – the white suit is an emblem of all that is sinisterly alien about science and modernity. The character of Sidney, once loveable as an underdog, now looms over the tiny form of Mrs Watson, his face in dark shadow, as the suit which is 'wearing him' takes control and attempts, like the artificial life-form in *Quatermass*, to survive and replicate itself.

As well as commenting on the danger threatened by the thoughtless onrush of technological innovation, *The White Suit* was responding to a growing crisis in the real world of textile manufacture. The post-war slump caused by continuing rationing, recession and unemployment resulted in mass lay-offs of workers in Lancashire; in the summer of 1952, 33 per cent of spinning operatives and 22 per cent of weaving operatives were either unemployed or on short time.[95] The 'textiles crisis', as it became known, prompted Sir Raymond Streat, chairman of the Cotton Board, to call an international conference at Buxton in September which concluded that the low demand was caused by a combination of 'not just increasing Japanese competition, but also Korean War stockpiling, import controls in Australia and untimely price-fixing arrangements by the Yarn Spinners' Association'.[96] A US productivity team that toured the industry in the same year found large elements of both management and labour dominated by an inertia which prevents them from seeing the future clearly... Their main effort at the moment seems to be directed towards the protection of the least efficient producers and the preservation of antiquated arrangements.[97]

As David Kynaston has written:

> The 1952 textiles crisis was a clear signal that it was time to stop privileging the great nineteenth-century export staples – coal, cotton, steel – and instead start prioritising the new, scientific, high-tech industries that could realistically be seen as having a future.[98]

The shift in perspective towards technology and synthetic fabrics had begun during the Second World War; in the face of maritime attacks on supply lines, the importance of local sources of essential materials became apparent – materials which could be developed out of the new synthetic substances that had been discovered in the previous decade. The invention of PVC in 1933 was followed two years later by polyethylene, discovered by chance at ICI.[99] Nylon also came onto the market in 1935, and polystyrene in 1937; once the war began, these timely materials were readily put to use in radar sets, parachutes, insulators and much else. After the war, acrylics such as Dralon and polyester fabrics, marketed as Dacron and Terylene, promised a utopian combination of utility, cheapness and modern, vibrant colours. In her work on the Festival Pattern Group, which created textile designs for the 1951 Festival of Britain based on atomic structures revealed by x-ray crystallography, the design historian Mary Schoeser traces the process by which science inserted itself into everyday material culture. She cites not only the invention of artificial fibres like nylon and terylene, but the invention of cyclamates (artificial sugar substitutes) in 1937 and the introduction of the first credit card (the Diners Club card) in 1950, and locates these developments within a wider context in the 1950s, which saw both the 'natural' order and the old political order being challenged, via developments as diverse as the first embryo transplant for cattle (1950) and the creation of NATO (1949). But for individuals creating costumes and settings for themselves on the domestic stage, technologically enhanced fabrics also promised to overturn the social codes governing the status of materials. The introduction of rotary screen printing in the 1950s (replacing the use of copper engraved rollers) meant that dye could be applied to the fabric in layers, creating 'fine lines and crisp textural effects' such as chevrons, herringbones and tweeds – texture which 'disguises cheap cloth'.[100] In 1956, the former mining company 3M began marketing Scotchgard and for the first time it became practical to put printed fabrics on furniture, too, in order to emulate more expensive weaves. Whereas Quentin Bell in the late 1940s had unquestioningly asserted that the sumptuosity of a fabric could never be usurped as the key marker of taste and value, new synthetic fabrics and technological innovations were indeed about to displace the idea that 'a cheap material cannot please'. But it was not just the cheapness of a printed tweed – or the disposability of the plastic mackintoshes worn by the Coronation watchers in 1953 – that offered a new understanding of how clothing might transform its wearer. The ascent of Mount Everest showed that technical fabrics had the power to transport the human subject into hitherto inaccessible realms.

THE CRUCIFIX AND THE CLOTH CAT: DISPUTED MATERIALS ON THE SUMMIT OF EVEREST

In one sense, the Everest expedition was a riposte to the idea that the British were no longer capable of grand adventures, and no longer valued the individual achievements of an elite. The *Spectator*, in a review of *Gloriana* which Wiebe perceptively calls a 'thinly veiled attack on Britten's homosexuality', had accused the opera of betraying

> those magnificent Renaissance creatures, the Elizabethans, with their pride and ambitions, their reckless intrigues and their fierce contempt of death. The authors have not convinced us that they have really grasped the great heart of the Renaissance individualist; the whole man, hard and sensitive, artist and warrior in one.[101]

Everest seemed to provide proof that the new Elizabethans could be as magnificent, reckless, individualistic and relentlessly heterosexual as their mythical forebears, and could seize new realms of experience in their manly grasp. And the fact that the 'conquest' was a symbolic one, rather than a military invasion, meant it could be enjoyed without disturbing the narrative of progress that had left the empire behind. The inconvenient detail that neither of the two men to attain the summit, Edmund Hillary and Norgay Tenzing, was British tended to be swept aside in celebrations of an expedition which was planned and executed by a largely British team, and led by the British army officer John Hunt. Recent accounts – like Peter H. Hansen's – of the ascent have seen the party's international flavour as suggestive that 'Britain was attempting to redefine the "British Empire" as a "Commonwealth of Nations".'[102]

> When Tenzing reached the summit of Everest, he waved from his ice-axe four flags representing Nepal, India, Britain and the United Nations ... That Hunt chose Hillary and Tenzing for the summit party reflects not only a recognition of their abilities but also an inclusive definition of "Britishness" consistent with the expansive definition of the Commonwealth articulated at the time of the coronation.[103]

Hunt's own account of the expedition, published in the *Geographical Journal* in December 1953, does indeed emphasise the meritocratic system of selection he employed when recruiting members of the team, although this mainly applied to the Sherpas, who were whittled down to a select few during the long march through Nepal and the preparatory climbs during which the camps along the ascent route were established and stocked with supplies. Hunt's language certainly smacks of imperial entitlement; he writes of the Sherpa men: 'We had arranged for twenty of these splendid little men to do the most arduous carrying on the higher part of the climb',[104] and during the early stages of the expedition remarks that 'the marches were short, owing to the slow progress of our laden coolies, and we had time to bathe as we waited for our cook Thondup to prepare breakfast'.[105]

While he does not stint in his praise for the bravery and strength of Tenzing and the other Nepali climbers who reached the final stages, he did not, as Hansen implies, select Hillary and Tenzing as the intended summit party; the first attempt on the peak was tried by an English scientist, Tom Bourdillon, and a Welsh doctor, Charles Evans. Indeed, Tenzing's strength and stamina meant that he alone was originally intended to take part in both the first and the second attempts – first as part of the support team for Bourdillon and Evans, and only secondly as a climber attempting the actual ascent. In the end, he was too ill to form part of the first support team – and he was not alone among the Sherpa men to suffer from exhaustion. When he and Hillary did make their ascent, Hillary recalled, 'the high-altitude Sherpas chosen to carry our camp high up the south-east ridge had all fallen ill except Ang Nyma, so there was nothing for it but to carry everything ourselves'.[106] Clearly, the idea that the Everest expedition was a utopia of post-colonial fraternity is over-simple; but another important shift in British self-image can be traced through the clothes and equipment that enabled the climb to succeed. Significantly, the 1953 expedition was the first to embrace nylon's combination of lightness, strength and resistance to moisture. Whereas the unsuccessful Swiss attempt in 1952 had been equipped with various combinations of cotton, wool, silk and other traditional fabrics, Hunt's expedition adopted nylon-lined smocks and trousers, tents of a nylon-cotton mix and sleeping bags with nylon outer layers.[107]

Later, when news of the success of the venture reached Britain, accounts of the ascent came close to equating the contribution of British manufacturers with the climbers' heroic qualities, emphasising that the novel equipment was 'manufactured after careful proving and experiment in conditions similar to those encountered or expected at high altitude'.[108] But another piece of specialist technological apparel made an even more crucial difference: masks delivering supplementary oxygen to the climbers. Michael Ward, who was expedition doctor in 1953, was clear about the benefits:

> Pre-war climbers at extreme altitude had suffered from hallucinations due to hypoxia; some had died from cold injury; hemiplegia had been reported; dehydration was extreme, fatigue overwhelming, and loss of weight severe. Muscle wasting was great: F. S. Smythe in 1933 could almost encircle the muscles of his thigh with the fingers of one hand. Fourteen deaths had been recorded on Everest up to 1952.[109]

But the introduction of technological enhancements did not necessarily imply a cancellation of hierarchies. Hillary's account of the climb participates in a narrative of technological dominance by describing how he had to intervene paternalistically in order to help Tenzing with his oxygen:

> I suddenly noticed that Tenzing, who had been going very well, was starting to drag. When he approached me I saw that he was panting and in some distress. I examined his oxygen set and, finding that the exhaust outlet from his mask was blocked with ice, was able to give him immediate relief.[110]

Tenzing's autobiography takes issue with this account – and other claims Hillary made about having to help him as he struggled up the mountain – in offended terms:

> Every so often, as had happened all the way, we would have trouble breathing, and have to stop and clear away the ice that kept forming in the tubes of our oxygen-sets. In regard to this, I must say in all honesty that I do not think Hillary is quite fair in the story he later told, indicating that I had more trouble than he with breathing, and that without his help I might have suffocated. In my opinion our difficulties were about the same – and luckily never too great – and we each helped and were helped by the other in equal measure.[111]

When Tenzing and Hillary reached the top of the mountain, they removed their masks for the 15 minutes they spent there, in order to conserve oxygen – and perhaps also to reassert their humanity at the moment of their triumph. The removal of the breathing apparatus, like the removal of the queen's wig in *Gloriana*, serves as a reminder that power is mapped onto the body of the human subject by a dialectical production of meaning contingent upon the placement, fit and operation of a prosthetic object. But the two men also divested themselves of some other symbolic things during their short stay on the summit. Reuters reported that 'along with Sherpa Tenzing's gifts of sweets to the mountain gods, Sir Edmund Hillary left a small fibre crucifix at the summit of Mount Everest'. This synthetic crucifix, made of an early form of plastic derived, like rayon, from cellulose, had reportedly been given to John Hunt by a monk at the Benedictine abbey of Ampleforth, and was passed in turn to Hillary to be taken to the summit. Its symbolism and status was always contested, however: Hillary's first account of the incident, given to reporters, only mentioned that he had buried an envelope in the snow, and he later explained that he thought it was up to Hunt to say what was in it.[112] Neither Hillary nor Hunt was religious, and arguably it was the object's manmade material which carried its primary symbolism: of conquest over the natural world. However, Tenzing's account emphatically denies any knowledge of this crucifix:

> From my pocket I took the package of sweets I had been carrying. I took the little red-and-blue pencil that my daughter, Nima, had given me. And, scraping a hollow in the snow, I laid them there. Seeing what I was doing, Hillary handed me a small cloth cat, black and with white eyes, that Hunt had given him as a mascot, and

I put this beside them. In his story of our climb Hillary says it was a crucifix that Hunt gave him, and that he left on top; but if this was so I did not see it. He gave me only the cloth cat. All I laid in the snow was the cat, the pencil and the sweets.[113]

This childish piece of cloth is contrasted, in Tenzing's account, both with the four flags he carried tied to his ice-axe, and with the red scarf which he wore to the summit: fabric materialisations of profound notions of loyalty and identity. The scarf and been given to him by the Swiss expedition leader Raymond Lambert, with whom he had attempted to scale Everest the previous year. These two men had enjoyed a close and equal friendship which Tenzing pointedly contrasts with his relationship with the British party, who always drew 'a line between them and the outsider, between sahib and employee'.[114] Just before the expedition set off, he had had to quell serious unrest among the other Sherpas, who disliked the idea that they were only being loaned their clothes and apparel by the British, whereas other nations had given them their equipment outright as part of their wages. But for his part, Tenzing's clothes and equipment declared his refusal to be entirely inducted into the British party:

> My boots, as I have said, were Swiss; my wind-jacket and various other items had been issued by the British. But the socks I was wearing had been knitted by Ang Lahmu. My sweater had been given to me by Mrs Henderson, of the Himalayan Club. My woollen helmet was the old one that had been left to me by Earl Denman. And, most important to all, the red scarf round my neck was Raymond Lambert's.[115]

Tenzing's resistance to the uniform dress code of the British expedition acknowledges the symbolic potency of clothing and its implicit challenge to human agency and identity. Hunt and the rest of the Everest party wished to construct a narrative of post-colonial equality enabled by futuristic technology, which would erase the resentments of an imperial past; instead, they found themselves trapped within old power structures which the technology only served to reinforce. In Coronation year, an ancient idea of British monarchy was produced by the symbols of status as a kind of dream, phantasmagoria or fiction. Almost simultaneously on the other side of the world, a dream of the future was being produced by the symbols of science and progress – a new phantasmagoria, but a familiar fetishisation of power. Yet technology's darker aspect was already threatening an even greater and more troubling incursion into humanity's nightmares. In the next chapter, we will see how atomic power came close to abolishing the hierarchy which put subjects in control of the object.

NOTES

1 'First royal masque since 1636', *The Times*, 26 May 1948, p. 4.
2 For an account of the influence of Festival style, see for instance William Feaver, 'Festival Star' in Banham and Hillier, *Tonic*, pp. 40–57.

3 *Family Portrait*, dir. by Humphrey Jennings (Wessex Film Productions, 1950).
4 'Princess at Oxford', *The Times*, 26 May 1948, p. 4.
5 'First royal masque since 1636', p. 4.
6 Michael Powell, *A Life in Movies: An Autobiography* (London: Faber and Faber, 2000) p. 651.
7 Powell, *A Life in Movies*, pp. 650–51.
8 Powell, *A Life in Movies*, p. 650.
9 Powell, *A Life in Movies*, p. 653.
10 See Andrew Moor, *Powell and Pressburger: A Cinema of Magic Spaces* (London: I.B. Tauris, 2005), p. 204.
11 *The Tales of Hoffmann*, dir. by Michael Powell and Emeric Pressburger (The Archers and Vega Film Productions, 1951).
12 Jonathan Faiers, *Dressing Dangerously: Dysfunctional Fashion in Film* (New Haven: Yale University Press, 2013), p. 6.
13 Faiers, *Dressing Dangerously*, pp. 6–7.
14 Faiers, *Dressing Dangerously*, p. 7. Although mentioned in Lacan's *The Four Fundamental Concepts of Psychoanalysis*, the theory of the suture was elaborated in detail in Jacques-Alain Miller, 'Suture (Elements of the Logic of the Signifier)', *Screen* 18:4 (1977–78) [original French publication 1966]. See also Jean-Pierre Oudart, 'Cinema and Suture', *Screen* 18:4 (1977–78) [originally published in *Cahiers du cinema* 211 and 212 (April and May 1969)].
15 *Corridor of Mirrors*, dir. by Terence Young (Apollo Films, 1948).
16 Walter Benjamin, 'Unpacking my Library', in *Illuminations*, pp. 61–69 (p. 69).
17 Benjamin, 'Unpacking my Library', p. 62.
18 Benjamin, 'Unpacking my Library', p. 64.
19 Chris Massie, *Corridor of Mirrors* (London: Faber and Faber, 1941), p. 46.
20 Iris Murdoch, *Under the Net* (London: Vintage, 2002).
21 See Ludwig Wittgenstein, *Tractatus Logico-Philosophicus*, trans. David Pears and Brian McGuinness (London: Routledge, 2003), E-book http://search.ebscohost.com/login.aspx?direct=true&db=nlebk&AN=97973&site=ehost-live. [accessed 28 January 2018], 6.341.
22 Murdoch, *Under the Net*, p. 40.
23 Murdoch, *Under the Net*, p. 42.
24 Murdoch, *Under the Net*, p. 44.
25 Murdoch, *Under the Net*, p. 43.
26 Murdoch, *Under the Net*, p. 44.
27 Murdoch, *Under the Net*, p. 47.
28 Murdoch, *Under the Net*, p. 94.
29 Murdoch, *Under the Net*, p. 52.
30 Murdoch, *Under the Net*, p. 159.
31 Murdoch, *Under the Net*, p. 107.
32 Murdoch, *Under the Net*, p. 168.
33 Murdoch, *Under the Net*, p. 168.
34 Murdoch, *Under the Net*, p. 23.
35 Murdoch, *Under the Net*, p. 169.
36 Murdoch, *Under the Net*, p. 171.
37 Murdoch, *Under the Net*, p. 53.
38 Murdoch, *Under the Net*, p. 283.

39 Quentin Bell, *On Human Finery: The Classic Study of Fashion Through the Ages* (London: Allison & Busby, 1992), p. 62.
40 Bell, *On Human Finery*, p. 20.
41 Bell, *On Human Finery*, p. 153.
42 Bell, *On Human Finery*, p. 31.
43 Bell, *On Human Finery*, p. 17.
44 Bell, *On Human Finery*, p. 23.
45 Maurizia Boscagli, *Stuff Theory: Everyday Objects, Radical Materialism* (New York: Bloomsbury, 2014), p. 82.
46 Boscagli, *Stuff Theory*, p. 88.
47 Boscagli, *Stuff Theory*, p. 93.
48 Boscagli, *Stuff Theory*, p. 91.
49 Boscagli, *Stuff Theory*, pp. 107–08.
50 'Three girls made the queen's dream dress', *Daily Express*, 2 June 1953, p. 1.
51 Brown, 'The Tyranny of Things', p. 446.
52 Brown, 'The Tyranny of Things', p. 457.
53 Brown, 'The Tyranny of Things', p. 457.
54 David Cannadine, 'The Context, Performance and Meaning of Ritual: The British Monarchy and the "Invention of Tradition", c.1820–1977', in Eric Hobsbawm and Terence Ranger, eds., *The Invention of Tradition* (Cambridge: Cambridge University Press, 1983), pp. 101–64 (p. 133).
55 'Informal scenes in the Annexe', *The Times*, 3 June 1953, p. 6.
56 'Informal scenes in the Annexe', p. 6.
57 Cannadine, 'The Context, Performance and Meaning of Ritual', p. 125.
58 Violet Bonham Carter, *Daring to Hope: the Diaries and Letters of Violet Bonham Carter, 1946–1969*, ed., Mark Pottle (London: Weidenfield & Nicholson, 2000), p. 213
59 'Night vigil in the streets', *The Times*, 3 June 1953, p. 6.
60 Quoted in Sylvia Townsend Warner, *The Diaries of Sylvia Townsend Warner*, ed., Claire Harman (London: Chatto and Windus, 1994).
61 Carol Dyhouse, 'Skin Deep: The Fall of Fur', *History Today*, 61:11 (November 2011), www.historytoday.com/carol-dyhouse/skin-deep-fall-fur [accessed 28 January 2018].
62 'Colourful outlook for rainy days', *The Times*, 17 October 1955, p. 11.
63 Eve Perrick, 'Eve Perrick had a £30 point of view – and still she got wet, cold and tired', *Daily Express*, 3 June 1953, p. 2.
64 Margaret Thatcher, *The Path to Power* (London: Harper Press, 1995), p. 78.
65 Robert Cannell, 'TV millions saw more than the Abbey peers', *Daily Express*, 3 June 1953, p. 2.
66 Angus Wilson, 'There's nothing like a Coronation to test's one's scepticism, one's innate Republicanism', *New Statesman*, 13 June 1953, www.newstatesman.com/print/archive/2013/06/13-june-1953-theres-nothing-coronation-test-ones-scepticism-ones-innate-republicanis [accessed 28 January 2018].
67 William Plomer, 'Let's Crab an Opera', in *Electric Delights* (London: Jonathan Cape, 1978), pp. 180–85 (p. 180).
68 See Peter F. Alexander, 'The Process of Composition of the Libretto of Britten's *Gloriana*', *Music & Letters*, 67:2 (April 1986), 147–58 (p. 150); Lytton Strachey, *Elizabeth & Essex: A Tragic History* (London: Chatto and Windus, 1930).
69 Charles Moore, *Double Harness* (London: Weidenfeld & Nicholson, 1976), pp. 239–40.

70 Benjamin Britten, *Opera Guide 24: Peter Grimes/Gloriana* (London: John Calder, 1983), p. 118.
71 Walter Bagehot, *The English Constitution* (London: Chapman and Hall, 1867), p. 86.
72 Plomer, 'Let's Crab an Opera', p. 181.
73 Plomer, 'Let's Crab an Opera', pp. 181–82.
74 Plomer, 'Let's Crab an Opera', p. 182.
75 Britten, *Gloriana*, p. 111.
76 John W. Klein, 'Some Reflections on *Gloriana*', *Tempo*, 29 (Autumn 1953), 16–21 (p. 17).
77 Britten, *Gloriana*, p. 112.
78 Britten, *Gloriana*, p. 116.
79 Britten, *Gloriana*, p. 118.
80 Britten, *Gloriana*, p. 117.
81 See Strachey, *Elizabeth & Essex*, p. 163.
82 See Peter F. Alexander, 'The Process of Composition of the Libretto of Britten's *Gloriana*', p. 152.
83 Heather Wiebe, '"Now and England": Britten's *Gloriana* and the "New Elizabethans"', *Cambridge Opera Journal*, 17:2 (July 2005), 141–72 (pp. 144–45).
84 Wiebe, 'Now and England', p. 145. For an example of such right-wing commentary, see Philip Gibbs, *The New Elizabethans* (London: Hutchinson & Co, 1953).
85 Wiebe, 'Now and England', p. 150.
86 Wiebe, 'Now and England', p. 150.
87 Britten, *Gloriana*, p. 110.
88 Wiebe, 'Now and England', pp. 170–71.
89 Christopher Breward and Ghislaine Wood, 'In the Service of the State: Change and Continuity in Design', in Breward and Wood, eds., *British Design from 1948: Innovation in the Modern Age* (London: V&A, 2012) pp. 40–63 (p. 53).
90 Breward and Wood, 'In the Service of the State', p. 53.
91 Breward and Wood, 'In the Service of the State', p. 53.
92 Breward and Wood, 'In the Service of the State', p. 53.
93 *The Man in the White Suit*, dir. by Alexander Mackendrick (Ealing Studios, 1951).
94 H.G. Wells, *The Invisible Man* (London: Penguin, 2005).
95 See David Kynaston, *Family Britain 1951–57* (London: Bloomsbury, 2010), p. 118.
96 Kynaston, *Family Britain*, p. 120.
97 Kynaston, *Family Britain*, p. 120.
98 Kynaston, *Family Britain*, p. 121.
99 Daniel R. Headrick, 'Botany, Chemistry, and Tropical Development', *Journal of World History*, 7:1 (Spring, 1996), 1–20 (p. 11).
100 Mary Schoeser, 'The Appliance of Science', in Elain Harwood and Alan Powers, eds., *Twentieth Century Architecture 5: Festival of Britain* (London: Twentieth Century Society, 2001), p. 124.
101 A Special Correspondent (Frank Howes), '*Gloriana*: A Great Event in English Music', *The National and English Review*, 141 (1953), p. 35; Wiebe, 'Now and England', p. 156.
102 Peter H. Hansen, 'Coronation Everest', in Stuart Ward, ed., *British Culture and the End of Empire* (Manchester: Manchester University Press, 2001), pp. 57–72 (p. 58).
103 Hansen, 'Coronation Everest', pp. 61–62.

104 John Hunt and Edmund Hillary, 'The Ascent of Mount Everest', *Geographical Journal*, 119:4 (December 1953), 385–99 (p. 386).
105 Hunt and Hillary, 'The Ascent of Mount Everest', p. 387.
106 Hunt and Hillary, 'The Ascent of Mount Everest', pp. 395–96.
107 See John Hunt, 'Return to Everest: II – new equipment for the British expedition', *The Times*, 3 February 1953, p. 9.
108 'Equipment for Everest: British industry's contribution', *The Times*, 9 June 1953, p. 4.
109 Michael Ward, 'The First Ascent of Mount Everest', *British Medical Journal*, 306 (May 29 1993), 1455–58 (p. 1457).
110 Hunt and Hillary, 'The Ascent of Mount Everest', p. 398.
111 James Ramsey Ullman, *Man of Everest: The Autobiography of Tenzing* (London: Reprint Society, 1956) p. 260.
112 See Hansen, 'Coronation Everest', p. 271.
113 Ramsey Ullman, *Man of Everest*, p. 267.
114 Ramsey Ullman, *Man of Everest*, p. 221.
115 Ramsey Ullman, *Man of Everest*, p. 257.

6

BOMBS, PROSTHETICS AND MADNESS: THE PAINFUL NEARNESS OF THINGS

A summer's day in 1940. The Brown family are at home in their neatly kept terraced house. They are all together in the sitting room: the children putting a record on the gramophone, the parents relaxing in armchairs, reading or knitting. Quietly and without fuss, they happen to notice that an incendiary bomb has fallen through their roof and landed in the bedroom upstairs. It nestles among their plain wooden furniture and begins to burn. Calmly, a voiceover explains:

> It burns very violently for the first minute but after that it *can* be tackled. Brown goes to ascertain the damage and goes to Smith next door for the pump they share. There's no panic. A bucket, always kept full, is placed outside the front door. Miss Smith arrives. She has received training from the local authorities which you too can receive. Brown decides to operate the pump away from the heat and smoke. You'll notice how Miss Smith keeps as near the floor as possible and plays a jet of water at the heart of the fire to get it under control. Brown Junior calls the Fire Brigade just in case.[1]

In this public information film, *How You Can Deal with Incendiary Bombs*, the image of the stable family unit and the cosy division of labour is part of a soothing propaganda rhetoric: under the patriarchal guidance of Mr Brown and the local authorities, even young women and children can tackle enemy bombs easily. These small incendiary devices are merely uninvited guests in the family home, unwelcome in the intimate context of the bedroom, but familiarly domestic in scale.

This early version of cosy wartime bomb-encounters did not go unchallenged. Later the same year, during the intense weeks of night-time air raids starting on 7 September 1940, Humphrey Jennings collected dramatic footage of specifically domestic disruption for the Crown Film Unit's propaganda short *London Can Take It!*[2] Tailored for the American market, it made a point of showing plucky Londoners giving up their right to a private home life, donning ARP uniforms after a hard day's work, or queuing quietly outside public shelters. A voiceover, by US reporter Quentin Reynolds, described them as 'the greatest civilian army ever assembled': 'I have watched them stand by their homes. I have seen them made homeless, I have seen them move to new homes, and I can assure you there is no panic, no fear, no despair in London Town.' This rapid shift in emphasis from small bombs absorbed into and neutralised by the family circle, to large bombs battering the home front and expelling people from their domestic lives – if not through violent destruction then through their own sense of civic duty – acknowledged changing attitudes to the real devastation suffered by London on the 76 nights of the Blitz. But as the war progressed and the air raids became more sporadic and geographically diffuse, the large-scale vision of public heroism against a dramatic nightscape, as promoted by Jennings's films, contracted back down to the level of the hand-sized, daytime object; but this time there was no soothing suggestion that they could be neutralised with a homely bucket and pump. Two more Ministry of Information films warned against the domestication of unfamiliar things: *Butterfly Bomb* (1944) shows a young boy in his family's garden, picking up one of the harmless-looking booby-traps – officially called SD2 bomblets – which were routinely dropped over communities in the north of England.[3] The boy is instantly killed as his mother watches in horror. *Dangerous Trophies: Unexploded Bombs* (1945) depicts a man cycling down a country road and stopping to pick up what he assumes is a dud device.[4] Despite being warned of the danger by a wise passer-by, he resolves to keep it as a souvenir; promising glibly to 'take the fuse out when I get home', he pedals off with it, promptly exploding a few feet down the lane.

In wartime, the public were repeatedly warned that the danger of these death-dealing things depended on their small scale and apparent harmlessness; such objects invited domestication, only to reveal their true scope and agency once they had achieved close contact with their human victim. In bombs, the thing-world offers a treacherous intimacy, and it was this intimacy which was repeatedly examined and interrogated in the culture of the immediate post-war period. By then, the war was over but another type of weapon was threatening the integrity of the human subject: the atomic bomb. This new technology redefined deadly intimacy; after the first blast had obliterated the area surrounding its point of impact, the bomb continued to kill insidiously, via radiation which could invisibly penetrate and poison the body. At the same time, despite its ubiquity in the political discourse of the Cold War, this was a bomb with which few were intimately acquainted, since its power lay in its abstract potential for devastation rather than its immediate physical presence in everyday life. This retention of potential and the suppression of the object's definitive conclusion finds echoes in the absences and narrative ruptures which characterise the post-war period's treatment of bombs as cultural objects. In this chapter I will argue that atomic culture resonates with anxieties about objects and intimacy, and that this motif crosses and re-crosses the threshold between traditional explosives and nuclear technology. In the first chapter of this book, we saw how bombs created new ecosystems of undead life, and left behind object-witnesses and rubble that told human stories. This final chapter shows how a very different understanding of bombs developed as the Second World War was replaced by the Cold War. In films including Powell and Pressburger's *The Small Back Room* (1949), the Boulting brothers' *Seven Days To Noon* (1950), and Michael Anderson's *The Dam Busters* (1955); as well as C.P. Snow's novel *The New Men* (1954) and Marghanita Laski's play *The Offshore Island* (1954), bombs leave no ruins behind them; instead, they take on a gothic aspect through their own ambiguous materiality, invading and compromising the fractured and ruined human body and giving birth to an uncanny absence and sterility.

'NOW YOU SEE INTO THE ATOMS THEMSELVES': SCALE AND THE PROBLEM OF NEARNESS

In 1946, the *Daily Express* released a polemical warning about the danger of the new bomb technology in a film, *The Atomic Age*.[5] It was released after the tests at Bikini Atoll in July that year, when two atomic bombs were detonated in order to test their effects on naval ships. The film consists of footage from the two Pathé reports of the tests, spliced together with a voiceover which swings between horrified accounts of the uncanny power of these weapons, and hopeful speculation that the science behind them will provide benefits to health and industry. A rolling title at the start of the film indicates its uneasy ambiguity:

> The *Daily Express* presents these Pathé newsreels as a reminder that a menacing shadow lies across the vista of a world enriched by man's fabulous discovery.
> Here we see once more the monstrous first-born child of the atomic age which in a moment of time, blotted out a great city and seared 92,000 people into oblivion. Yet it is still only a child, no more than eighteen months old...

The conjunction of nightmarish destruction with the image of a small child echoes the code name of the nuclear bomb dropped on Hiroshima, 'Little Boy', and is later reiterated by the voiceover's description of the bombed ships lying 'devastated and toylike in a boiling ocean'. By evoking the reckless destructive energy of a toddler, the image does not so much excuse the atom bomb's mindlessness as warn against the idea that it is susceptible to reason, and suggest that it is all the more fearful because it touches the heart of family reality. While footage of the American tests safely distances the mushroom clouds by filming them from miles away, Japanese footage of the casualties of Hiroshima and Nagasaki, also included in the film, emphasise the bodily intimacy of the damage inflicted: a woman's skin is marked with the pattern of the dress she wore when the bomb was dropped; a man's wristwatch is removed to show that it has left a paler area on his badly burned skin; someone places their feet in the shadow footprints left by a man apparently vaporised in the blast, to show the exact posture of the victim at the moment of his death.

Repeatedly, the point is made that London or another city close to home could suffer the same fate:

> One bomb would kill 50,000 people, 400,000 would be made homeless. Many would die a slow death, as atom test animals are now dying at Bikini. We cannot afford to drift, as the clouds are drifting, into an atomic war. Here is the true challenge of our time: whether science is to be used to destroy us, or by releasing new sources of power, lighten the daily work of every one of us.

In fact, even advocates of the peaceful applications of atomic energy found it hard to deploy the idea of homely usefulness as an argument; it was to become increasingly important to stress that the technology could never be scaled down for personal use. In 1947, Professor J.D. Cockcroft, director of the Harwell atomic research and development plant in Berkshire, gave a talk to the Institution of Mechanical Engineers in which he felt it necessary explicitly to spell out the incompatibility of the technology with homely and familiar spaces:

> Speaking of the possibilities of using nuclear energy for heat and power production, he said that owing to the intense radio activity in atomic piles cement shields had to be used to protect the workers. There had been much talk about an atomic motor-car, but one of 30 hp [horse power] would need a 6ft concrete shield. An atomic propelled aircraft of 10,000 hp would need a 100ft shield.
> He said he would not recommend small atomic piles for central heating.[6]

Instead, it was made clear to the public that atomic technology can occupy only one of two possible non-domestic spaces: either it must be strictly corralled inside purpose-built silos inaccessible to unauthorised personnel, or it will drift dangerously through the air in a deadly cloud. Thus, the figure of the 'bomb' was utterly transformed: the unassuming domestic invader had become an object of technological – and bureaucratic – alienation.

The conceptual impact of nuclear weaponry is firstly one of dizzying scale – the vast zone of potential obliteration unleashed from the unimaginably tiny atom produces a kind of nausea which seems to challenge the concept of space and time as parameters defined by and arranged around the human. At the Festival of Britain Science exhibition in 1951, an introductory display plunged visitors into an immersive encounter with the new scale of the atomic age, where objects are not only unseeable but are on the brink of the unknowable. As the guide-catalogue described it:

> You come into the exhibition through five rooms which take you, step by step, into the heart of the matter. Going through these rooms you seem to shrink like Alice in Wonderland, and the things round you seem to grow larger and larger. There are pencil and paper in the first room. Now you find yourself apparently shrinking, first to the size of the pencil, and then to the thickness of the paper ... Another step, another thousand times smaller, and you see the structure of the graphite

crystals which make up the pencil lead. And then the last step, you are ten thousand times smaller than you began, and now you see into the atoms themselves.[7]

This journey into the nuclear wonderland attempted to domesticate the atomic uncanny by framing it in terms of humble daily objects like pencil and paper, but it also acknowledged the strangeness of this conceptual leap. Writing implements also contain other worlds – they combine haptic familiarity with a creative potential to conjure up enormous vistas of new ideas. In *On Longing*, Susan Stewart describes how the human subject is reconstituted by exposure to things that are very small or very big: 'While the miniature represents a mental world of proportion, control, and balance, the gigantic presents a physical world of disorder and disproportion.'[8] The new technology encompassed both extremes. It wasn't just the gigantic potential of these new bombs that the post-war imagination had to reconcile with the unimaginable miniaturisation of the atom itself. Atoms might appear in disguise, presenting themselves as compact, even domestic, objects like pen and paper, and then reveal themselves to be incomprehensibly bigger on the inside.

Within this dialectic of scale, it was the giganticism of nuclear explosions which first attracted philosophical exploration. In his 1950 lecture 'The Thing', Heidegger begins with the observation that modern technology has abolished distance in both time and space, yet 'the frantic abolition of all distances brings no nearness'.[9] Heidegger assumes that new technologies make intimacy impossible, and he attempts to find consolation for this by contemplating the atom bomb not as an anomaly but as an exemplary object, the perfect Thing. Because its implosive force both gathers together matter and throws it violently outwards, it sums up the Thing's uncanny distancelessness which is 'more unearthly than everything bursting apart':[10]

> Man stares at what the explosion of the atom bomb could bring with it. He does not see that the atom bomb and its explosion are the mere final emission of what has long since taken place, has already happened.[11]

The bomb's violent scope and instantaneous effect make notions of relative time and space irrelevant; thus, the very existence of the atom bomb means that the absence of nearness should be contemplated philosophically rather than fearfully:

> What is this helpless anxiety still waiting for, if the terrible has already happened? The terrifying is unsettling; it places everything outside its own nature. What is it that unsettles and thus terrifies? It shows itself and hides itself in the *way* in which everything presences, namely, in the fact that despite all conquest of distances the nearness of things remains absent.[12]

The atomic bomb abolishes distance by expanding so rapidly that it accomplishes the feat of being in two places at the same time – it repels the human subject by 'placing everything outside its own nature'. For Heidegger, the Thing is that which gathers meaning and identity into itself, while simultaneously defining and excluding the human subject. In this, he was accessing a philosophical debate, about how technology altered subject–object relations, which had exercised modernist thinkers earlier in the twentieth century.

In 1928's *One Way Street*, for instance, Walter Benjamin had described the relationship between workers and technology as a compensatory one:

> Warmth is ebbing from things. Objects of daily use gently but insistently repel us. Day by day, in overcoming the sum of secret resistances – not only the overt ones – that they put in our way, we have an immense labour to perform. We must compensate for their coldness with our warmth if they are not to freeze us to death, and handle their spiny forms with infinite dexterity if we are not to bleed to death.[13]

These 'spiny forms' gesture towards Schopenhauer's 'Porcupine Problem' – the dilemma of spiny creatures who need to stay together for warmth yet are forced to keep away from each other's quills. The porcupines 'were tossed between two evils, until they had discovered the proper distance from which they could best tolerate one another'.[14] Benjamin extrapolates this problem of intimacy onto relations between soft, warm humans and cold, sharp things. Describing the modern condition of urban and industrial workers who can expect no comfort from each other, but rather 'feel themselves to be the representatives of a refractory material world', he identifies a sense of hopeless yearning for union with the inanimate world that the human subject experiences as part of the metropolitan struggle for survival. In this version of modernity, ignoring these cold things is not an option: while they repel us, objects also have us in their grasp. People are slaves; they must labour to compensate for the impossibility of intimacy with the object world.

By the 1950s, however, intimacy with things was not only possible, it had become a new problematic and a different kind of work. Benjamin's workers were modernist subjects – fractured, alienated and reified by the mechanisms of modernity – but after the war, this version of subjectivity was already transforming into what would become known as the post-modern subject – contingent, conflicted and fluid. The reification critiqued by Benjamin and Georg Lukács yielded to an internalised relation between the subject and the object which would later become the basis for Bruno Latour's concept of the quasi-object and Gilles Deleuze and Félix Guattari's idea of networked and entangled human-object assemblages.[15] For Heidegger, however, the intimate compensations which Benjamin's workers were obliged to undertake were redrawn as a serene reflection of the self in the thing-world.

Yet the atom's giganticism had a political aspect which made serenity impossible. The terror inspired by the intimate complication of human and technological agency was more than a primal emotional response. The concept of deterrence was beginning to create a dialectic of absence and action; a nuclear bomb's mere existence, its mere *potential* for devastating action, was supposed to balance the existence and potential of an equal and opposite nuclear bomb on the other side. It was into this uneasy tension between inscrutable, ontologically unstable objects that the human somehow had to be inserted.

'IT WAS A PERSONAL MATTER': PUTTING THINGS IN THEIR PLACE

At first glance, Powell and Pressburger's 1949 war drama *The Small Back Room* does not appear to be an atomic film, but its central narrative about a physically and emotionally damaged bomb disposal expert provided an opportunity to examine problems of intimacy and distance in relationships between the human and the thing which resonated with the era's growing atomic anxiety.[16] Based on Nigel Balchin's 1943 novel of the same name, the film follows a scientist, Sammy Rice, who works for a small team at the cutting edge of weapons research at the height of the Second World War. The film's plot concerns his quest to understand a new type of German booby-trap bomb which has been killing children because it looks harmless but explodes as soon as it is touched. He speculates that, like the 'butterfly' bomblets in the public information film discussed earlier in this chapter, these may look deceptively domestic – 'I should think the blasted things are mocked up as teddy bears or candy bars!' – but this turns out not to be the case: the device Sammy is finally called upon to defuse achieves a different kind of intimacy. It gets close to him not by invading his domestic existence literally, but by coming to symbolise everything – every Thing – that is haunting and sabotaging him with its uncanny agency and quasi-subjectivity. Sammy is troubled not just by the enigmatic maguffin he must find and defuse (for most of the film, the bomb is materially absent, since no one has found an unexploded example) but by several other inanimate but uncannily powerful things: a brandy bottle he keeps on his desk at home to remind himself of his potential for alcoholism; the telephone which constantly interrupts and intervenes in his life; and a prosthetic 'tin' foot which causes him great pain and constantly tempts him to reach for the analgesic of alcohol. Foot, bottle and bomb conspire to frustrate him with their distanceless absence; each 'presences' as something that does not exist, or cannot be allowed to take place. Sammy's foot-pain is a phantom, the projection of flesh-and-blood feeling into a metal prosthesis, and it can only be alleviated by the obliteration of consciousness nestling within the forbidden bottle. Once unleashed, the alcohol will destroy Sammy's mental clarity and steady hand, which he will need if he is to defuse the bomb. The 'presencing' of the prosthetic foot (in the form of pain) threatens to set off a chain reaction of presence ending with the ultimate assertive 'presencing' of the bomb as it fulfils its function with its 'final emission'. This presence, in Heidegger's terms, exemplifies the cancellation of nearness: both the bomb and anything within its scope will become instantly absent.

Tim Armstrong, in *Modernism, Technology and the Body: A Cultural Study*, describes how pre-war modernism adopted the idea of prosthesis to conceptualise the increasingly elided boundary between the machinic and the human which arose from the incursion of technology into everyday life.[17] In particular, he argues that the twin impacts of war and advertising produced the modernist body as fragmented object, a 'zone of deficits in terms of attributes (strength, skill, nutrition), behaviours (sleep, defecation, etc.), with matching remedies'.[18] Meanwhile, Vivian Sobchack has written about the tropological resonance of the post-modern prosthesis as an aspect of theories of cyborg or post-human cultural theory, and questioned whether it represents a lost ideal of wholeness: 'Those who successfully *incorporate* and *subjectively live* the prosthetic ... sense themselves neither as lacking something nor as walking around with some "thing" that is added onto their bodies.'[19] It is interesting to consider *The Small Back Room* in the light of these earlier and later cultural turns. Whereas the explicit and provocative otherness of the modernist prosthetic could be used to illuminate and understand the modern 'body-in-crisis',[20] and the post-modern cyborgian prosthesis is a visible challenge to outmoded categorical boundaries, during the mid-century it was the prosthetic's *dual* potential both to disrupt the body, and to disappear into it, which became a locus of gothic unease.

Only when Sammy has put the bomb in its place as an object to be decoded and dismantled, can his 'tin' foot achieve its proper nearness; by the end of the film he has accepted it as part of himself. This prosthetic nearness becomes indistinguishable from absence. Rather like the dirty window which Bill Brown has used as the archetypal object of Thing Theory,[21] the thingliness of a prosthetic is only apparent when it causes difficulty or ceases to be transparent. The film is full of reminders of what human feet feel and do: Sammy conducts a crucial conversation about the bomb's fuse in a basement room which resounds to the pounding of footsteps above, while the feet are also seen as shadowy forms passing overhead on a translucent grating. Likewise, he has a regular date at a jazz club with his girlfriend Sue, where he sits by the raised dancefloor, surrounded by other people's feet, but cannot join the dance.

Sammy's friction with the material world reaches a crisis at the start of the film's final act, when his most potent things close in on him in his domestic retreat. Plagued by the pain emanating from his prosthesis, he succumbs at last to the bottle of brandy, in an incongruous Expressionist dream-sequence in which a giant bottle looms over him and threatens to crush him. This sequence foregrounds the artificial and technological quality of film itself, as if to problematise the notion of a seamless conjunction between human and thing-world;

and it is at this very moment that the telephone rings with news that two unexploded specimens of the mystery bomb have finally been discovered. The solution to Sammy's personal conflict lies in successfully confronting this deadly technology; he travels to Chesil Bank, where he learns that his colleague has been killed while attempting to defuse the first bomb. The second lies half-buried in the shingle, and in the film's tense finale, Sammy grapples with it both physically and mentally: first struggling to loosen the cap that seals it, and then making a leap of deduction about its deceptively engineered interior. By correctly decoding the bomb's structure, Sammy's identity and sense of 'wholeness' are recuperated, but at a cost: this act of defusing the bomb is not just an intellectual challenge but a sweatily physical and intimate encounter. 'It was a personal matter,' he tells the army officer supervising the operation when he emerges victorious from the struggle.

As I have argued in Chapter 3, *A Matter of Life and Death*, with its preoccupation with transmissions of various kinds, sees Powell and Pressburger tackling questions of dematerialisation and spectrality within the ongoing trauma of the Second World War. *The Small Back Room*, on the other hand, seems rather to look forward to the Cold War, where the culture and spectre of dematerialisation is represented by the threat of nuclear obliteration and the penetrative transmission of radiation. *The Small Back Room* ends with very different representation of the idea of transmission, as part of an exposé of the reification and fragmentation implied by the potential obliteration of space and time, life and death. Here, radio does not reach out to infinity, but seeps into the most intimate articulations of personhood. When Sammy arrives at Chesil Bank for his climactic battle, he must first receive the posthumous report of his colleague, Dick Stewart, who – working alone to protect others in the event of an explosion – transmitted a running commentary, via the field telephone, of his unsuccessful attempt to defuse the bomb. This was recorded in shorthand by a young ATS corporal, and in an excruciatingly poignant scene she reads it out to Sammy – complete with Stewart's witty quips and asides – in an increasingly halting and broken voice. When it is Sammy's turn to attempt to defuse the second bomb, he performs the same feat of ventriloquism as his dead comrade, relaying his own thoughts and memoranda via field telephone to the same young woman, who listens on headphones before speaking his words for the rest of the waiting army officers to hear. This unnamed female corporal becomes aligned to, if not actually part of, the technology of Sammy's professional life. In a reversal of the technological interface which, for Kittler, would characterise the media age as one in which the apparatus intervenes in the transmissions of the body, the ATS corporal becomes incorporated into the apparatus, first as a human phonograph and then as a human loudspeaker. But while she models for Sammy a technophiliac ideal of perfect assimilation of the human into the thing, this is not the solution he must access in order to stand on his own two feet as a whole man. Powell's handwritten screenplay emphasises the triumph of his reintegrated subjectivity: 'He looks just like any happy man with two feet ... No longer outside the world, but in it: no longer talking to a man in uniform, but with him, as an equal.'[22] The importance Powell placed on this moment of bodily reintegration becomes clear when the film's final scene is compared to the climax of Balchin's novel, in which Sammy can't find the strength he needs to unscrew a vital component of the bomb and is forced to ask for help from the military officer supervising the operation. Despite the bomb's successful neutralisation and the fact that Sammy's brilliant analysis was the crucial intervention, he feels unmanned by personal failure. As the book closes he is left hunched in despair on a park bench back in London, watching the moon set:

> I sat and watched it going and I knew there was no answer. If I'd been a bit sillier or a bit more intelligent, or had more guts, or less guts, or had two feet or no feet, or been almost anything definite, it would have been easy. But as it was, I didn't like what I was, and couldn't be what I liked, and it would always be like that.[23]

Balchin's Sammy remains an unhappy hybrid, certain that his prosthesis denies him access both to a fully human sensibility and to the implacable disinterestedness of material objects. For Powell and Pressburger's Sammy, on the other hand, integration and acceptance of his metal foot depends on his ability to discriminate between different types of thing. By decoding and defusing the bomb, he has located the boundary between the transparent, incorporated prosthesis and the alien, technological Other – the same distinction Sobchack was to reiterate half a century later. By putting a limit on the troubling intimacy of a dangerously assertive Thing, Sammy attempts to put the thing-world back in its place and re-establish the possibility of distance which Heidegger would declare irrevocably lost.

'SHOCKED OUT OF SPEECH': FRAGMENTATION AND INTEGRATION IN *THE UNDEFEATED*

The Small Back Room was not the only film of this period to examine the encounter between human and prosthesis. Paul Dickson's 1950 docu-drama *The Undefeated*, made to promote the work of the Ministry of Pensions, stages one war veteran's experience of the compensatory power of replacement limbs overtly in terms of a psychological recuperation.[24] The film's protagonist, Joe Anderson, had been a wartime glider pilot whose legs were amputated after a crash, and who now also suffers from post-traumatic loss of speech. The voiceover informs us that the recuperation of his physical abilities must precede his mental recovery:

> He didn't speak about it because he couldn't. He'd been shocked out of speech by something that happened in the crash – something that only Joe knew about. The doctors would have given a lot to know it too, but that would take time. Now the important thing was that Joe should walk again.

His rehabilitation begins when he is fitted with a pair of prosthetic legs and inducted into a tough physiotherapy regime to teach him how to use them. But his recovery is not complete until his doctor arranges a meeting with Joe's former co-pilot, Lofty, whom Joe believes had been killed in the crash. Seeing this man return, as it were, from the dead, enables Joe to return to life too – he breaks his silence to call out Lofty's name.

But as well as making the point that psychic integrity depends on the physical synthesis of body and material prosthesis, the film suggests a further relationship between human and technology. Joe is detached from his voice by the film's very structure; the voiceover narrating his story is presented as belonging to an unseen welfare officer in the Ministry of Pensions who remembers Joe's case – a man represented by a first-person camera which moves through London's streets and around the corridors of the Ministry, but is never seen. Only at the end of the film does the narrator reveal that he *is* Joe Anderson, that he is no longer a patient but now works as a welfare officer, and that the story he has been telling is his own. This moment of self-naming mirrors Joe's naming of Lofty and produces a moment of radical integration of fragments: subject and object merge as the narrator and his protagonist align, and when the narrator is reunited with his/Joe's body, Joe finds his voice a second time as his newly vocal mouth synchronises with the voiceover to say the words 'Joe Anderson'. This merging also fuses two actors together: Gerald Pearson, a real-life amputee who has played Joe's mute body, and the Oscar-nominated professional Leo Genn, who supplied the voice.

As in *The Small Back Room*, prosthetics have stood in, not simply for the human limbs they replace, but for the thing-world of technology in general; and like the Powell and Pressburger film, *The Undefeated* presents its audience with various paradigms of disembodiment and incorporation in order to explore the new object relations arising from the incursions of material agents into human discourse. The fact that Joe's glider, like Sammy Rice's bomb, is an explosive weapon of war underlines the anxiety that such incursions inspired. The crash scene is re-enacted by cutting from blurry actualité footage of a glider coming down, to a crisp and carefully staged scene of devastation. The camera roams across the wreckage, first lingering on sleek metal canisters – possibly ordnance of some kind – that the glider was carrying among its troop-supply cargo, and then moving to some scraps of paper bearing the remains of technical or navigational diagrams. Only then does it find Joe's agonised form, enmeshed in the twisted remains of his aircraft, which seems attached to his torso like a nightmarish prosthetic appendage. Joe's struggle to reframe prosthesis as a benign incorporation is key to the film's purpose, yet it is constantly sabotaged by the mechanics of the film itself, which violates its subject's integrity at every turn by dismembering Joe into his constituent parts – voice/body, narration/silence, first person/third person, brisk official/

wounded victim, Gerald Pearson/Leo Genn – tricks which film alone can formally achieve, and which therefore tend to stress the specifically *filmic* nature of the narrative.

The Undefeated carefully layers its subject/object divisions and elisions, and brings the audience into the equation as an equally unstable third term: the film invites us to experience the world through the narrator's eyes in the first-person-camera sequences, suggesting that we share a surgical distance from Joe as an object/patient, while denying us access to the internal consciousness of Joe-as-narrator and the crucial information that it is the *patient's* point of view that we are sharing, even as we observe him *observing himself* going through his ordeal. For an amputee like Joe, the integrity of a synaesthetic system, extending beyond the body into the external world of stimulus, is interrupted by the permanently 'anaesthetised' prosthetic limb, and not until this sensorial blockage is overcome can the dynamic interchange between subject and object be restored.[25]

For audiences, Sammy Rice's fragile victory may have offered a comforting resolution to the kinds of neurological shocks which for Benjamin categorised modern life, and which would certainly have been acknowledged by a population still learning to live both with real Blitz damage and potential nuclear devastation. But Powell and Pressburger's film, with its curious Expressionist interlude at its heart, also highlights the artificiality of cinematic rhetoric at the very moment when Sammy succumbs to the anaesthetic intervention of the brandy bottle, and makes a point of shaking us out of any phantasmagoric stupor. Similarly, research conducted by the Central Office of Information records that audiences watching *The Undefeated* were both troubled and stirred into a new kind of wakefulness:

> About a quarter of the audiences found that the film made them feel in some degree uncomfortable or ill at ease ... Many seemed to regard these feelings as salutary, in that it gave them an opportunity for expressing sympathy and gratitude in respect of men who, they thought, might be too easily forgotten.[26]

Thus the film serves as a cognitive prosthesis, supporting audiences in the proper remembrance of the dismemberments and amputations of the war; but it is a prosthetic that insists on its presence as an artefact, reminding them also that a technological thing-world is occupying the absences of human aesthetic experience. In Benjamin's terms, the film distracts this forgetful audience even while supposedly reminding them of their forgetfulness:

> Reception in distraction – the sort of reception which is increasingly noticeable in all areas of art and is a symptom of profound changes in apperception – finds in film its true training ground. Film, by virtue of its shock effects, is predisposed to this form of reception ... because it encourages an evaluating attitude in the audience but also because at the movies, the evaluating attitude requires no attention. The audience is an examiner, but a distracted one.[27]

The creeping 'metalisation of the human body' celebrated in the Futurist manifesto became an urgent cultural problem in the bomb-films of the post-war period, not just because of the ongoing industrialisation and reification which Benjamin hoped would be exploded by film's prosthetic access to the 'optical unconscious', but because a new category of thing – the tiny atom with its vast scope nestling within it – was manifesting a different kind of thingly agency, as well as a surgical ability to intervene in the human body.[28] At the same time, the concept of deterrence was beginning to create a new dialectic of agency and action; a thing's mere existence, and its potential for devastating action, was supposed to make its potential action a political impossibility. Unfortunately, the icy paradox of mutually assured destruction depends on the sterile purity of machine logic – and atomic culture began to create new stories about what would happen when human subjectivity was re-inserted into the zero-sum equation.

'IF I'D KNOWN IT WAS GOING TO BE LIKE THIS, I'D NEVER HAVE STARTED': BOFFINS AS HUMAN PROSTHESIS

The Boulting brothers' 1950 film *Seven Days To Noon* seems to scrutinise such concerns about deterrence and human agency.[29] It concerns a nuclear research scientist, Professor Willingdon, who is appalled by the implications of his own work and steals a nuclear bomb with the intention of blackmailing the government into declaring a programme of unilateral disarmament. He carries the bomb in a small, plain suitcase: a visual signifier which mirrors the autotelic self-containment of the reified human agent who carries it. Willingdon himself is a blank. His past life and motivations remain unexplored and his robotic adherence to the concept of deterrence is presented as a monomania which cuts him off from considerations of the interests of his fellow human beings: in trying to end the possibility of nuclear war, he has put himself at the mercy of the very object he claims to detest, and sacrificed his own agency in order to carry, hide and further the interests of the suitcase bomb.

As well as emptying Willingdon of his humanity, the film focuses on another kind of absence: the gradual emptying out of London as martial law is declared and evacuation enforced. Anti-nuclear films like Pathé's *The Mighty Atom* had visualised the destructive power of atomic weapons by showing a map of London with a four-mile circular area marked on it to indicate how much of the city would be vaporised if a bomb were dropped on Tower Bridge; *Seven Days To Noon* employs a similar image in a scene in which a committee of military and political leaders plan their response to Willingdon's threat. Blankness, absence and obliteration infuse every aspect of the film. Even at a narrative level, it refuses to deliver any of the usual markers of the thriller genre in terms of fast-paced incident, ratcheting tension or complex characterisation; scenes repeatedly fizzle out, their dramatic potential nullified. Instead, the film lingers on the details of the city's rapid militarisation, and the brutality of the evacuation, which is enforced via house-to-house inspections performed at gunpoint. In one scene a man takes advantage of the dark, deserted city to rob a jeweller's shop; picked out by a spotlight while making his escape, he is summarily executed by an army sniper.

The emotionless mechanism of bureaucratic diktat emerges as the most chilling protagonist in the piece; here it is the human which presences as absence when the timid and misguided scientist displays his mindless lack of agency, and becomes the bomb's reified human prosthesis, an inhumanity which is echoed by the cold logic of the state. In *One Way Street*, Benjamin had already outlined the tendency of objects to enlist the human as a kind of flesh-and-blood prosthesis, compensating for their lack of warmth; similarly, the loneliness of the enslaved human subject is at the heart *Seven Days To Noon*, and Professor Willingdon becomes like Benjamin's 'bus conductors, officials, workmen, salesmen' who 'feel themselves to be the representatives of a refractory material world'.[30] The cold aloofness of the bomb's inhuman logic is finally penetrated by Willingdon's daughter, who approaches him during his final desperate stand-off with the authorities and appeals to his memory of family life. That this climactic scene takes place in a Blitz-ruined church is also significant: the tottering walls of the ruin remind us, as they did in the bombsite texts examined in Chapter 1, that brute materiality can be inimical to the human subject. Willingdon's fantasy of a totalising and hermetic one-ness between him and the bomb he carries is a dangerous delusion.

The figure of the obsessive scientist as a gothic figure meddling with forces beyond human understanding can be traced, via Stevenson's Dr Jekyll, to Mary Shelley's Victor Frankenstein. By the mid-1950s, the boffin had begun increasingly to co-exist with the soldier as the archetypal human forced to grapple with the thing-world. Whereas Joe Anderson was a military man who had to put his trust in the scientific theories of his doctors, and Sammy Rice was a technical expert whose conflicts with the military would be resolved by the end of the film, Professor Willingdon was finally hunted down and disarmed by men in uniform who relished the chance to return the city to the state-controlled certainties of a wartime footing. In 1955 the two figures of scientist and soldier were again brought together in Michael Anderson's *The Dam Busters*.[31] On the surface, this film provides an image of perfect co-operation between the two archetypes, with the eccentric inventor Barnes Wallis reliant on the dashing heroics of Wing Commander Guy Gibson in order to bring his theory about the bouncing bomb to fruition. But, like *Seven Days To Noon*, this is also a film about the way martial technology creates lacunae in human relations which the thing-world then fills.

Like Willingdon, Barnes Wallis has an idyllic home life which the film sketches in during the early scenes, only to show him rejecting it and leaving it behind. Like Willingdon, too, Barnes Wallis's mental health is shown to be jeopardised by his work, although in this case his obsession is successfully harnessed to the war effort. His progression away from home and family is clearly signposted: his early experiments with his bomb concept are conducted on a domestic scale with the help of his children, using a catapult and a water-filled trough. As the film progresses, the setting of his tests becomes further and further removed from the quaint English cottage in which we first see him: first he transfers his prototype into an industrial space full of technicians and equipment providing precise measurements, then he moves to Chesil Bank (scene of Sammy Rice's personal battle with a bomb) for full-scale testing under military supervision.

By the time Wallis has been entirely swallowed by the military environment of the Bomber Command airfield, all suggestions of domesticity have been replaced by an atmosphere of public-school banter and an ascetic lifestyle of communal meals and plainly furnished barracks. The one discordant note of warmth and affection is sounded, not by a human, but by Guy Gibson's dog. It is the dog which greets Gibson when we first glimpse him, climbing out of his aeroplane after a successful mission; it is the dog who sits at a table opposite him in his room while he relaxes and reads a newspaper. This faithful companion stands in for the wifely domesticity which Gibson denies himself; the rest of the men in his company must make do with letters from home. These missives are matched by the unopened valedictory letters left behind by the men killed in the bouncing bomb mission at the end of the film, and by the killed-in-action letters Gibson declares he is going off to write just before the credits roll. The absence of these dead airmen is represented only by words and by the material signifiers they leave behind: it is the dog's death, not theirs, which is described and lingered over. As the men receive their final briefing for the Dam Buster mission, the dog is seen roaming around the base looking for Gibson, and being turned away at every door. Finally the weary dog reaches the outer gate of the airfield and is killed by a speeding car which rushes on without stopping. When the news is brought to Gibson he immediately links the dog's death with the mission ahead: 'I'd like you to bury him at midnight on the grass verge outside my office,' he orders. 'I'd like you to do it then, just about the time we're going into the job over there.'

The film's heavy emphasis on the death of the dog is a counterweight to the lightness with which the deaths of the men are brushed off; it is as if the dog stands in for a natural life which must be repressed if the men are to be subsumed into the autotelic technology of war. The motif is again of a troubling intimacy with things which fill in the absence of human relations: while Barnes Wallis works feverishly in his role as the bomb's proxy and human agent, the airmen succumb to a prosthetic attachment to their planes and weaponry, typified by the face-masks they wear which mediate their communications with each other and with the men in other planes. Without these masks, they are as mute as Joe Anderson, and they are silent in another crucial way too: the mission and the new technology is shrouded in secrecy. The men in the elite Dam Buster squadron are socially and physically cut off from their comrades by this need for confidentiality, and the silent scenes at the end of the film, where the camera lingers on the dead men's abandoned possessions, is the logical conclusion of this severing of humanity and language. The film's ambivalence towards the military technology which it is supposedly glorifying is expressed by the very man who invented the bomb, in the final conversation between Wallis and Gibson. 'Is it true? All those fellows lost?' Wallis asks. 'Fifty-six men! If I'd known it was going to be like this, I'd never have started.' Gibson, the trained soldier, recommends a dulling of the senses as the remedy for this human feeling: 'You mustn't think that way ... Why don't you go and find the doctor and ask for one of his sleeping pills?'

Just as in *The Undefeated* and *The Small Back Room*, however, the anaesthetic regime of medicine, narcotics or jingoism is undermined by the film's own determination to remind the audience of its fictivity. Barnes Wallis's bouncing bomb, the essential object driving the narrative, never manages to insert itself frictionlessly into the cinematic world, but is represented by a combination of mismatched actualité footage and special effects in which the bomb has clearly been painted onto the negative by hand – a measure demanded by the Ministry of Defence in order to preserve the finer details of its design. This cartoon bomb gives rise to explosions created by bluescreen matting, with a 'hole' introduced into the footage of the detonation site, through which an image of an explosion is projected. Thus the key moment in the film – the destruction of the German dam – is framed by clear markers of artifice and artificiality. Wallis's homely garden experiment has culminated in a phantasmagoria of patriotic triumphalism, but that phantasmagoria has been 'exploded' – in Benjamin's terms – by 'the dynamite' of film and its undisguised technological manipulation of space and time.[32]

'DOING WHAT THE MACHINE WANTS': C.P. SNOW'S *THE NEW MEN*

Film's attraction to narratives of prosthetic intimacy and cinema's potential for thingly self-commentary explains the prevalence of this medium in cultural responses to mid-century technological anxiety. One writer who did attempt to address these questions in a novel was C.P. Snow. *The New Men* (1954) is narrated by a staid and passionless civil servant, Lewis Eliot, and it tells the story of the rise of his younger brother, Martin, a second-rate nuclear physicist who reaches the heights of his profession at a secretive nuclear research plant through a ruthless willingness to capitalise on the mistakes of his colleagues.[33] Martin is one of the 'new men': an 'alien' as Lewis describes him, able to 'accept secrets, spying, the persistence of the scientific drive, the closed mind, the two world-sides, persecution, as facts of life'.[34] Snow repeatedly links this new mindset – which combines Machiavellian politicking with unreflective devotion to scientific progress – with a kind of mechanistic lack of humanity. 'People who know about government machines all end up by doing what the machine wants, and that is the trouble we have got ourselves in today,' says Arthur Mountenay, an older scientist whose qualms about the use of nuclear weapons mean he is gradually pushed out of the sphere of influence.[35]

When a scandal erupts about physicists who have been spying for the Soviets, Martin seizes his chance to demonstrate that he has absorbed the new realpolitik of nuclear research, while his maverick boss Walter Luke only absorbs the radiation that arises from their deadly work. During Walter's first attempt to synthesise plutonium, one of the protective concrete containers cracks, exposing him to a radioactive leak. Visiting Luke in hospital, Lewis is struck by his deathly appearance:

> For a moment I remembered him as I had first met him ... Then he had been ruddy, well fleshed, muscular, brimming with a young man's vigour ... Now he was pale, not with an ordinary pallor but as though drained of blood; he was emaciated, so that his cheeks fell in and his neck was like an old man's; there were two ulcers by the left-hand corner of his mouth; bald patches shone through the hair on the top of his head.[36]

Unlike the amputees in *The Undefeated* or *The Small Back Room*, Luke has not lost a part which can be prosthetically added back onto his body, but has been subtracted – 'drained' – by the vampiric, intangible thing which he has incorporated. Although able to say a few words, he is mostly silent and uncommunicative ('Luke lay quiet, his face so drawn with illness that one could not read it') and his primary worry is that he will be made sterile.[37] The myth of autogenesis celebrated by Futurism finds its opposite in the broken figure of Walter Luke – not a warrior but an intellectual; not encased in metal but all too porous; not capable of expression and self-reproduction, but silent and non-reproductive.[38] Instead, it is the 'breeder' reactor which is capable of creating something other than itself, and which capitalises on human greed, curiosity and ambition to build an environment inimical to human life:

> Martin led me to the hangar. It was empty, not a single human being in sight; it was noiseless, the pile standing silent in the airy space ... He did not see the curious, sinister emptiness of the place ... He took me to the control room, a cubbyhole full of shining valves with one kitchen chair placed, domestic and incongruous, in front of a panel of indicators.[39]

The incongruity of the domestic chair emphasises the alienation demanded by this technological regime, and while Martin embraces his role as a 'new man' early in the book, it takes a cult-like initiation in the auratic presence of plutonium for Lewis to access this new form of inhuman intimacy. Martin lets him into the innermost heart of the research plant and shows him 'a floppy bag' with 'one corner ... weighed down, as though by a small heavy object, it might have been a lead pellet'.[40] For Lewis this is a moment of unexpected, life-affirming intimacy:

> [Martin] looked at the bag with a possessive, and almost sensual glance.
> I had seen collectors look like that.
> 'Touch it,' he said.
> I put two fingers in the bag and astonishingly was taken into an irrelevant bliss.
> Under the bag's surface, the metal was hot to the touch – and, yes, pushing under memories, I had it, I knew why I was happy. It brought back the moment, the grass and earth hot under my hand, when Martin and Irene told me she was going to have a child ... I had been made a present of a Proustian moment, and the touch of the metal, whose heat might otherwise have seemed sinister, levitated me to the forgotten happiness of a joyous summer night.[41]

What are we to make of this peculiar appropriation of Proust's sensory epiphany? While Lewis accepts this joy as a gift, the reader is clear that something sinister has indeed happened here, some annexation of the human via the hot touch of metal. Benjamin's workers in *One Way Street* had had to compensate for the coldness of industrial things, but in the atomic age it is an uncanny warmness and intimacy that threatens the human. Lewis is tricked by the tactility of the plutonium pellet – he has been transported to a moment quickening with new life, but it is infertility and death that the plutonium is really gestating.

' "OR SOMETHING" DOESN'T EXIST': USE-VALUE AS RESISTANCE IN *THE OFFSHORE ISLAND*

Marghanita Laski's play *The Offshore Island*, written for the BBC in 1954, also relies on the medical and metaphorical sterility of atomic self-reproduction in order to highlight a heroic and 'natural' human quality which is under threat.[42] It uses the setting of a group of nuclear survivors to argue for a pure essence of humanity which emerges once commodity capitalism, technology, and geopolitical concerns have been removed. Over three acts, it depicts the attempts of the Verney family – Rachel and her teenage children James and Mary – to hold onto the small pocket of uncontaminated land which they have nurtured for ten years since a nuclear war destroyed most of Europe. When American soldiers arrive, the family are told that they are being rescued and will be taken to the consumer paradise of the United States; by the end of the play, it is clear that this is a lie: American and Russian armies have in fact joined forces to cleanse Britain of any last survivors and plan to drop more bombs in a scorched-earth agreement designed to make sure that the territory is of no use to either side. Far from being saved, the Verneys gradually learn that they, along with any other 'contaminated persons', must either die where they are or be deported, forcibly sterilised and incarcerated in 'reservations' in remote parts of North America.

Dramatically, the play fails to rise above its strident political agenda, but it is of interest in the context of other mid-century attempts to assimilate the threat of atomic apocalypse into the prevailing culture of progress and consumer desire. When placed next to Laski's *The Victorian Chaise-Longue*, it highlights an implicit connection between new patterns of consumption emerging in the 1950s, and the annihilation of all consumption which seemed to be the inevitable outcome of the Cold War. In Laski's novella, Melanie's gentrified junk had insisted on the recursiveness of history and refused to succumb to the social amnesia of commodities severed from their origins. In *The Offshore Island*, a pure kind of use value has been restored, since every precious manmade object is tracked precisely by the resourceful survivors, who exploit the ontological fluidity of things liberated from economic exchange, and are thus capable of endlessly and freely repurposing them. In the opening scene, for instance, James and Mary argue over a knife which James is using to cut out pieces of a rubber tyre he has salvaged. 'Couldn't you have used your penknife or something?' Mary asks. 'My penknife has become a screwdriver, and "or something" doesn't exist,' he replies.[43] In this radical return of wartime make-do-and-mend, the family recycle the component parts of old commodities like their car, television set and telephone, which no longer serve their original function. These things take on the gothic attributes of uncanny revenance which the play's sentimentalist, Mary, finds uncomfortable; she wishes these commodity 'skeletons' could remain 'alive as themselves' rather than reappearing in pieces, their parts given new uses and meanings.[44] James, the pragmatist, argues that an object is only 'alive because it's being used'.[45] Like the shattered bodies of those who have been injured by conventional bombs, the repurposed commodities can overcome their dismemberment by rematerialising in new forms; but neither James nor Mary has come to terms with the atomisation produced by nuclear weapons, which radically disincorporate and reincorporate bodies and things at a molecular level. They are presented with only two options by the American invaders: either succumb to their alienating system of control and industrial incarceration, or become so much atomic dust. Yet as a conversation between two of the soldiers makes clear, this latter option has been chosen by all the survivors they have met.

It is Mary who is most tempted by the Americans' offer; as she did with Melanie Langdon, Laski is interested in critiquing the role of women as the primary targets of, and conformists to, the fantasy that material objects can communicate personality or confer status. Pathetically, Mary has learned these norms only imperfectly, from old magazines; nevertheless, when she exchanges her string of pearls for a necklace made of shells, she has to be reminded that 'they're both valuable now, aren't they, shells and pearls alike, according to how much you fancy them'.[46] The honest, post-technological shell-necklace is contrasted with the 'long glittering ear-rings' presented to Mary by the Americans in an attempt to win her over to the idea of going with them – a gift Rachel sharply refers to as 'beads for the savages'. The provenance of these ear-rings is not made clear, but when, in the final act, the Americans cynically relieve Mary of the mink coat she has produced in an effort to impress them, there is a strong suggestion that such relics are routinely confiscated from the intransigent 'contaminated persons' who have chosen death rather than resettlement in camps.

In the end, however, both the Verneys' survivalist tools and the Americans' seductive commodities are overshadowed by the sterilising immensity of absence promised by the atom bomb which has been sent to disinfect the space of both natural and cultural productiveness. Infertility is a constantly reiterated theme of the play: Rachel and her occasional partner Martin – the Verneys' distant neighbour who visits twice a year to barter food and information – discuss the lack of successful pregnancies among the survivors, as well as the three miscarriages Rachel has had after Martin's visits; despairingly, they make plans for Mary to move to Martin's small community and for James to become a partner for Martin's daughter. These plans would be futile even without the Americans' enforced sterilisation programme, however: fallout from the original war has made procreation impossible. Just as in *Seven Days To Noon*, the atom bomb has incorporated the human subject in order to reproduce only its own inherent blankness.

Laski has set up two opposing thing-worlds in the play: the empty glitter of commodity culture and the threadbare dignity of utopian self-sufficiency. But the Americans' surprise entrance at the end of Act 1, wearing face masks and protective suits and communicating with an unseen authority via radio equipment, emphasises their disalignment from any kind of human system and their assimilation into a radically alienated thing-world. Set against this terrifying inhumanity, mere reification and commodification seem quaint. Laski wants to present commodities, with their supple ability to tap into hidden channels of desire, as the deceptive gateway to the cold intimacy of the nuclear object. Benjamin meditated on the 'spiny forms' of the industrial thing-world which require human agents to warm them up; mid-century writers were fearful of being ineluctably subsumed into an enveloping cold.

'STOP WORRYING': PHALLIC WEAPONS AND COMIC BOMBS

The sterilisation policy of Laski's sinister Americans, and the prison camps set up for contaminated Europeans, of course evoke the Holocaust's combination of eugenics and mass slaughter; for Laski, atomic weapons were allied not only with sterility and a facelessly destructive bureaucracy, but with fascism and Nazism too. This ideological othering of atomic weaponry was characteristic of the moment when atomic research ceased to be, culturally speaking, the preserve of scruffy, lab-crazed boffins driven by obsession and intellectual pride, and instead became associated with megalomaniacs inside window-less, technologically advanced lairs, cut off from reality and the lives of their millions of potential victims. Ian Fleming – politically as far removed as possible from the left-wing, CND-supporting Laski – was one of the first to codify this formula in popular culture. In his 1955 James Bond thriller *Moonraker* he describes the ideal spatial and ideological environment for a rogue nuclear warhead: an underground plant built by a diehard Nazi, carved into a cliff face and lined with concrete and gleaming steel, where monk-like, shaven-headed technicians in identical uniforms labour to bring the ultimate weapon to life.[47] Inside this sterile space, the Moonraker atomic rocket represents a fantasy of sexualised machinery, ready to seed the world with death:

> For several minutes [Bond] stood speechless, his eyes dazzled by the terrible beauty of the greatest weapon on earth ... Up through the centre of the shaft, which was about thirty feet wide, soared a pencil of glistening chromium ... The shimmering projectile rested on a blunt cone of latticed steel which rose from the floor between the tips of three severely back-swept delta fins that looked as sharp as surgeons' scalpels. But otherwise nothing marred the silken sheen of the fifty feet of polished chrome.[48]

The evil mastermind behind this bomb, Hugo Drax, has been posing as an English philanthropist who survived a near-fatal explosion during the war. In fact, we learn that the German bomb which disfigured and nearly killed him was planted by his own men, and when his wounded body was mistaken for that of an English soldier, he opportunistically adopted this false identity as cover for his elaborate atomic plot. Much of his wickedness, Fleming implies, derives from his perversion of the heroic narrative epitomised by *The Undefeated*: he is a lover of bombs, not their victim, and his chosen prosthesis is not a complex assemblage of human and technology, but a monstrously phallic agent of revenge. His secret target is London, but as Bond's sidekick Gala reflects, it is obliteration and absence that Drax truly desires:

> The thin needle of the rocket. Dropping fast as light out of a clear sky. The crowds in the streets. The Palace. The nursemaids in the park. The birds in the trees. The great bloom of flame a mile wide. And then the mushroom cloud. And nothing left. Nothing, nothing, nothing.[49]

In order to defeat Drax, Bond and Gala must negotiate an industrialised space which is designed to repel the human: they must crawl through painfully narrow ducts, swing from gantries and tolerate blasts of heat and steam before Bond can achieve his intimate encounter with the bomb itself. When he reaches it, he renders it harmless by re-setting its gyroscopic navigation system in a surgical operation which is reminiscent of – but more triumphantly straightforward than – Sammy Rice's tense excision of the booby-trap's fuse in *The Small Back Room*. For both men, implacable technology can only be countered by manual labour: they must use their hands to disrupt the inner workings of an outwardly inscrutable object. While Sammy's hands compensated for his missing foot, Bond begins the scene with his hands themselves disabled: Drax has bound them with rope before leaving Bond and Gala to die in the rocket's blast-zone. In one of his less plausible feats of physical prowess, Bond escapes this bondage by means of a blowtorch which he operates with his teeth; once free, his warm hands can touch the cold bomb and force it to accommodate the human.

Towards the end of the Cold War in 1984, Jacques Derrida wrote an emotive essay, 'No Apocalypse, Not Now (Full Speed Ahead, Seven Missiles, Seven Missives)' which yoked nuclear weapons and language together to express the void of meaning at the heart of deconstruction and différance.[50] For Derrida, nuclear war is 'a phenomenon whose essential feature is that of being *fabulously textual*, through and through':

> Nuclear weaponry depends, more than any weaponry in the past, it seems, upon structures of information and communication, structures of language, including non-vocalizable language, structures of codes and graphic decoding. But the phenomenon is fabulously textual also to the extent that, for the moment, a nuclear war has not taken place: one can only talk and write about it.[51]

He goes on to argue that literature is uniquely threatened by the 'remainderless' annihilation of mutually assured destruction because it is the most purely technological (that is, textual) form of expression: 'That is why deconstruction … belongs to the nuclear age.'[52]

As I have argued, however, nuclear narratives of the 1950s addressed this fabulous quality of presence and absence as much through gothic overdetermination as through a post-modern deferral of signification – or rather, it might be said that the links between gothicism and post-modernity can be clearly traced in the narratives of the mid-century. The tension between two ways of understanding a nuclear bomb – as an all-too-present autotelic object preparing to breed death, or an absent, coded symbol of codedness itself, is demonstrated by the two iterations of Peter George's 1958 novel *Red Alert* (aka *Two Hours To Doom*), which mark a transition in the cultural treatment of bombs-as-things at the start of the 1960s.[53] George's earnest thriller concerns an unhinged general, Quenten, who deliberately orders an unauthorised nuclear strike on Russia in the paranoid belief that it is the only way to vanquish America's enemy. This scenario was freely adapted by Stanley Kubrick for the 1964 satire *Dr Strangelove, or How I Learned to Stop Worrying and Love the Bomb*.[54] In George's original, the emphasis is on the chain of command which Quenten has imposed on the B-52 bomber wing under emergency 'Plan R'. This plan makes all communication with the bombers impossible without a code which only they and Quenten know, which means that it is impossible for anyone else to tell them to abort their mission after the initial order is given. As in *Seven Days To Noon* and *The New Men*, the bomb has co-opted a human agent as a kind of prosthetic extension of itself, inspiring a cold-blooded obsession that obliterates warmth, compassion or reason. However, it is Quenten's own hand that defeats him: after he commits suicide, his secret code is deciphered just in time by Major Howard, who interprets the general's doodles on a notepad:

> It was funny, he thought, flipping the pages and glancing idly at the scrawls and doodles there, how much of a man's subconscious is revealed when he scrawls on a pad. His conscious mind may be busy with other things. But his subconscious often prompts him to scrawl thoughts which are hidden deep beneath the surface.[55]

As in *The Undefeated* and perhaps *The Small Back Room*, human psychology is both the cause of, and the solution to, the object-world's attempts to commandeer human agency and make it subservient to techno-logic. But in *Red Alert*, the bomb itself, as a thing, barely makes an appearance except as an abstract threat, whereas by the time Kubrick came to adapt the novel, the missile's stubborn thingliness was placed firmly at the centre of the action. He turns a minor incident in the novel, in which a missile temporarily sticks in the damaged bomb-release mechanism of the B-52, into the film's mock-triumphant finale, as the bomber's cowboy commander Major 'King' Kong rides the missile, whooping, into oblivion.

Meanwhile, the character of Strangelove – entirely the invention of Kubrick and the actor Peter Sellers – represents an ironic resolution of the conflict between warm hands and cold technology. Strangelove's attempt to disguise his fascist sympathies is continually subverted by his 'alien limb' – not a prosthesis but a disobedient, Nazi-saluting arm which insists on its own version of history; its fascist eruptions clearly signal Kubrick's unease about the uncanny agency of the objects of war. In the War Room, technology is overtly fetishised; the politicians and generals sit in front of giant screens, while communication with the Russians – necessary to avert global apocalypse – is mediated by the mechanised interventions of a telephone hotline. Indeed, the idea of telephonic interventions into human communication, so central to the dénouement of *The Small Back Room*, is curiously echoed at the start of *Dr Strangelove* when army chief General Turgidson communicates with the Pentagon from the lavatory in his bunker by shouting his answers to his bikini-clad girlfriend, who then relays them into the phone, listens to the responses, and then shouts them back to Turgidson. The mediation of *The Small Back Room*'s corporeal/corporal girl/phone apparatus was a chilling reminder of the creeping otherness which the thing-world was seeking to impose on the human subject. By 1964, this prosthetic incursion could be played for laughs, but it also serves to foreground Kubrick's decision to return to the thing and insist that his audience contemplates its potential for intervention. In the figure of the Strangelove – whose very name suggests an alien intimacy – we find a filmic riposte to Heidegger: to accept philosophically the atom bomb's inevitable presencing – to 'stop worrying and love the bomb' – is presented as the idea of a fascist madman.

Kubrick's comic treatment of Cold War atomic politics was symptomatic of a general shift in attitudes towards the uncanny objects of modernity. The 1960s thing-world was, in a sense, just as threatening to the human subject as it had been in the immediate post-war period, and perhaps more so; but as the century matured and consumerism took hold, gothic warnings about the animation of the inanimate lost their sense of deep unease and became more playful.

NOTES

1 *How You Can Deal with Incendiary Bombs* (British Pathé, 1940).
2 *London Can Take It!*, dir. by Humphrey Jennings (Crown Film Unit, 1940).
3 *Butterfly Bomb* (Ministry of Information, 1944).
4 *Dangerous Trophies: Unexploded Bombs* (British Pathé, 1945).
5 *The Atomic Age* (British Pathé and *Daily Express*, 1946).
6 'Obstacles to use of nuclear energy', *The Times*, Wednesday, Jun 11, 1947, p. 3.
7 *1951 Exhibition of Science South Kensington: Festival of Britain*, pp. 8–9.
8 Susan Stewart, *On Longing: Narratives of the Miniature, the Gigantic, the Souvenir, the Collection* (Durham, NC: Duke University Press, 1993), p. 74.
9 Martin Heidegger, 'The Thing', in *Poetry, Language, Thought*, trans. Albert Hofstadter (New York: Harper Perennial Classics, 2001), pp. 161–84 (p. 163).
10 Heidegger, 'The Thing', p. 164.
11 Heidegger, 'The Thing', p. 164.
12 Heidegger, 'The Thing', p. 164.
13 Walter Benjamin, *One Way Street*, in *Selected Writings Vol 1, 1913–1926*, trans. Marcus Bullock and Michael W. Jennings (Cambridge, MA: Harvard University Press, 1996), pp. 444–88 (pp. 453–54).
14 Arthur Schopenhauer, *Parerga and Paralipomena: Short Philososphical Essays Vol 2*, trans E.F.J. Payne (Oxford: Oxford University Press, 1974), pp. 651–52.
15 Bruno Latour, *We Have Never Been Modern* (Cambridge, MA: Harvard University Press, 1993); Gilles Deleuze and Félix Guattari, *A Thousand Plateaus* trans. Brian Massumi (London: Continuum, 2004).
16 *The Small Back Room*, dir. by Michael Powell and Emeric Pressburger (The Archers, 1949).
17 Tim Armstrong, *Modernism, Technology and the Body: A Cultural Study* (Cambridge: Cambridge University Press, 1998).
18 Armstrong, *Modernism, Technology and the Body*, p. 98.

19 Vivian Sobchack, 'A Leg to Stand On', in Marquard Smith and Joanne Morra, eds., *The Prosthetic Impulse: From a Posthuman Present to a Biocultural Future* (Cambridge, MA: MIT Press, 2006), pp. 17–38 (p. 22), emphasis in the original.
20 Armstrong, *Modernism, Technology and the Body*, p. 98.
21 See Brown, 'Thing Theory', p. 4. 'The interruption of the habit of looking *through* windows as transparencies enables the protagonist [of A.S. Byatt's *The Biographer's Tale*] to look *at* a window itself in its opacity.'
22 Quoted in Moor, *Powell and Pressburger*, p. 162.
23 Nigel Balchin, *The Small Back Room* (London: Cassell, 2000), p. 192.
24 *The Undefeated*, dir. by Paul Dickson (Central Office of Information, 1950).
25 For a fascinating discussion of the overlapping notions of aesthetics, synaesthetics and anaesthetics, see Susan Buck-Morss, 'Aesthetics and Anaesthetics: Walter Benjamin's Artwork Essay Reconsidered', *October*, 62 (Autumn, 1992), 3–41 (pp. 29–30).
26 Quoted in Katy McGahan, *Land of Promise: The British Documentary Movement, 1930–1950* (London: BFI, 2010), booklet accompanying DVD, p. 69.
27 Benjamin, 'The Work of Art', p. 269.
28 Futurist manifesto quoted in Buck-Morss, 'Aesthetics and Anaesthetics', p. 4.
29 *Seven Days To Noon*, dir. by John Boulting and Roy Boulting (London Films, 1950).
30 Benjamin, *One Way Street*, p. 454.
31 *The Dam Busters*, dir. by Michael Anderson (ABPC, 1955).
32 Benjamin, 'The Work of Art', p. 265.
33 C.P. Snow, *The New Men* (London: Stratus, 2001).
34 Snow, *The New Man*, p. 231.
35 Snow, *The New Man*, p. 160.
36 Snow, *The New Man*, p. 137.
37 Snow, *The New Man*, p. 138.
38 Buck-Morss, 'Aesthetics and Anaesthetics', p. 7.
39 Snow, *The New Man*, p. 122.
40 Snow, *The New Man*, p. 217.
41 Snow, *The New Men*, p. 217.
42 Marghanita Laski, *The Offshore Island* (London: Cresset, 1959).
43 Laski, *The Offshore Island*, p. 2.
44 Laski, *The Offshore Island*, p. 6.
45 Laski, *The Offshore Island*, p. 6.
46 Laski, *The Offshore Island*, p. 27.
47 Ian Fleming, *Moonraker* (London: Penguin, 2004).
48 Fleming, *Moonraker*, pp. 108–09.
49 Fleming, *Moonraker*, p. 179.
50 Jacques Derrida, 'No Apocalypse, Not Now (Full Speed Ahead, Seven Missiles, Seven Missives)', *Diacritics*, 14:2 (Summer, 1984), 20–31.
51 Derrida, 'No Apocalypse, Not Now', p. 23, emphasis in the original.
52 Derrida, 'No Apocalypse, Not Now', p. 27.
53 Peter George [aka Peter Bryant], *Red Alert* (New York: Rosetta, 2000).
54 *Dr Strangelove, or How I Learned to Stop Worrying and Love the Bomb*, dir. by Stanley Kubrick (Columbia Pictures and Hawk Films, 1962).
55 George, *Red Alert*, p. 124.

CONCLUSION: BEYOND THE MID-CENTURY

> There was no end to the ways in which nice things are nicer than nasty ones.
>
> Kingsley Amis, *Lucky Jim* (1954)[1]

In the course of this book I have argued for the existence of a post-war moment, lasting roughly ten years from 1945 to 1955, which was distinct from the later 1950s and the emerging cultures of youth, protest and neophilia which flowered in the 1960s. What, then, became of mid-century gothic? If its stories of alien objects capable of infiltrating and intervening in the human realm contained a warning against the creeping interchangeability of people and the consumer goods which offered to define and placate them, then this warning was often drowned out by the normative bellow of advertising and mass culture. As the 1950s progressed, and the Cold War made great geopolitical struggles a question of abstract, bureaucratic concern rather than a 'personal matter', a new appetite for distracting pleasures took hold. The heroes (and, more rarely, heroines) of literature's Angry Young Men movement and cinema's New Wave refused to be bullied by over-assertive objects, and instead set out to prove that they could seize hold of them and repurpose them at will. An early example of this new attitude can be seen in Kingsley Amis's *Lucky Jim* (1954). Jim Dixon's epiphanic realisation that 'nice things are nicer than nasty ones' marks the moment when this turn begins in British literature. Amis presents his banal observation as a revolutionary insight because he wishes to make explicit his own rejection of the norms against which Dixon – a stroppy young historian – is rebelling; yet, as the examples discussed in previous chapters show, there was already a strong antinomian impulse in mid-century gothic's interest in recalcitrance. *Lucky Jim* makes its point by retrospectively defining the post-war decade as an era of dull conformity and excessive obedience, when in fact – as Doris Lessing observed in the quotation from *The Four-Gated City* cited in the Introduction – really 'the air had cleared well before'.[2] Perhaps the more telling cultural difference between the earlier and later periods is the way non-commodities receded from view as objects worth paying attention to. The mechanism of shifting desire and partial satisfaction can already be seen in Dixon's proto-countercultural rebellion, which is expressed in terms of a restless need for personal fulfilment, rather than any considered position of political dissatisfaction.

At one of the key points of the novel, Dixon is invited to a social weekend by the head of his university department, and disgraces himself by sneaking off to get drunk in the local pub and then setting fire to his bed by falling asleep with a lit cigarette. The house of his host, Professor Welch, is replete with the solid English furniture and folksy knick-knacks which had represented bohemian good taste to the previous generation; Dixon literally burns through these layers of cultural sediment and awakens the next morning with a hangover but a characteristic lack of angst. Buoyed by the attention of a pretty girl who offers to help him, he approaches the task of disposing of the charred remains with glib pragmatism, cutting away the burnt areas of sheets and blankets with a razor blade, repositioning an expensive rug in order to disguise the scorch marks, and hiding a damaged table among the other junk in a nearby lumber room:

> He unrolled a handy length of mouldering silk and spread it over the table-top; then arranged upon the cloth thus provided two fencing foils, a book called *The Lesson of Spain*, and a Lilliputian chest-of-drawers no doubt containing sea-shells and locks of children's hair; finally propped up against this display a tripod meant for some sort of telescopic or photographic tomfoolery. The effect, when he stepped back, was excellent; no observer could doubt that these objects had lived together for years in just this way.[3]

Dixon's ad-hoc curation of this mismatched set of objects is intended only to conjure up a sense of random junk gathered together for no purpose; unlike, say, the objects assembled for Jones's *Black Eyes and Lemonade*, or the bombsite debris collected by Henderson and Paolozzi for *Patio and Pavilion*, Dixon's exhibits are designed specifically to discourage the 'tomfoolery' of close looking. Instead, the mere fact of their superannuation is enough to provide camouflage for the recent conflagration. Dixon is the archetype of a generation entirely unburdened by post-war trauma; moreover, he is the opposite of Benjamin's revolutionary dreamer, awakened into consciousness by the piled wreckage of history. Dixon is a chimera, prone to pranks and disguises, and his drunken sleep does not provide access to dreams of radical rupture but merely catapults him into a scene of meaningless devastation which is all too easily consigned to an irrelevant past. Far from being haunted by uncanny debris, he is himself the impish spectre invading the Welches' personal and domestic space with his own mischievous and destructive agenda.

While mid-century gothic depended on a particular anxiety about time, Dixon's decision to live for the pursuit of 'nice things' coincides with his stark rejection of history, both as an academic career and as a force acting upon his inner life: he ends the book on a moment of triumphant laughter which openly mocks the past and its claims to ongoing relevance. This kind of ahistorical insistence on grasping the available pleasures of the now was precisely the impulse which also interested Roland Barthes from 1954 to 1956, when he was writing the essays on consumer culture which would be collected as *Mythologies*. Myth, Barthes wrote,

> abolishes the complexity of human acts, it gives them the simplicity of essences, it does away with all dialectics, with any going back beyond what is immediately visible, it organises a world which is without contradictions because it is without depth, a world open and wallowing in the evident, it establishes a blissful clarity: things appear to mean something by themselves.[4]

This view contradicts Adorno and Horkheimer's more gothic reading of mythology in *Dialectic of Enlightenment*, where enchantment was understood as both the precursor of and potential antidote to rationalism and reification, continually redefined in order to subsume each newly superannuated layer of the once-cutting-edge. For Barthes, mythology does away with such dialectical complexity, coating mass culture with an approachable veneer of quasi-natural contemporaneity. His essay on the *Blue Guide* book on Spain notes that 'History is hardly a good bourgeois' and is therefore without traction in commodity culture; he proposes that more up-to-date guidebooks should ignore old churches and monuments in favour of 'the urbanism, the sociology and the economy which trace today's actual and even most profane questions'.[5] A guide to modern culture, he argues, must primarily track and critique the workings of the dominant system of consumption; it can safely ignore the past, and indeed is required to do so in order to illuminate the eternal now of mass commodification.

Whereas, in mid-century gothic, human subjects struggled to assert their individuality through their relationships with variously uncanny, recalcitrant or inscrutably technological objects, Barthes describes a mediation of the human which depends on the abolition of individuality and the triumph of a system of communal preferences encoded and regulated by consumerism. His review of the 1955 Citroën DS car, for instance, treats it as a magical object 'from another world' which seems to have no origin or history, and is outside the system of production and capital. Yet while seeming entirely new on the outside, inside it conquers the potential aggressiveness of its technological futurism by assuming a familiar domesticity: 'The dashboard looks more like the worktable of a modern kitchen than a factory control room'.[6] Provocatively, he calls this car 'the almost exact equivalent of the great Gothic cathedral', not for any ambition towards grandeur and sublimity but for the anonymity of its artists and the fact that it is 'consumed in its image, if not in its use, by an entire populace'.[7] Of course Gothicism, in its original medieval form, as well as in later revivals, was always defined by a shocking unruliness rather than by the kind of glassy smoothness that characterised the Citroën car, but Barthes's evocation of the gothic in this essay, and the implication that the same class hierarchies are at work in the reception of luxury consumer durables as operated in premodern monumental architecture, suggests that mid-century unease could still be discerned by the attentive critic, even in the shiny dreamworld of the automobile showroom.

In 1944, Elizabeth Bowen had observed Blitz survivors piecing themselves together by collecting old fragments from the rubble; in 1964, Herbert Marcuse noted: 'The people recognise themselves in their commodities; they find their soul in their automobile, hi-fi set, split-level home, kitchen equipment.'[8] *One-Dimensional Man*, his influential study of consumerism and its ability to penetrate the personal, shows how the new became more important than the old during the intervening decades, yet his study echoes many of the concerns which underpinned mid-century gothic's unease about the thing-world.

Clearly, despite the new attitudes represented by the likes of Jim Dixon, such disquiet persisted into the 1960s. It is there, too, in Harold Pinter's 1960 play *The Caretaker*, although it has lost its gothic overtones in favour of a sense of the absurd. The eternal present of consumerism, which pretends to solve any longing for a better future by proffering an endless supply of fleeting pleasures, is crucial to the sense of temporal and spatial dislocation in the play. Pinter depicts three men locked in an endless battle to define themselves and each other, who are thwarted by their inability to come to terms with the past, present and future. Davies the tramp constantly refers back to his difficult past; because he has become untethered from his possessions, and from the crucial 'papers' he left in Sidcup, he has lost his identity and can only piece himself together temporarily via a series of found objects which (he frequently complains) never quite fit him properly. Aston, who offers him shelter, is suffering from the cognitive effects of shock therapy and lives only in the present because he can no longer organise his thoughts with sufficient clarity to remember the details of the past, nor to progress with his modest future plan to build a shed in the garden. Aston's brother Mick, in contrast, confidently expresses his vision of the future, although that vision changes from moment to moment. He makes extravagant claims about the transformation he will work on the flat they share, in terms culled from interior decoration magazines:

> Yes. Venetian blinds on the window, cork floor, cork tiles. You could have an off-white pile linen rug, a table ... in afromosia teak veneer, sideboard with matt black drawers, curved chairs with cushioned seats, armchairs in oatmeal tweed, a beech frame settee with a woven sea-grass seat, white-topped heat-resistant coffee table, white tile surround.[9]

This is an unattainable fantasy: instead of such harmoniously assembled furnishings, replete with their fetishised material attributes, Mick's flat is in fact piled with old rubbish, as described in Pinter's at-rise description of the stage setting:

> To the right of the window a mound: a kitchen sink, a step-ladder, a coal bucket, a lawn-mower, a shopping trolley, boxes, sideboard drawers ... a couple of suitcases, a rolled carpet, a blow-lamp, a wooden chair on its side, boxes, a number of ornaments, a clothes horse, a few short planks of wood, a small electric fire and a very old electric toaster.[10]

Like *Lucky Jim*'s Dixon, Mick is hoping to consign such old junk to a forgotten past, but he is finding it hard to extricate himself and his flat from this mound of stuff. Pinter shows how human relationships break down in the context of material uncertainty and inadequacy of meaning. Uncanniness and overdetermination are ratcheted up into an insistent, baffling irrationality – an effect that is just as shocking and frightening as a gothic intervention. Individual agency is compromised on an intimate level by forces seemingly outside, and yet intimately imbricated with, the human.

Post-war things seemed remarkable in their ability to anchor themselves in space and time, creating vortices in the flow of history. Yet if an object's tangible presence might be assumed to be a marker of its incontrovertible reality, what happens when it has to express the future, not the past, and becomes the inadequate avatar of unattainable desire? The past can sometimes be held in the hand as a relic, and the present is at hand all the time; but the future has no materiality; and when an attempt is made to materialise it, something else happens: its promise melts away or stagnates clumsily, so that the object is always unsatisfactory, disruptive. As the twentieth century progressed, the uncanny was increasingly associated with a technological other, and science fiction took the place of gothic as the genre which critiqued the totalisation of mass culture. In contemporary culture, with the emergence of autonomous digital objects, the twenty-first century has searched for new ways of understanding the thingliness of things and their relationship with the human. Yet by paying attention to the mid-century's preoccupation with nasty things, we can regain a useful perspective on the power of nice things to shock and unsettle us. Uncanny agency and alien intimacy continue to focus our sense of unease wherever the animate and inanimate come together.

NOTES

1 Kingsley Amis, *Lucky Jim* (London: Penguin, 2000), p. 243.
2 Lessing, *The Four-Gated City*, pp. 307–08.
3 Amis, *Lucky Jim*, p. 74.
4 Roland Barthes, *Mythologies*, trans. Richard Howard and Annette Lavers (New York: Hill and Wang, 2013) p. 256.
5 Barthes, Mythologies, p. 137; p. 136.

Conclusion

6 Barthes, *Mythologies*, p. 171.
7 Barthes, *Mythologies*, p. 169.
8 Herbert Marcuse, *One-Dimensional Man: Studies in the Ideology of Advanced Industrial Society* (Oxford: Routledge, 2002), p. 11.
9 Harold Pinter, *The Caretaker* (London: Methuen, 1985), p. 60.
10 Pinter, *The Caretaker*, p. 6.

BIBLIOGRAPHY

BOOKS AND ARTICLES

Adorno, Theodor, *Minima Moralia: Reflections on a Damaged Life*, trans. E.F.N. Jephcott (London: Verso, 2005)
—— *The Culture Industry*, trans. J.M. Bernstein (London: Routledge, 2001)
Adorno, Theodor W. and Max Horkheimer, *Dialectic of Enlightenment*, trans. John Cumming (London: Verso, 1997)
Alexander, Peter F., 'The Process of Composition of the Libretto of Britten's *Gloriana*', *Music & Letters*, 67:2 (April 1986), 147–58
Alloway, Lawrence, 'Dada 1956', *Architectural Design* (November 1956), 374
Amis, Kingsley, *Lucky Jim* (London: Penguin, 2000)
Armstrong, Isobel, *Victorian Glassworlds: Glass Culture and the Imagination 1830–1880* (Oxford: Oxford University Press, 2008)
Armstrong, Tim, *Modernism, Technology and the Body: A Cultural Study* (Cambridge: Cambridge University Press, 1998)
Bachelard, Gaston, *The Poetics of Space*, trans. Maria Jolas (Boston: Beacon, 1964)
Bagehot, Walter, *The English Constitution* (London: Chapman and Hall, 1867)
Balchin, Nigel, *The Small Back Room* (London: Cassell, 2000)
Ballaster, Ros, *Fabulous Orients: Fictions of the East in England 1662–1785* (Oxford: Oxford University Press, 2005)
Banham, Mary and Bevis Hillier, eds., *A Tonic to the Nation: The Festival of Britain 1951* (London: Thames & Hudson, 1976)
Banks, Paul, ed., *Britten's Gloriana: Essays and Sources* (Woodbridge: Boydell, 1993)
Banton, Michael, *The Coloured Quarter: Negro Immigrants in an English City* (London: Cape, 1955)
Barthes, Roland, *Mythologies*, trans. Richard Howard and Annette Lavers (New York: Hill and Wang, 2013)
Baudrillard, Jean, *The System of Objects*, trans. James Benedict (London: Verso, 2005)
Bell, Quentin, *On Human Finery: The Classic Study of Fashion Through the Ages*, rev. edn. (London: Allison & Busby, 1992)
Benjamin, Walter, *The Arcades Project*, trans. Howard Eiland and Kevin McLaughlin (Cambridge, MA: Harvard University Press, 1999)
—— *Illuminations*, trans. Harry Zorn (London: Random House, 1999)

―― *Selected Writings*, trans. Marcus Bullock and others, 4 vols (Cambridge, MA: Harvard University Press, 1996–2003)
Bentley, Nick, *Radical Fictions: The English Novel in the 1950s* (Oxford: Peter Lang, 2007)
Bhabha, Homi, 'Of Mimicry and Man: The Ambivalence of Colonial Discourse', *October*, 28 (Spring 1984), 125–33
Black, Misha, 'Architecture, Art and Design in Unison', in Mary Banham and Bevis Hillier, eds., *A Tonic to the Nation: The Festival of Britain 1951* (London: Thames & Hudson, 1976), pp. 82–85
Bluemel, Kristin, ed. *Intermodernism: Literary Culture in Mid-Twentieth-Century Britain* (Edinburgh: Edinburgh University Press, 2009)
Bonham Carter, Violet, *Daring to Hope: the Diaries and Letters of Violet Bonham Carter, 1946–1969*, ed. Mark Pottle (London: Weidenfeld & Nicholson, 2000)
Boscagli, Maurizia, *Stuff Theory: Everyday Objects, Radical Materialism* (New York: Bloomsbury, 2014)
Botting, Fred, *Gothic* (London: Routledge, 1996)
Bowden, B. V., ed., *Faster Than Thought: A Symposium on Digital Computing Machines* (London: Pitman, 1953)
Bowen, Elizabeth, *The Collected Stories of Elizabeth Bowen* (London: Random House, 1999)
―― *The Demon Lover and Other Stories* (London: Jonathan Cape, 1952)
―― *The Heat of the Day* (London: Vintage, 1998)
―― *People, Places, Things: Essays by Elizabeth Bowen* (Edinburgh: Edinburgh University Press, 2008)
Breward, Christopher and Ghislaine Wood, eds., *British Design from 1948: Innovation in the Modern Age* (London: V&A, 2012)
Britten, Benjamin, *Opera Guide 24: Peter Grimes/Gloriana* (London: John Calder, 1983)
Brown, Bill, 'Thing Theory', *Critical Inquiry*, 28:1 (Autumn 2001), 1–22
―― 'The Tyranny of Things (Trivia in Karl Marx and Mark Twain)', *Critical Inquiry*, 28:2 (Winter 2002), 442–69
Bruce-Mitford, R.L.S., ed., *Recent Archaeological Excavations in Britain* (London: Routledge & Kegan Paul, 1956)
―― 'The Sutton Hoo Ship-Burial', *Scientific American*, 184:4 (April 1951), 24–30
Buck-Morss, Susan, 'Aesthetics and Anaesthetics: Walter Benjamin's Artwork Essay Reconsidered', *October*, 62 (Autumn 1992), 3–41
Calder, Angus, *The Myth of the Blitz* (London: Random House, 1992)
Care Evans, Angela, *The Sutton Hoo Ship Burial* (London: British Museum, 1986)
Carrington, Noel and Clarke Hutton, *Popular Art in Britain* (London: Penguin, 1945); the cover gives the title as *Popular English Art*
Carroll, Lewis, *The Annotated Alice*, ed. Martin Gardner (London: Penguin, 2000)
Cary, Joyce, *Triptych* (Harmondsworth: Penguin, 1985)
Casson, Hugh, Brenda Colvin and Jacques Groag, *Bombed Churches as War Memorials* (Cheam: Architectural Press, 1945)

Christie, Ian and Andrew Moor, eds., *The Cinema of Michael Powell: International Perspectives on an English Film Maker* (London: BFI, 2005)

Coase, R.H., *British Broadcasting: A Study in Monopoly* (London: Longmans, 1950)

Cohen, Gerard Daniel, *In War's Wake: Europe's Displaced Persons in the Postwar Order* (Oxford: Oxford University Press, 2012)

Cohen, Margaret, *Profane Illumination: Walter Benjamin and the Paris of Surrealist Revolution* (Berkeley: University of California, 1993)

Conekin Becky E., *'The Autobiography of a Nation': The 1951 Festival of Britain* (Manchester: Manchester University Press, 2003)

Coven, Frank, ed., *Daily Mail Television Handbook* (London: Associated Newspapers, [1949])

de Balzac, Honoré *The Wild Ass's Skin*, trans. Herbert J. Hunt (London: Penguin, 1977)

Deleuze, Gilles and Félix Guattari, *A Thousand Plateaus*, trans. Brian Massumi (London: Continuum, 2004)

Derrida, Jacques, 'No Apocalypse, Not Now (Full Speed Ahead, Seven Missiles, Seven Missives)', *Diacritics*, 14:2 (Summer 1984), 20–31

Descartes, René, *Treatise of Man* (Cambridge, MA: Harvard University Press, 1972)

Durgnat Raymond, *A Mirror for England: British Movies from Austerity to Affluence* (London: Faber and Faber, 1970)

Dyhouse, Carol, 'Skin Deep: The Fall of Fur', *History Today*, 61:11 (November 2011), www.historytoday.com/carol-dyhouse/skin-deep-fall-fur [accessed 28 January 2018]

Elen, Richard G., 'TV Technology 5: Magic Rays of Light', www.screenonline.org.uk/tv/technology/technology5.html [accessed 28 January 2018]

Eliot, T.S., *Notes Towards the Definition of Culture* (London: Faber and Faber, 1948)

Esty, Jed, *A Shrinking Island: Modernism and National Culture in England* (Princeton: Princeton University Press, 2004)

Fabre, Michel, 'Samuel Selvon: Interviews and Conversations', in Susheila Nasta, ed., *Critical Perspectives on Sam Selvon* (Washington DC: Three Continents Press, 1988)

Fagg, William, *Traditional Sculpture from the Colonies* (London: Colonial Office, 1951)

Faiers, Jonathan, *Dressing Dangerously: Dysfunctional Fashion in Film* (New Haven: Yale University Press, 2013)

Fisher, Mark, *The Weird and the Eerie* (London: Repeater, 2016)

Fleming, Ian, *Moonraker* (London: Penguin, 2004)

Foster, Hal, 'The Archive without Museums', *October*, 77 (Summer 1996), 97–116

Foucault, Michel *Discipline and Punish: The Birth of the Prison*, trans. A. Sheridan (London: Allen Lane, 1977)

Freedgood, Elaine, *The Ideas in Things: Fugitive Meaning in the Victorian Novel* (Chicago: University of Chicago Press, 2006)

Freud, Sigmund, *The Uncanny*, trans. David McLintock (London: Penguin, 2003)

George, Peter (aka Peter Bryant), *Red Alert* (New York: Rosetta, 2000)

Gibbs, Philip, *The New Elizabethans* (London: Hutchinson, 1953)
Glass, Ruth, ed., *London: Aspects of Change, Centre for Urban Studies Report No 3* (London: MacGibbon & Kee, 1964)
Grey Walter, William, *The Living Brain* (London: Penguin, 1961)
―― 'A Machine that Learns', *Scientific American*, 185.2 (August 1951), 60–63
―― 'An Imitation of Life', *Scientific American*, 182.5 (May 1950), 42–45
Harwood, Elain and Alan Powers, eds., *Twentieth Century Architecture 5: Festival of Britain* (London: Twentieth Century Society, 2001)
Headrick Daniel R., 'Botany, Chemistry, and Tropical Development', *Journal of World History*, 7:1 (Spring 1996), 1–20
Heidegger, Martin, *Poetry, Language, Thought*, trans. Albert Hofstadter (New York: Harper Perennial Classics, 2001)
Hershberg, David, ed., *Perspectives on Contemporary Literature: Literature and the Historical Process* (Lexington: University Press of Kentucky, 1987)
Highmore, Ben, 'Hopscotch Modernism: On Everyday Life and the Blurring of Art and Social Science', *Modernist Cultures*, 2:1 (Summer 2006), 70–79
―― 'Something out of nothing: concretising the immaterial in Brutalism', plenary at 'Objects of Modernity', 23–24 June 2014, University of Birmingham
Hobsbawm, Eric and Terence Ranger, eds., *The Invention of Tradition* (Cambridge: Cambridge University Press, 1983)
Hodges, Andrew, *Alan Turing: The Enigma* (London: Vintage, 2014)
Hoffman, E.T.A., *Tales of Hoffmann* (London: Penguin, 1982)
Hornsey, Richard, *The Spiv and the Architect: Unruly Life in Postwar London* (Minneapolis: University of Minnesota Press, 2010)
Hunt, John and Edmund Hillary, 'The Ascent of Mount Everest', *The Geographical Journal*, 119:4 (December 1953), 385–99
Jäger, Lorenz, *Adorno: A Political Biography*, trans. Stewart Spencer (New Haven: Yale University Press, 2004)
Jarvis, Alan, *The Things We See: Indoors and Out* (Harmondsworth: Penguin, 1946)
Johnston, John, *The Allure of Machinic Life* (Cambridge, MA: MIT Press, 2008)
Jones, Barbara, 'Popular Art', handwritten draft, Whitechapel Gallery archive (undated)
―― *The Unsophisticated Arts* (London: Architectural Press, 1951)
―― *English Furniture at a Glance* (London: Architectural Press, 1954)
Kelly, Edward H., 'The Meaning of "The Horse's Mouth"', *Modern Language Studies*, 1:2 (Summer 1971), 9–11
Kittler, Friedrich, *Gramophone, Film, Typewriter*, trans. Geoffrey Winthrop-Young and Michael Wutz (Stanford: Stanford University Press, 1999)
―― *Optical Media: Berlin Lectures 1999*, trans. Anthony Enns (Cambridge: Polity, 2010)
Kjellman-Chapin, Monica, ed., *Kitsch: History, Theory, Practice* (Newcastle Upon Tyne: Cambridge Scholars, 2013)
Klein, John W., 'Some Reflections on *Gloriana*', *Tempo*, 29 (Autumn 1953), 16–21

Kynaston, David, *Austerity Britain 1945–51* (London: Bloomsbury, 2007)
—— *Family Britain 1951–57* (London: Bloomsbury, 2010)
Lacan, Jacques, *The Four Fundamental Concepts of Psycho-Analysis*, trans. Alan Sheridan (London: Karnac, 1977)
—— *Seminar of Jacques Lacan, Book II: The Ego in Freud's Theory and in the Technique of Psychoanalysis 1954–1955*, trans. Sylvana Tomaselli (Cambridge: Cambridge University Press, 1988)
Lamb, Jonathan, 'Modern Metamorphoses and Disgraceful Tales' *Critical Inquiry*, 28 (Autumn 2001), 133–66
—— *The Things Things Say* (Princeton: Princeton University Press, 2011)
Larkin, Philip, *The Less Deceived* (London: Marvel, 1977)
Laski, Marghanita, *Little Boy Lost* (London: Persephone, 2001)
—— *The Offshore Island* (London: Cresset Press, 1959)
—— *The Victorian Chaise-Longue* (London: Persephone, 1999)
Latour, Bruno, *We Have Never Been Modern* (Cambridge, MA: Harvard University Press, 1993)
Lefebvre, Henri, *The Production of Space*, trans. Donald Nicholson-Smith (Maiden, MA: Blackwell, 1991)
Leslie, Esther, *Walter Benjamin: Overpowering Conformism* (London: Pluto, 2000)
Lessing, Doris, *The Four-Gated City* (London: Paladin, 1990)
Luckhurst, Roger, *The Mummy's Curse: The True History of a Dark Fantasy* (Oxford: Oxford University Press, 2014)
Lukács, Georg, *History and Class Consciousness*, trans. Rodney Livingstone www.marxists.org/archive/lukacs/works/history/ [accessed 28 January 2018]
MacKay, Marina, *Modernism and World War II* (Cambridge: Cambridge University Press, 2007)
Macaulay, Rose, *The Pleasure of Ruins* (London: Weidenfeld & Nicholson, 1953)
—— *The World My Wilderness* (London: Collins, 1950)
Malraux, André, *The Voices of Silence*, trans. Stuart Gilbert (London: Secker & Warburg, 1956)
Marcuse, Herbert, *One-Dimensional Man: Studies in the Ideology of Advanced Industrial Society* (Oxford: Routledge, 2002)
Marx, Karl, *Capital Volume 1*, trans. Ben Fowkes (London: Penguin, 1990)
Marx, Karl and Friedrich Engels, *Manifesto of the Communist Party*, trans. Samuel Moore, www.marxists.org/archive/marx/works/1848/communist-manifesto/ch01.htm#007 [accessed 28 January 2018]
Massey, Anne, *The Independent Group: Modernism and Mass Culture in Britain, 1945–59* (Manchester: Manchester University Press, 1995)
Massie, Chris, *Corridor of Mirrors* (London: Faber and Faber, 1941)
McGahan, Katy, *Land of Promise: The British Documentary Movement, 1930–1950* (London: BFI, 2010); booklet accompanying DVD
McLuhan, Marshall, *The Mechanical Bride: Folklore of Industrial Man* (New York: Vanguard, 1951)

Mellor, David 'Mass-Observation: The Intellectual Climate', *Camerawork*, 11 (September 1978), 4–5
Mellor, Leo, *Reading the Ruins: Modernism, Bombsites and British Culture* (Cambridge: Cambridge University Press, 2011)
Melville, Robert, 'Exhibitions', *Architectural Review*, 120 (November 1956), 332–34
Meynell, Alix, *Public Servant, Private Woman* (London: Victor Gollancz, 1988)
Miller, Jacques-Alain, 'Suture (Elements of the Logic of the Signifier)', *Screen*, 18:4 (Winter 1977–78), 24–34
Mitchell, W.J.T., *What Do Pictures Want? The Lives and Loves of Images* (Chicago: University of Chicago Press, 2005)
Moberly, L.G., 'Inexplicable', in Jack Adrian, ed., *Strange Tales from the Strand* (Oxford: Oxford University Press, 1992), pp. 183–96
Moor, Andrew, *Powell and Pressburger: A Cinema of Magic Spaces* (London: I.B. Tauris, 2005)
Moore, Charles, *Double Harness* (London: Weidenfeld & Nicholson, 1976)
Moore, Thomas, *Intercepted Letters; or, The Two-Penny Postbag* (London, 1813)
Moriarty, Catherine, *Drawing, Writing, Curating: Barbara Jones and the Art of Arrangement. An Essay to Accompany the Exhibition* (London: Whitechapel Gallery, 2013)
Msiska, Mpalive-Hangson, 'Sam Selvon's *The Lonely Londoners* and the Structure of Black Metropolitan Life', *African and Black Diaspora: An International Journal*, 2:1 (January 2009), 5–27
Mulvey, Laura, 'Visual Pleasure and Narrative Cinema', *Screen*, 16:3 (Autumn 1975), 6–18
Murdoch, Iris, *Under the Net* (London: Vintage, 2002)
Orwell, George, *Complete Works*, ed. Peter Davison, 20 vols. (London: Secker & Warburg, 1986–98)
—— *Essays* (London: Penguin, 1984)
—— *Nineteen Eighty-Four* (London: Penguin, 2013)
Oudart, Jean-Pierre, 'Cinema and Suture', *Screen*, 18:4 (Winter 1977–78), 35–47
Packard Vance, *The Hidden Persuaders* (London: Penguin, 1960)
Paravisini-Gebert, Lizbeth, 'Colonial and Post-Colonial Gothic: The Caribbean', in Jerrold E. Hogle, ed., *The Cambridge Companion to Gothic Fiction* (Cambridge: Cambridge University Press, 2002)
Pearson, Lynn, '"Roughcast Textures and Cosmic Overtones": A Survey of British Murals 1945–1980', *Decorative Arts Society 1850–the Present*, 31 (2007), 116–37
Pinter, Harold, *The Caretaker* (London: Methuen, 1985)
Plomer, William *Electric Delights* (London: Jonathan Cape, 1978)
Powell Michael, *A Life in Movies: An Autobiography* (London: Faber and Faber, 2000)
Powell Michael and Emeric Pressburger, *The Life and Death of Colonel Blimp* (London: Faber and Faber, 1994)
Priestley, J.B. *The Other Place and Other Stories of the Same Sort* (London: William Heinemann, 1954)

Priestley, J.B. and Jacquetta Hawkes, *Journey Down a Rainbow* (London: Heinemann-Cresset, 1955)
Proust Marcel, *The Way by Swann's*, trans. Lydia Davis (London: Penguin, 2003)
Riquelme, John Paul, ed., *Gothic and Modernism: Essaying Dark Literary Modernity* (Baltimore: Johns Hopkins, 2008)
Royle, Nicholas, *The Uncanny* (Manchester: Manchester University Press, 2003)
Russell, Gordon, *The Things We See: Furniture* (Harmondsworth: Penguin, 1953)
Ryle, Gilbert, *The Concept of Mind* (London: Penguin, 2000)
Sansom, William, *The Blitz: Westminster at War* (Oxford: Oxford University Press, 1990)
—— *Something Terrible, Something Lovely* (London: Hogarth Press, 1948)
—— *Stories* (London: Hogarth Press, 1963)
Schopenhauer, Arthur, *Parerga and Paralipomena: Short Philosophical Essays*, Vol. 2, trans. E.F.J. Payne (Oxford: Oxford University Press, 1974)
Sconce, Jeffrey, *Haunted Media: Electronic Presence from Telegraphy to Television* (Durham, NC: Duke University Press, 2000)
Selvon, Sam, *The Lonely Londoners* (London: Penguin, 2006)
—— *Ways of Sunlight* (London: Hodder Education, 2015)
Selzer, Alvin J., 'Speaking Out of Both Sides of "The Horse's Mouth": Joyce Cary vs. Gulley Jimson', *Contemporary Literature*, 15:4 (Autumn 1974), 488–502
Sextus Empiricus, *Outlines of Pyrrhonism*, trans. R.G. Bury (Cambridge, MA: Harvard University Press, 1933)
Shelley Mary, *Frankenstein* (London: Everyman, 1963)
Sinfield, Alan, *Literature, Politics, and Culture in Postwar Britain* (Berkeley: University of California Press, 1989)
Smith, Marquard and Joanne Morra, eds. *The Prosthetic Impulse: From a Posthuman Present to a Biocultural Future* (Cambridge, MA: MIT Press, 2006)
Smithson, Alison and Peter, *Changing the Art of Inhabitation* (London: Ellipsis, 1994)
Snow, C.P., *The New Men* (London: Stratus, 2001)
Stewart, Susan, *On Longing: Narratives of the Miniature, the Gigantic, the Souvenir, the Collection* (Durham, NC: Duke University Press, 1993)
Stonard, John-Paul, 'Pop in the Age of Boom: Richard Hamilton's "Just What is it That Makes Today's Homes So Different, So Appealing?"', *Burlington Magazine* (September 2007), 607–20
Strachey, Lytton, *Elizabeth & Essex: A Tragic History* (London: Chatto and Windus, 1930)
Taylor, Basil, *The Festival of Britain* (London: Lund Humphries, 1951)
Thatcher, Margaret, *The Path to Power* (London: Harper Press, 1995)
Thomas, Dylan, *Quite Early One Morning* (New York: New Directions, 1954)
Thompson, Michael, *Rubbish Theory: The Creation and Destruction of Value* (Oxford: Oxford University Press, 1979)
Townsend Warner, Sylvia, *Diaries*, ed. Claire Harman (London: Chatto and Windus, 1994)
Tubbs, Ralph, *Living in Cities* (Harmondsworth: Penguin, 1942)

Turing, Alan, 'Computing Machinery and Intelligence', *Mind* 49 (October 1950), 433–60
—— 'Intelligent Machinery, a Heretical Theory', Turing digital archive, AMT/B/20, www.turingarchive.org/viewer/?id=474&title=6 [accessed 28 January 2018]
Ullman, James Ramsey, *Man of Everest: The Autobiography of Tenzing* (London: Reprint Society, 1956)
Walpole, Horace, *The Castle of Otranto: A Gothic Story* (Oxford: Oxford University Press, 1996)
Walsh, Victoria, *Nigel Henderson: Parallel of Life and Art* (London: Thames & Hudson, 2001)
Ward, Michael, 'The First Ascent of Mount Everest', *British Medical Journal*, 306 (29 May 1993), 1455–58
Ward, Stuart, ed., *British Culture and the End of Empire* (Manchester: Manchester University Press, 2001)
Warner, Marina, *Stranger Magic: Charmed States and the Arabian Nights* (London: Chatto and Windus, 2011)
Warner Lewis, Maureen, *Guinea's Other Suns: The African Dynamic in Trinidad Culture* (Dover, MA: Majority Press, 1991)
Wasson, Sara, *Urban Gothic of the Second World War: Dark London* (Basingstoke: Palgrave Macmillan, 2010)
Waters, Catherine, *Commodity Culture in Dickens's 'Household Words': The Social Life of Goods* (Aldershot: Ashgate, 2008)
Waugh, Evelyn, *Brideshead Revisited: The Sacred and Profane Memories of Captain Charles Ryder* (London: Penguin, 2000)
Weidenfeld, A.G., ed., *The Changing Nation: A Contact Book* (London: Contact, 1948)
Wells, H.G., *The Invisible Man* (London: Penguin, 2005)
Whitworth, Lesley, 'Inscribing Design on the Nation: The Creators of the British Council of Industrial Design', *Business and Economic History*, 3 (2005), www.thebhc.org/sites/default/files/whitworth.pdf [accessed 28 January 2018]
Wiebe, Heather, '"Now and England": Britten's *Gloriana* and the "New Elizabethans"', *Cambridge Opera Journal*, 17:2 (July 2005), 141–72
Willis, Corin, 'Meaning and Value in *The Jazz Singer*', in John Gibbs and Douglas Pye, eds., *Style and Meaning: Studies in the Detailed Analysis of Film* (Manchester: Manchester University Press, 2005)
Woolf, Virginia, 'Solid Objects', in David Bradshaw, ed., *The Mark on the Wall and Other Short Fiction* (Oxford: Oxford University Press, 2001), 54–59

PAMPHLETS, CATALOGUES AND EXHIBITION GUIDES

1951 Exhibition of Science South Kensington: Festival of Britain, guide-catalogue (London: HMSO, 1951)
Black Eyes and Lemonade, exhibition catalogue (London: Whitechapel Gallery, 1951)

Faster than Thought: The Ferranti Nimrod Digital Computer. A Brief Survey of the Field of Digital Computing with Specific Reference to the Ferranti Nimrod Computer (Hollinwood: Ferranti, 1951), www.goodeveca.net/nimrod/booklet.html [accessed 28 January 2018]

Nigel Henderson: Photographs of Bethnal Green 1949–1952, exhibition catalogue (Nottingham: Midland Group, 1978)

South Bank Exhibition London: Festival of Britain, guide-catalogue (London: HMSO, 1951)

This Is Tomorrow, exhibition catalogue (London: Whitechapel Gallery, 1956)

Traditional Sculpture from the Colonies, exhibition catalogue (London: Colonial Office, 1951)

FILMS AND TELEVISION PROGRAMMES

The Atomic Age (British Pathé and *Daily Express*, 1946)

Brief City: The Story of London's Festival Buildings, dir. by Jacques B. Brunius and Maurice Harvey (Observer Films, 1952)

Bristol's Robot Tortoises Have Minds of Their Own (BBC newsreel, 1950)

Butterfly Bomb (Ministry of Information, 1944)

Citizen Kane, dir. by Orson Welles (RKO Radio Pictures and Mercury Productions, 1941)

Corridor of Mirrors, dir. by Terence Young (Apollo Films, 1948)

The Dam Busters, dir. by Michael Anderson (ABPC, 1955)

Dangerous Trophies: Unexploded Bombs (British Pathé, 1945)

The Dead of Night, dir. by Alberto Cavalcanti, Charles Crichton, Basil Dearden, Robert Hamer (Ealing Studios, 1945)

Dr Strangelove, or How I Learned to Stop Worrying and Love the Bomb, dir. by Stanley Kubrick (Columbia Pictures and Hawk Films, 1962)

Family Portrait, dir. by Humphrey Jennings (Wessex Film Productions, 1950)

Fathers of Pop, written and narrated by Reyner Banham (Arts Council Film, 1979)

Free Cinema (BFI, 2006); DVD

How You Can Deal with Incendiary Bombs (British Pathé, 1940)

Hue and Cry, dir. by Charles Crichton (Ealing Studios, 1947)

The Jazz Singer, dir. by Alan Crosland (Warner Brothers and Vitaphone, 1927)

Land of Promise: The British Documentary Movement, 1930–1950 (BFI, 2010); DVD

Later with Jools Holland (Episode 31.5, BBC, 2008), www.youtube.com/watch?v=zFWHudQQ82A [accessed 28 January 2018]

The Life and Death of Colonel Blimp, dir. by Michael Powell and Emeric Pressburger (The Archers, 1943)

London Can Take It!, dir. by Humphrey Jennings (Crown Film Unit, 1940)

The Man in the White Suit, dir. by Alexander Mackendrick (Ealing Studios, 1951)

A Matter of Life and Death, dir. by Michael Powell and Emeric Pressburger (The Archers, 1946).

The Quatermass Experiment (BBC, 1953)
The Red Shoes, dir. by Michael Powell and Emeric Pressburger (The Archers, 1948)
Seven Days To Noon, dir. by John Boulting and Roy Boulting (London Films, 1950)
The Small Back Room, dir. by Michael Powell and Emeric Pressburger (The Archers, 1949)
Tales of Hoffmann, dir. by Michael Powell and Emeric Pressburger (The Archers and Vega Film Productions, 1951)
Together, dir. by Lorenza Mazzetti (Harlequin Productions and BFI, 1956)
The Undefeated, dir. by Paul Dickson (Central Office of Information, 1950)

NEWSPAPER AND MAGAZINE ARTICLES AND REVIEWS

'A mystery burial ship: treasures without a body', *The Times*, 23 February 1940, p. 6
'A new tool for the research scientist', *Scientific American*, 135:6 (1 December 1926), www.scientificamerican.com/magazine/sa/1926/12-01/ [accessed 28 January 2018]
'Accurate bombing through cloud', *The Times*, 28 November 1944, p. 4
'Adrift in Europe', *The Times*, 8 February 1945, p. 5
'Anglo-Saxon burial ship: treasures found in excavation on Suffolk estate', *Manchester Guardian*, 31 July 1939, p. 13
'Bargepole – please do not touch', *Evening News*, 8 September 1951, p. 13
'Barracking shadows', *The Times*, 29 December 1948, p. 5
Barry, Gerald, 'A tonic to the nation', *Daily Mail Preview & Guide to the Festival of Britain*, May 1951, p. 3
'Blues History' an interview with Chris Barber in *fROOTS Magazine*, August/September 2005, www.chrisbarber.net/archives/froots/froots.htm [accessed 28 January 2018]
'Bombing through clouds: A British target-finding invention', *Illustrated London News*, 6 December 1944, p. 689
'Brutal televised plays', *The Times*, 21 March 1950, p. 7
Cannell, Robert, 'TV millions saw more than the Abbey peers', *Daily Express*, 3 June 1953, p. 2
'Colourful outlook for rainy days', *The Times*, 17 October 1955, p. 11
'Decline of the junk shop', *The Times*, 28 April 1952, p. 9
'Discoveries at Sutton Hoo: Anglo-Saxon art', *Manchester Guardian*, 27 September 1939, p. 6
'Displaced persons for England: women of Baltic states', *The Times*, 24 July 1946, p. 4
Dixon, Bryony and Christophe Dupin, 'Soup dreams', *Sight & Sound*, March 2001, pp. 28–30
'Equipment for Everest: British industry's contribution', *The Times*, 9 June 1953, p. 4
'Exiles in Britain: flourishing Slav settlements in our midst', *The Times*, 20 June 1953, p. 7
'First royal masque since 1636', *The Times*, 26 May 1948, p. 4

'Future of the city churches: commission's final report', *The Times*, 22 October 1946, p. 7

'Homeless people of Europe: UNO committee's work ending', *The Times*, 1 June 1946, p. 4

'Home Office and Mr Power: Kitchener allegations refuted', *The Times*, 10 September 1926, p. 9

Howes, Frank (credited as 'A Special Correspondent'), '*Gloriana*: A Great Event in English Music', *The National and English Review*, 141 (1953), 35

Hunt, John, 'Return to Everest: II – new equipment for the British expedition' *The Times*, 3 February 1953, p. 9

'Informal scenes in the Annexe', *The Times*, 3 June 1953, p. 6

Lambert, Gavin, 'Free cinema', *Sight & Sound*, Spring 1956, pp. 173–77

Laski, Marghanita, 'The visionary gleam: thoughts on the South Bank Exhibition', *Vogue*, June 1951, pp. 73–78

'London's museums renewed and rising popular demand: the aftermath of war', *The Times*, 7 June 1946, p. 7

Merrill Robert, 'Dr William D. Coolidge and his new magic ray', *Salt Lake Telegram*, Nov 21 1926, p. 12

'New homes for 893,000 refugees', *The Times*, 28 March 1951, p. 3

'Night vigil in the streets', *The Times*, 3 June 1953, p. 6

'Nineteen Eighty-Four and all that', *The Times*, 16 December 1954, p. 9

'Obstacles to use of nuclear energy', *The Times*, 11 June 1947, p. 3

O'Donovan, Patrick, 'Black eyes and lemonade', *The Observer*, 16 September 1951, p. 8

Perrick, Eve, 'Eve Perrick had a £30 point of view – and still she got wet, cold and tired', *Daily Express*, 3 June 1953, p. 2

'Princess at Oxford', *The Times*, 26 May 1948, p. 4

'Review of R.H. Coase, "British Broadcasting: A Study in Monopoly"', *Times Literary Supplement*, 14 April 1950, p. 223

Robertson, Bryan, 'Parallel of life and art', *Art News and Review*, 19 September 1953, p. 6

'Ruined city churches: preservation as memorials', *The Times*, 15 August 1944, p. 5

'Ruined churches as memorials: the emotional effect', *The Times*, 22 August 1944, p. 2

'Ruins of bombed churches', *The Times*, 19 August 1944, p. 5

Shadwick, Alan, 'Collector's piece', *Manchester Guardian*, 30 December 1948, p. 3

'Ship burial in Suffolk: jury's finding on gold and silver, not "treasure trove"', *The Times*, 15 August 1939, p. 9

'Surplus population of Europe: help for migrants', *The Times*, 7 December 1953, p. 6

'Televised plays', *The Times*, 22 March 1950, p. 7

'Those who are left', *The Times*, 8 March 1956, p. 11

'Three girls made the queen's dream dress', *Daily Express*, 2 June 1953, p. 1

Wallis, Nevile, 'Taste in art', *The Observer*, 19 Aug 1951, p. 6

Wilson, Angus, 'There's nothing like a Coronation to test's one's scepticism, one's innate Republicanism', *New Statesman*, 13 June 1953, www.newstatesman.com/print/archive/2013/06/13-june-1953-theres-nothing-coronation-test-ones-scepticism-ones-innate-republicanis [accessed 28 January 2018]

Whittet, G.S., 'London commentary', *Studio International*, November 1951, p. 154

INDEX

Note: literary works can be found under authors' names.

40,000 Years of Modern Art 59, 72

Adorno, Theodor 3, 23, 27
  Dialectic of Enlightenment 9, 23, 27, 210
  'How to look at television' 110–11
  and Max Horkheimer 9, 23, 27, 210
  Minima Moralia 1, 9
Aldiss, Brian 99, 104
Amis, Kingsley
  Lucky Jim 208–10, 212
Anderson, Michael 185
Andrews, Michael 63–64
Angry Young Men 4
animals 56, 158
  see also dogs; taxidermy
Armstrong, Isobel 9–10, 94
Armstrong, Tim 8–9, 190
atom 187, 188, 195
Atomic Age, The 185–86
atomic bomb *see* bombs

Bachelard, Gaston
  Poetics of Space, The 34
Balchin, Nigel 189
Banton, Michael
  Coloured Quarter, The 61–62, 69, 71
Barthes, Roland
  Mythologies 210–11

Baudrillard, Jean
  System of Objects, The 124–25
BBC 3, 36, 82–83, 108–09, 111–13, 200
Beaton, Cecil 171
Bell, Quentin
  On Human Finery 159–61, 174
Benjamin, Walter 123, 209
  Arcades Project, The 6, 53, 141–42, 153
  One Way Street 188, 196, 202
  'Unpacking My Library' 153
  'Work of Art in the Age of Mechanical Reproduction, The' 28, 84, 143, 194
Bhabha, Homi 70
Bikini Atoll 185–86
Black Eyes and Lemonade 51, 52–61, 65, 156, 209
Black, Misha 2, 43, 157
Blake, William 21, 24
Blitz, the 17–20, 28, 34, 184, 196, 211
bombed waste 139
bombs 19, 155, 183, 185, 186, 189, 191–92, 201, 203, 205
  atomic 184, 187, 202
  bouncing 196–98
  domestic detonator 157
  incendiary 183
  nuclear 185, 189, 195, 204
  V2 rocket 87
bombsite 19, 73, 196

Bowen, Elizabeth 8, 34
  Demon Lover and Other Stories, The 126–27, 211
  'English Fiction at Mid-Century' 12n.28
  Heat of the Day, The 121, 127–32, 134
brain-scanning *see* electroencephalography
Brief City 44
Britten, Benjamin
  Gloriana 146, 167–71, 175
Brown, Bill
  'Thing Theory' 10, 190
  'The Tyranny of Things' 13n.38, 162
Butterfly Bomb 184

Cannadine, David 162–63
Carroll, Lewis 97
Cary, Joyce
  Horse's Mouth, The 20–29, 34
Casson, Hugh 164
  Bombed Churches as War Memorials 33–38, 39
  and Festival of Britain 42
cathode ray 82, 98
  screen 81, 84, 96
  tube 80, 83, 84, 97, 105
cenotaph 50, 52, 57
clothes 149, 152–53, 155
  see also costume
Cohen, Margaret 6
Cold War 184, 191, 201, 204, 208
colonialism 58, 60, 68
  see also empire
computers 81, 95, 102
  'Nimrod' 105–06
Coronation 161, 163–64, 171
  gown by Norman Hartnell 162
  as television spectacle 166
coronets 151, 163
Corridor of Mirrors 152–54, 155, 157
costume 146, 151, 152, 164, 169, 170, 174
crown 155, 162, 169
cybernetics 53, 81, 96, 105

Daily Mail Television Handbook 89, 108, 109
Dam Busters, The 185, 196–98
Dangerous Trophies: Unexploded Bombs 184
Dead of Night, The 123
dogs 11, 56, 70, 130, 155, 158, 197
Dr Strangelove, or How I Learned to Stop Worrying and Love the Bomb 205–06
duffel coats 164–65

electroencephalography (EEG) 96–97
Eliot, T.S. 33
  Notes Towards the Definition of Culture 4, 36
Elizabeth I 167–71
Elizabeth II 146, 147–48, 163
empire 51, 59, 164, 171, 175
  see also colonialism
Enlightenment 6, 9, 80
Everest 146, 175–78

Family Portrait 147
fascism 28, 203, 205, 206
Festival of Britain 1, 42–44, 59, 147
  Dome of Discovery 1–3, 157
  Exhibition of Science 99, 186–87
  Homes and Gardens Pavilion 43
  Regatta Restaurant 3, 42–43
  Skylon 1
  South Bank Exhibition Guide 3, 50
Fisher, Mark
  Weird and the Eerie, The 7
Fleming, Ian
  Moonraker 203
Freud, Sigmund 7, 81, 101, 137
  'Uncanny, The' 7, 83–84, 85, 95, 121, 123, 125, 162
Futurist 28, 195

gentrification 133–35
glass 57, 64, 81, 83, 85, 86, 90, 92–94, 150, 162, 165

Glass, Ruth
   Aspects of Change 133–34
Grey Walter, William 81, 96–101
   Living Brain, The 96
   'Machine That Learns, A' 100

Hamer, Robert 124
Hamilton, Richard
   Just what is it that makes today's home so different, so appealing? 74–75
'Haunted Mirror, The' 123–24
Heidegger, Martin
   'Thing, The' 187–88, 206
Henderson, Judith 72
Henderson, Nigel 72–74
   Parallel of Life and Art 72–73
   Patio and Pavilion 73–74
Hepworth, Barbara 3
Highmore, Ben 5, 73
Hillary, Edmund 175–78
Hoffmann, E.T.A.
   'Sandman, The' 7, 84
Holocaust, the 11, 202
Horkheimer, Max *see* Adorno, Theodor
Hornsey, Richard 5
horror 20, 38, 49, 51, 53, 57, 68, 70, 107, 111, 112, 122, 153
How you can deal with incendiary bombs 183
Hunt, John 175–76, 177

Independent Group 71–75

Jazz Singer, The 74
Jennings, Humphrey 147, 183–84
Jones, Barbara 38, 51–52, 64, 73
   English Furniture at a Glance 141
   as illustrator 38
   Unsophisticated Arts, The 53, 57, 58
   see also Black Eyes and Lemonade
junk 8, 11, 73, 89, 130, 139, 140–42, 156, 201, 209, 212
   junk shop 23, 25, 60, 90–93, 100, 122, 132, 135–37, 140, 142

Kittler, Friedrich 191
   Optical Media 87
Kneale, Nigel 113
Korda, Alexander 148, 150

Lacan, Jacques 81, 98, 101–02, 124, 151
Larkin, Philip 33
Laski, Marghanita
   Little Boy Lost 10–11
   Offshore Island, The 185, 200–02
   Victorian Chaise Longue, The 90, 121, 132–43, 201
   'Visionary Gleam, A' 11
Lessing, Doris
   Four-Gated City, The 4, 208
London Can Take It! 183–84
Lukács, Georg 5

Macaulay, Rose
   Pleasure of Ruins, The 39
   World My Wilderness, The 34, 38–42
Mackendrick, Alexander 172
McLuhan, Marshall 74
Man in the White Suit, The 146, 172–73
Marx, Karl 23, 136
Marxism 6
masks 155, 156, 176–77, 198, 202
Masque of Hope, The 146, 147–48, 167, 169
Mazzetti, Lorenza 34, 62–64
Mighty Atom, The 195
mirrors 94, 97, 100, 124, 152, 155
   see also Corridor of Mirrors; 'Haunted Mirror, The'
Mitchell, W.T.J. 82, 90–91
Moberly, L.G.
   'Inexplicable' 122–23, 134
modern art 28
modernism 3, 4, 18, 147
Momma Don't Allow 62, 74
mummies 51, 52
Murdoch, Iris
   Under the Net 146, 154–59

Nazi 203, 205
nostalgia 30, 32, 37, 50, 55, 58, 90, 142

nuclear energy 186
nuclear war 195, 200, 204
nuclear weaponry 186, 191
　see also bombs, nuclear
nylon 174, 176

Obeah 68–69
Orwell, George 121
　'Just Junk' 92
　Nineteen Eighty-Four 81, 87, 88–92,
　　95, 103, 107
　'Poetry and the Microphone' 88

Packard, Vance 6
Paolozzi, Eduardo 63–64, 71
　Bunk! 71
　Dr Pepper 71
　Parallel of Life and Art 72–73
　Patio and Pavilion 73–74, 209
Paravisini-Gebert, Lizbeth 50, 68
Pasmore, Victor 43
Pinter, Harold
　Caretaker, The 211
Piper, John 35
　Englishman's Home, The 43–44
plastic 65, 73, 135, 158, 164, 165, 175, 177
Plomer, William 168
plutonium 199, 200
Powell, Michael 85, 148
　and Emeric Pressburger 85, 112, 146,
　　148–50, 170, 185, 189, 191–94
　Matter of Life and Death, A 85–87,
　　93, 191
　Red Shoes, The 146, 148–51, 152, 170
　Small Back Room, The 185, 189–92
　Tales of Hoffmann, The 85
Pressburger, Emeric *see* Powell,
　Michael
Priestley, J.B.
　Gravity's Rainbow 5
　'Uncle Phil on TV' 107–09
prosthetic 177, 189–90, 193–94, 198
Proust, Marcel 93, 200

Quatermass Experiment, The 112, 173

radar 81, 87, 97, 112, 174
radio 86, 88, 90, 202
regalia 160, 163, 171
reification 5, 9, 27, 67, 153, 188, 202, 210
Reisz, Karel 62–63
robots 98, 99–102
Royal College of Art 53, 172
rubble 1, 8, 18, 20, 27, 34, 35, 39, 128,
　　185, 211
ruins 6, 18, 29–30, 31, 32–42, 44, 71, 72,
　　134, 142, 185, 196
Russell, Gordon 125, 140
Ryle, Gilbert 95–96, 102, 110

Sansom, William 17–20, 26, 40
　Blitz: Westminster at War, The 17
　Fireman Flower 20
　*Something Terrible, Something
　　Lovely* 44n.8
　Stories 45n.12
Second World War 5, 17, 30, 58, 87, 185,
　　189, 195
Selvon, Sam 62
　Lonely Londoners, The 52, 65–68,
　　69–71
　'Obeah in the Grove' 68–69
Seven Days to Noon 185, 202, 205
skin 52, 58
　bearskin 159
　see also tattoos; taxidermy
Shearer, Moira 149–50
Shelley, Mary 101, 102–03
Smithson, Alison and Peter 72–73
Snow, C.P.
　New Men, The 198–200, 205
Spencer, Stanley 27
sterility 185, 200, 203
Sutton Hoo 48–51, 75

tattoos 58
taxidermy 56, 57, 74
　stuffed pike 135
　stuffed snake 155, 156
　Walter Potter 57
telephone 189, 191, 205–06

television 75, 80–89, 93, 94–95, 96, 98, 107–13, 121, 140, 166
Tenzing, Norgay 175–78
textiles 164, 172
  crisis 173–74
  synthetic 164–65, 172, 174–75
This Is Tomorrow 73–74
Thomas, Dylan 3
Thompson, Michael
  Rubbish Theory 134–35
Together 34, 62, 63–64
Turing, Alan 81
  'Computing Machinery and Intelligence' 102–05
  'Digital Computers Applied to Games' 106
  at Festival of Britain 104–05
  'Intelligent machinery, a heretical theory' 105
  willingness to believe in extra-sensory perception 106–07
Twain, Mark
  Prince and the Pauper, The 162, 163

Undefeated, The 192–94, 203, 205

Virilio, Paul 87
Vogue (magazine) 11

Walpole, Horace 121
  Castle of Otranto, The 7
Waugh, Evelyn 35
  Brideshead Revisited 29–33, 34, 50, 134
waxworks 53, 152–53
Whitechapel Gallery 51, 52, 53, 73
wig 167–68, 171
Woolf, Virginia
  Solid Objects 8

EU authorised representative for GPSR:
Easy Access System Europe, Mustamäe tee 50,
10621 Tallinn, Estonia
gpsr.requests@easproject.com